THE ADMIRAL
AND THE AMBASSADOR

One Man's *OBSESSIVE SEARCH* for the *BODY* of
JOHN PAUL JONES

Scott Martelle

CHICAGO
REVIEW
PRESS

Copyright © 2014 by Scott Martelle
All rights reserved
Published by Chicago Review Press Incorporated
814 North Franklin Street
Chicago, IL 60610
ISBN 978-1-61374-730-8

Library of Congress Cataloging-in-Publication Data
Martelle, Scott, 1958–
    The admiral and the ambassador : one man's obsessive search for the body of
John Paul Jones / Scott Martelle.
        pages cm
    Includes bibliographical references and index.
    ISBN 978-1-61374-730-8
    1. Jones, John Paul, 1747–1792—Death and burial. 2. Jones, John Paul, 1747–
1792—Tomb. 3. Porter, Horace, 1837–1921. I. Title.
    E207.J7M23 2014
    973.3'5092—dc23
                                        2014002307

Interior design: PerfecType, Nashville, TN

Printed in the United States of America
5 4 3 2 1

For Margaret, of course

Contents

INTRODUCTION

O N A SUNDAY MORNING in late January 1913, the US secretary of the navy, George von Lengerke Meyer, and Horace Porter, the former US ambassador to France, led a small group of political dignitaries on a thirty-mile train trip from Washington, DC, to the United States Naval Academy in Annapolis, Maryland. It was an unusually warm, spring-like day, and bright sunshine drenched the countryside as the train glided eastward, arriving a little before 11 AM. A small welcoming committee awaited them at the platform. After the dignitaries alit and introductions had been made, academy superintendent Captain John H. Gibbons escorted the group the few blocks to the college grounds for a brief ceremony that would be part funeral and part final chapter of a long and shifting story.[1]

As the dignitaries arrived, the academy's seven hundred uniformed midshipmen were already in place on an expanse of treed parkland between the domed, five-year-old chapel and a ship basin that had been carved into the bank of the Severn River at the northeast edge of the grounds. The grandiose, five-story Bancroft Hall, the cadets' palatial new dormitory, anchored the southeast corner of the park, and once the dignitaries had entered the chapel, a small detachment of midshipmen marched to an open stone courtyard at the foot of the broad staircase leading up to Bancroft Hall's main entrance.

A half dozen of the young men then split off and entered the hall, making their way beneath the grand staircase where they surrounded and carefully lifted a flag-draped coffin from a temporary bier of two sawhorses. The young pallbearers carried the body outside to a small caisson, then fell in behind the navy band and a double line of midshipmen for the short and somber parade to the chapel. While the dignitaries listened to a short service on the main floor, the pallbearers took the coffin down a short flight of stairs to a large room in the middle of the basement where they hoisted it into a massive twenty-one-ton marble-and-bronze sarcophagus supported by bronze dolphins. Workmen then winched the heavy lid into place and sealed the sarcophagus shut.

The ceremony in the church was short—just a few comments about the significance of the moment and some accolades for the man whose body was freshly placed in the basement crypt, closed out by a prayer. At its end, the celebrants descended the stairs to the basement, where they became the first tourists to visit the final resting place of Revolutionary War hero John Paul Jones. The moment was decidedly anticlimactic, but that shouldn't have been surprising for what was, in effect, Jones's fourth funeral.

Jones's arrival at his ornate crypt came more than 120 years after his death in Paris in 1792. France at that time was in the throes of its own revolution, and Jones's death—of natural causes—was quickly noted and even more quickly forgotten, an ignominious end for the man many people consider to be the father of the US Navy. Were it not for Horace Porter, one of the men on the Annapolis outing on that January day, Jones's body would likely still be buried deep beneath modern Paris instead of tucked into the basement of the Annapolis Chapel. How Porter found the hero's remains—which involved something of a historical detective story—is the subject of this book.

Jones was most famous for words he never uttered. According to legend, "I have not yet begun to fight" was his response to a demand that he "strike his colors"—surrender—by a British navy captain with whom his barely floating *Bonhomme Richard* was engaged in a deadly sea battle. What Jones actually said was closer to "I have not yet thought of it, but I am determined to make you strike!" Not quite as resonant or poetic, though equally emblematic of Jones's preternatural stubbornness and drive.

Over generations, such embellishments to Jones's life have helped create a legend that exceeds the scope of the man, which is fine; that is the nature of heroes and hero worship. The real Jones, though, was a fascinating figure without the embellishments. At times petulant and easily offended, at other times a masterful and intuitive naval strategist, Jones cut a wide swath through Revolutionary America and the salons of Europe. He liked women—especially, it seems, those already married. He liked receiving accolades. And he hungered for fame and acceptance from the rich and the powerful, an understandable character trait for the ambitious, lowborn son of a Scottish gardener.

In the course of his short life, Jones achieved much. He became a successful sea captain and expert navigator, a self-taught and prolific letter writer, a murderer, and a war hero. He was received at the courts of royalty in Paris and Saint Petersburg, was fluent in French, and counted among his friends and acquaintances a roster of America's founding fathers, including Thomas Jefferson, James Madison, and Benjamin Franklin.

He was the first American naval commander to receive a salute from a foreign power—France—while flying the new American flag, the Stars and Stripes, and showed through his cleverness, bravery, and will, that the eighteenth century British navy was not as formidable as it might have seemed. While Jones never acquired the kinds of riches he sought, he did amass a fortune large enough to make most men comfortable in that time.

Jones's story has been well chronicled in many splendid (and some not-so-splendid) biographies, led in 1959 by Samuel Eliot Morison's Pulitzer Prize–winning *John Paul Jones: A Sailor's Biography*, and followed more recently by Evan Thomas's well-turned *John Paul Jones: Sailor, Hero, Father of the American Navy* in 2003. Jones biographies invariably end with a full or partial chapter on how Jones's body went missing after his death, tacked on like an appendix, as though the author is saying, well, I've told you a story about this fascinating man and I guess I should tell you that here at the end of his life another little drama took place.

It's that last story that fascinates me most. There is something poignant about Jones's earthly afterlife. It speaks to our national impulse to elevate heroes—particularly military ones—but also our collective short memory and disregard for history. The genesis of this book was my chance encounter with an article, "Home Is the Sailor," by historian Adam Goodheart, in the April 2006 issue of *Smithsonian* magazine. The piece explored lingering uncertainty about whether the body in that Naval Academy crypt is indeed that of Jones. I believe it is and that the questions are more of the "what if" variety than serious doubts.

But the article introduced me to the man responsible for finding the body, Horace Porter, who achieved significant fame during his life but who has since faded into the shadows of history. Curiosity piqued, I began poking around to learn more about Porter and the obsession that led this confidante of presidents—himself a decorated Civil War hero who attained the rank of brigadier general—to spend several years and a small fortune trying to find the body of a man long dead.

As I worked, it became clear that the lives of Porter and Jones, taken together, were inextricably linked to some of the most significant events in the first half of the nation's history. Through them, we can see on a human scale the evolution of a nation from its birth in revolt against the British through the patriotic fervor and burgeoning militarism and imperialism that would make the twentieth century the American Century.

So this book begs a bit of indulgence. It proceeds largely chronologically and focuses primarily on Porter, but it also detours a bit into wars and assassinations, international exhibitions, and the frailties of human endeavors and egos. While this is not a biography of Jones or Porter, understanding who these men were and the times in which they lived is crucial to understanding why their deeds mattered. In some ways, it is a story of obsession, of small acts committed in times of great upheaval, and of lives dedicated both to personal success and to the well-being of the nation.

In that, it is at heart an American story. And America's story. But it begins more than 220 years ago in France, with a lonely and ailing man in the midst of another country's revolution.

1

Jones: A Hero Dies

Paris, July 18, 1792

John Paul Jones was gravely ill. He had always been a slender man, but over the last few months his body had slowly swelled, first the feet and legs, now the hands and abdomen. He was lethargic and had trouble walking around his Paris neighborhood. Slight exertions left him struggling for breath, and coughing fits punctuated his conversations. In recent days, his white skin had begun yellowing, and Jones was entertaining no delusions about how this precipitous decline in health was going to play out. Less than two weeks after his forty-fifth birthday, Jones was, he believed, dying.

Jones had spent a fair amount of time in Paris over the years, yet in his final days he only had a small circle of friends he could rely on. One of them, Samuel Blackden, an American businessman, had been quietly pressing the Scottish-born hero of the American Revolution to get his affairs in order. And that morning, Jones was finally ready. He sent word to Blackden and another friend, Gouverneur Morris, the US envoy to France, that he wanted to dictate his will and he wanted them to witness it.

The men arrived around five o'clock at Jones's third-floor apartment overlooking the Rue de Tournon, a block-long street on the Left Bank that ran north from the Palais de Luxembourg, once the home of art collections and royalty but now standing unused as the French Revolution gathered steam. Blackden arrived with Jean-Baptiste Beaupoil, a former aide to Jones's friend the Marquis de Lafayette, the French soldier and aristocrat who had helped the Americans during their revolution. Morris, the official face of the young United States, brought two French notaries to handle the legal requirements of recording the dying hero's last will and testament.[1]

The men found Jones "sitting in an easy chair, sick in body but of sound mind, memory, judgment, and understanding"—the prerequisites for writing a will. Despite his success as a sea warrior and his reputation as a captain to be feared by enemies and crewmen alike, Jones wasn't physically imposing. He was about five feet seven inches tall, with long dark hair rusted to gray at the temples. At sea, he often exploded in violent anger, but ashore he was usually courteous, gratingly so at times. But now he was all business, as though not wanting to waste breath on the inconsequential.

Amid his coughing fits, Jones itemized his possessions and told the men that he wanted his estate—including assorted debts that were owed him, property in the United States, some business investments and bank accounts—to go to his two sisters in Scotland and to their children. As Jones dictated, his cough worsened; the meeting was wearing him out. The notaries completed their work and left together with Morris. Blackden and Beaupoil lingered a few minutes, but then they left too, and Jones retired to his bedroom.

Paris at the time was filled with revolutionary fervor, and tension was building rapidly on the streets and in the salons. It was this, not Jones's failing health, that preoccupied Morris. He went from Jones's apartment to dine with the British ambassador to France, Lord Granville Leveson-Gower, and the ambassador's wife, Lady Susannah Stewart Sutherland, where they traded news of the day. It was not good. A month earlier, a mob had invaded the royal palace at the Tuileries and humiliated Louis XVI and his queen, Marie Antoinette, by, among other things, forcing the king to don a red hat—a symbol of the revolution—and drink a toast to the health of his subjects.

As word of the king's humiliation spread, royalists from around France converged on Paris to defend the realm. Supporters of the revolutionaries also made their way to the capital, drawn by the scent of radical change. The future of France, and of the rights of man, were being fought over by the ancien régime and those seeking to create a new society, one in which the people, rather than birthright and a kiss from God, would determine who ruled.

Sensing the looming violence, members of the Legislative Assembly, where royalist Feuillants were locked in raucous debate with the revolutionary Jacobins, began drifting away, not wanting to be caught up if the tensions broke into riots and bloodshed, arrests and guillotines. The struggle was changing Paris at its roots. The sprawling, three-story Palais de Luxembourg would soon become a prison, and in a few months' time, Louis XVI would lose his head at the freshly renamed la Place de la Révolution with thousands of Parisians cheering the executioner instead of their king. So there was much to concern the diplomats of the United States and England, much to discuss over their meal.[2]

Morris made a short evening of it. After dinner, he took his carriage to the home of his married mistress, Adélaïde-Emilie de Flahaut, and went with her to the nearby home of Dr. Félix Vicq d'Azyr, a member of the Académie française whose patients included the queen. The trio moved on to Jones's apartment. The commodore's valet let them in, telling them that Jones was in his bedroom. They opened the door to find a corpse. Jones was flopped face-first over the edge of the mattress, his booted feet still on the floor, as though life had left him a step short of his bed, or in the midst of a final prayer.

Jones died on his own time—a rare event in those guillotine-hungry days in Paris—but he did not die on his own terms. It was the last in a series of events over which Jones had lost all control, a poignant turn for a man accustomed to altering not only the course of a battle but the course of history as well.

Jones had arrived in Paris in May 1790 after a year of wandering Europe's capitals, hoping to resurrect a military career that had foundered badly in the service of Russia's Catherine the Great. Jones was a proven leader of men, or at least of sailors, and an accomplished naval strategist. During the American Revolution, he took the fight to England itself, raiding coastal villages and capturing British warships. The British, noting Jones's Scottish birth, branded him a pirate and a traitor.

Yet for all of Jones's cunning at sea, he was a failure at politics and the intrigues of royal courts. He had left Saint Petersburg in disgrace, the whispers of a tawdry sexual dalliance with a young girl rippling ahead of him. Once in Paris, he found the city remarkably changed from his previous visits, when he had been welcomed at the king's court. Now he was barely welcomed anywhere, in part because Paris itself was different. The American Revolution had been a fight for separation, a struggle for independence by colonies lying an ocean away from their ruler. In the end, governance had changed, but the social order had remained the same. The French Revolution was something altogether different, a vicious and unforgiving uprising of the masses, a true upending of the social order. Much of the aristocracy among whom Jones felt most comfortable had fled the city, some even the country, and others were in hiding. Even the king and his queen were at the mercy of their subjects, forced to live under house arrest at the Tuileries.

Against that backdrop, there was no room and little patience for Jones, an ego-driven man selling doomed schemes aimed at his naval resurrection. He had become a boor to his friends, and his failing health gave him a cadaverous look, like "a wine skin from which the wine has been drawn," as Thomas Carlyle later described him. The former commodore suffered from a nagging pneumonia, and his lungs were weakened. For months, Jones's ailing kidneys had been developing lesions and small fibrous masses, and scarring over, which interfered with their crucial biological functions. Slowly, they stopped working. The doctor who examined the body ruled the death natural, due to dropsy of the lungs. Jones the sailor had, in effect, drowned in his own fluids.

— ❖ —

The mortician and his assistants did their work with practiced efficiency. Two days after Jones's death, they placed the body on a table, stripped it, and then dressed it in a long linen shirt decorated with plaits and ruffles. They twisted the hair, more than two feet long, into a ball and tucked it inside a small linen cap at the nape. In the custom of the era, they covered Jones's hands and feet with foil and then wrapped the whole body in a long burial cloth with, inexplicably, the numeral 2 stenciled on the top.

When they were done, they carefully placed the body in an expensive lead-lined coffin and secured it in place with wads of straw in case the

Americans might someday send for the body. Or maybe Jones's family in Scotland would claim him. The orders were to prepare the body for days of jouncing and bouncing over roads to the coast and then over the seas to its final resting place, even though the coffin was scheduled to be dropped in the Parisian ground in a matter of hours.[3]

Once the body was secured, the rim of the lower half of the coffin was coated with solder; the top was slipped carefully into place and then sealed shut. Someone had drilled a hole in the lid near the head of the coffin, and now the mortician slowly poured in tiny streams of alcohol until the lead box was filled. A metal screw was twisted tightly into the hole and sealed with drops of molten lead, leaving a bumpy scar above the dead man's head.

A few hours later, as evening came on, the coffin was taken from Jones's apartment and slowly wheeled northward in a small funeral parade through the streets of Paris, across the Seine, and on out of the walled city. It continued on until it reached the only place around Catholic Paris in which a Protestant could be lawfully buried, the cemetery of Saint Louis, outside the l'Hôpital Saint-Louis. The distinguished but small crowd of about sixty mourners entered through the gate at Rue des Écluses-Saint-Martin and passed through a fruit garden, the leafy branches beginning to swell with apples and pears, and then another gate at the top of stairs that led eight feet down to the cemetery.

The mourners included Jones's friend François Pierre Simonneau, a royal bureaucrat who had covered the 462-franc cost of the burial out of his own pocket rather than see Jones's body heaved into a pauper's grave. It was Simonneau who thought that maybe someday the Americans might send for their war hero and so arranged for the lead coffin and the gallons of alcohol to preserve the body. And it was no small expense. Simonneau had paid more than triple the going rate for a traditional burial with a wooden coffin and contemporary embalming methods. (For the poor, whose unprotected bodies were dumped into the ground, the cost of a funeral was even less.) It wasn't that Jones didn't have money. He had left an estate of some $30,000, but nearly all of it was tied up in investments and debts owed him from elsewhere in Europe and in the United States. Gouverneur Morris, as the American representative in Paris, declined to front the cost of the funeral on behalf of the government or to assume the burial debts on behalf of Jones's estate. "Some people here who like rare shows wished him to have a pompous funeral," Morris wrote to a friend years later. "As I had no right to spend on such follies either the money of his heirs or that of the United States, I desired that he might be buried in a private and economical manner."

Simonneau was joined by a delegation of twelve members of the Legislative Assembly, which the day before—amid crucial debates over the future of France—had marked Jones's passing with a formal vote recognizing his life and long friendship with France. Other faces familiar about Paris at the time were at the graveside as well, including Jean-Baptiste Beaupoil, who had seen Jones on the day he died, and Louis-Nicolas Villeminot, who led a detachment of grenadiers to accompany the cortege. There were some Americans, too, who had crossed paths with Jones in Paris: Jones's friend Blackden; Reverdy Ghiselin of Maryland, who had recently arrived from Le Havre, where he was trying to establish business; and Thomas Waters Griffith, an American merchant who also became witness to the excesses of the French Revolution as he sought his own fortune.

The Reverend Paul-Henri Marron, a Swiss Calvinist who apparently had never met Jones, delivered a eulogy for the legend, not the man. Marron glossed over the sexual scandal and court intrigues that had driven Jones from Saint Petersburg and romanticized the dead man's motives, bathing him in a revolutionary light—fitting, for the time and the place. "Paul Jones could not long breathe the pestilential air of despotism," the minister said. "He preferred the sweets of a private life in France, now free, to the *éclat* of titles and of honors which . . . were lavished upon him by Catherine. The fame of the brave outlives him; his portion is immortality." Then the minister urged his fellow *citoyens* to let Paul be their inspiration. "What more flattering homage could we pay to . . . Paul Jones, than to swear on his tomb to live or to die free? It is the vow, it is the watchword for every Frenchman."

The grenadiers fired a salute into the air, and the small gathering broke up. The mourners began making their way south in the gathering dusk, back along the road to the walled city, to the lights, and to the revolution. The gravediggers turned to their final task, shoveling the rich French earth onto the coffin of the man who would become known as the Father of the American Navy, and whose grave would soon be lost in the tumult of war.

2

---------------- ☀ ----------------

A New President

Washington, DC, March 4, 1897

Horace Porter sat atop a parade stallion as he waited for a carriage to emerge from a nearby gate. It was a few minutes after 10 AM, and the blustery winds that ushered in the dawn had died down, leaving a pleasantly sunny but chilly day in Washington. Bad weather, of course, is bad news for a parade, so the clear skies gave Porter one less thing to worry about. It was his parade that was at stake on this late-winter morning, and he wanted everything to go according to plan. The celebration was the first of a series of high-profile events in which Porter would play a central role over the next few weeks, and while he wasn't a man prone to anxiety, one suspects he was well aware of what failure would mean for his reputation for probity, discipline, and reliability—even if no one truly expected him to control the weather.[1]

Porter's sixtieth birthday was a month away, and the years had left their marks. He was in fine health, but his hair and mustache had grayed, and his face sagged around the cheeks. Still, he maintained the military bearing learned a half century earlier as he rose to the rank of brigadier general in the Union Army and as a top aide to General Ulysses S. Grant. After the war, Porter followed Grant into politics. Although Porter had long ago moved into civilian life, on this morning he sported a full dress uniform: dark blue jacket and pants with a gold belt and oversized epaulets, a broad sash, medals on his chest, and a plumed black hat on his head. A new sword dangled in its scabbard at his side, a gift from his staff to commemorate this day for which they had planned and worked most of the previous four months.[2]

Porter's horse stood at the head of a small detachment of cavalrymen in the middle of Pennsylvania Avenue. Rows of forty-five-star flags flapped over the heads of thousands of people overflowing the sidewalks and spilling noisily into Lafayette Square. Porter ignored the human din and kept his eye on a nearby gate, waiting for a carriage to emerge bearing his friend Major William McKinley and President Grover Cleveland. The carriage would be Porter's cue to spur his horse and start his small squadron, the official escort on the short trip from the White House to the Capitol, where McKinley, an Ohio native and former Republican congressman and governor, would soon be sworn in as the twenty-fifth president of the United States.

The election had been groundbreaking for American politics, shifting tactics from old-style parades and rallies to a more media-savvy, and media-using, strategy. The main issue as the nation shouldered its way out of an economic depression had been money. McKinley ran on a "sound money" platform, pinning the value of the US dollar to a gold standard. Democrat William Jennings Bryan stood for "free silver," a policy that would have pegged the value of the dollar to silver, making goods more affordable and boosting the wealth of western silver miners. Gold won, but the real engine behind McKinley's victory was the maneuvering of his campaign manager, Ohio millionaire and powerbroker Mark Hanna, who built the campaign around letters, pamphlets, and books provided free to the voters. The material explained McKinley's monetary and trade polices—dry stuff in the best of times—but also reinforced McKinley's image as a sober and prudent leader, an attractive force of stability in times of financial upheaval and uncertainty. At the time, political radicals were turning to the gun and the bomb to try to overthrow capitalism, and labor activists were sparking strikes to wrest better wages and working conditions from men who were just as strident in their refusals to grant them.

Mounting such an "educational campaign" of literature, as McKinley's political advisors called it, took a lot of cash, and Porter, as it happened, was exceedingly good at raising money. Porter brought in hundreds of thousands of dollars in donations, underwriting a campaign that overwhelmed the Democrats and helped propel the Republican Party to national dominance, until the Great Depression caused another political realignment and sent Franklin Delano Roosevelt to the White House.[3]

While the 1896 election was significant for the nation, it was also a critical moment for Porter. He had been on the national political stage before— by now, in fact, he was an old and seasoned hand—but McKinley's victory would mark the start of a fourth chapter in his life and send him on an adventure to rival that of his war years.

---------------⚙---------------

Porter was born in Huntingdon, Pennsylvania, in 1837, the son of David R. Porter, a businessman turned politician who, two years later, would be elected governor of Pennsylvania. The elder Porter himself was the son of a Revolutionary War veteran, Andrew Porter, who began as a captain in the marines aboard the *Effingham* but then quickly transferred to the artillery. Eventually achieving the rank of colonel, Andrew Porter fought at the battles of Princeton, Brandywine, Germantown, and Trenton.

Before the war, Colonel Porter, who had a penchant for mathematics, ran his own small private school in Philadelphia, but after the war he settled into farming in Norristown, Pennsylvania, and eventually became a surveyor, helping establish the Pennsylvania state boundaries. His son David Porter, despite his success in politics, lost fortunes at least twice during economic depressions—first running ironworks, then as a railroad investor—but those troubles occurred before and after Horace, his sixth son and seventh child to survive into adulthood, was raised.[4]

Horace Porter grew up primarily in Harrisburg, attending school during the day and working at his father's ironworks in the after hours. A tinkerer, he created several small refinements to the machinery in the ironworks and developed an interest in engineering. As a governor's son, he also absorbed lessons in politics and military affairs. General Sam Houston was a friend of Porter's father and an occasional visitor, and the young Horace would listen to the famous Texan's stories of battles from the War of 1812 to the fight for Texas independence to the Mexican-American War. He also eavesdropped on the adults' debates over West Point (Houston disliked it) and slavery (Houston was for it).

The elder Porter also counted James Buchanan, then the US representative to the Court of St. James's in London, among his friends, and Horace, through their letters, "had his first glimpse of that European world to the problems of which he was later to give so much thought."[5] When he was thirteen years old, Porter was sent off to a boarding school in Lawrenceville, New Jersey, where he excelled academically—first in his class in Latin, French, and math—and also organized a small military company of students.

As he neared graduation, Porter sought an appointment to West Point but missed the cut. Porter enrolled in the Lawrence Scientific School at Harvard instead and tried again the next year for West Point, this time more forcefully. During his midwinter break, Porter traveled to Washington to lobby Ner Middleswarth, the congressman from his home district in Pennsylvania, for an appointment. It worked: Porter was admitted to West Point in 1855.

As a cadet, Porter studied engineering and trained in artillery and ordnance management. He was a generally good student in a class that faced severe erosion. Porter's entering class had eighty-one students; by graduation day five years later (one of only two West Point classes to follow a five-year program), fifty-five students were left.[6] Porter placed near the top across most of his subject areas, though he seemed to have trouble with French, placing thirteenth, then fifteenth, and then dropping to twenty-ninth. The cadet apparently hit the books, though, and by the 1857 term Porter was first in his French class too.

While Porter enjoyed the military training, he suffered the occasional mishap. During a horseback training drill, his mount reached out and bit the animal in front, which retaliated by kicking out a hind leg that "struck my right leg several inches above the ankle," opening up a deep gash that wouldn't heal, Porter wrote his sister on September 20, 1858, from a hospital bed. Porter spent more than a week in the hospital before he had recovered enough to rejoin training and his classes.[7]

West Point was an all-male bastion, but family members and girlfriends made regular visits and were quartered at the three-story West Point Hotel, fronted by a broad and deep wooden porch, which became the cadets' place to meet and woo young women. In the summer of 1859, Sophie McHarg, the daughter in a prominent Albany family, was staying at the hotel with a friend, Mary Satterlee, though the reason for their visit is unclear. Porter happened by while the two young women were on the porch, and was smitten with McHarg. They soon began courting, and after Porter graduated third in his class in July 1860, the couple became engaged. Porter spent the summer as an artillery instructor at West Point and that fall was assigned to the army's Watervliet Arsenal at Troy, just a few miles from Albany, a convenient posting for his romantic life. But his orders were soon to change.[8]

In April 1861 secessionist troops in South Carolina opened fire on the US government's military installation at Fort Sumter, launching the Civil War. Porter was overwhelmed at Watervliet as orders escalated for supplies and weapons to be shipped to different Union outposts. He was sent on one clandestine mission to Washington, DC, to deliver reports deemed too sensitive for the mail. Wearing civilian clothes, he took the steamer *Daylight*, along with a contingent of Union troops and military supplies, to Hampton Roads and then up the Potomac, where the ship made it past Confederate gun emplacements without incident. At Washington, the ship was boarded by William H. Seward, the secretary of state, and President Lincoln, who told those aboard he felt compelled to personally thank each of them for their efforts. Porter delivered his messages and made his way back to Watervliet.

By October, Porter had received orders to join an expedition sailing to Hilton Head, and almost immediately he was engaged in action as the

General Horace Porter during the Civil War.
Photo by Matthew Brady; National Archives, ARC identifier 529380 / local identifier 111-B-5276, item from record group 111, records of the Office of the Chief Signal Officer, 1860–1985

Union troops shelled a Confederate-held fort (with Porter running his own small battery of artillery), then seized the ground after the rebels retreated.

In April 1862 Porter was put in charge of ordnance for an attack on Fort Pulaski at the mouth of the Savannah River, which fell after a two-day bombardment. There the fight for the Carolinas bogged down, and in July Porter was ordered to assume command of the ordnance for the armies of Virginia under General George McClellan. "This is the greatest position a young man has ever held in this country," Porter boasted in a July 24 letter to his father. "I am very much gratified, but I will have an immense amount of work."

Porter's rise, though, was soon stymied by the politics and favoritism of McClellan's top command, and after the Battle of Antietam, Porter was transferred to Cincinnati and then Murfreesboro, Tennessee, where he was named chief of ordnance for the Army of the Cumberland, commanded by General William S. Rosecrans. Rosecrans was engaged in pursuing what he presumed to be rebels fleeing southward, and he became overextended. The rebels, under General Braxton Bragg, were actually regrouping, and on September 19, 1863, they launched an unexpected counteroffensive, engaging the Union troops at Chickamauga, just over the Georgia state line from Chattanooga.

The thinly spread Union troops crumbled and began retreating northward in complete disarray. In the ghastly two-day battle, some thirty-five thousand men on both sides were killed or wounded. As the Union troops were retreating, and in their confusion at the risk of slaughter and the loss of critical artillery guns, Porter rallied some one hundred soldiers to defend a small hill. The ferocity of Porter's efforts fooled the Confederates into believing a much larger force was holding the hill, delaying their advance long enough for the other Union troops to retreat safely with their arms. By the time the retreat was complete, more than half of Porter's men had been killed or wounded; Porter himself suffered a slight hand wound from an exploding shell fragment. The coverage of the retreat had come at a high cost, but Porter's actions likely averted an exponentially higher number of deaths.

The poor progress of the war for the North led to a change in the top command. On October 17, 1863, General Ulysses S. Grant was put in charge of the Military Division of the Mississippi, which included the armies of the Ohio, Cumberland, and Tennessee. A week later, Grant was in Chattanooga, where Porter and the retreating troops had stopped to regroup. One evening Porter was summoned to the headquarters of General George H. Thomas, whom Grant had named to replace Rosecrans after the Chickamauga debacle. It had been raining for two days, and Thomas's quarters, a small one-story wooden house, had a single fireplace to ward off the chill. Porter entered and found the room filled with officers; a soaked and exhausted-looking man sat near the fire.

"He was carelessly dressed, and his uniform coat was unbuttoned and thrown back from his chest," Porter would later recall.

> He held a lighted cigar in his mouth, and sat in a stooping posture, with his head bent slightly forward. His clothes were wet, and his trousers and top-boots were splattered with mud. General Thomas approached this officer, and, turning to me and mentioning my name, said, "I want to present you to General Grant." Thereupon the officer seated in the chair, without changing his position glanced up,

extended his arm to its full length, shook hands, and said in a low voice, and speaking slowly, "How do you do?" This was my first meeting with the man with whom I was destined afterward to spend so many of the most interesting years of my life.[9]

Porter was transferred to Washington in November 1863, but Grant intervened with a written request that Porter be reassigned to his staff. In the spring of 1864, Grant took charge of all the Union troops, and by May, Porter was at his side, where the young ordnance specialist would spend the rest of the war as one of the general's top aides. Wherever Grant went, Porter went, including Appomattox Court House in Virginia on April 9, 1865, when General Robert E. Lee signed the surrender papers. For years, Porter would keep in a small wooden box the nub of a pencil he claimed Lee had used that day to make some alterations to the agreement.[10]

In the months after the war, Porter continued to travel and work with Grant, and he became particularly useful as Grant was sought as a speaker across the northern states. Grant hated speechmaking. Porter, however, discovered that not only did he like it, but he was good at it as well, and so he was often put forward to deliver speeches in Grant's stead. When President Andrew Johnson, who assumed the office with Lincoln's assassination, appointed Grant acting secretary of war, Porter served as his assistant secretary of war. When Grant ran for president, Porter was part of his circle of political intimates and followed him into the White House as one of two personal secretaries.

Conducting a war and running a governmental bureaucracy were two very different things, and the Grant administration was rife with corruption, partly a function of Grant's deep loyalty to friends and aides, which made him slow to respond to reports of malfeasance. Porter was drawn into two of the scandals through accusations by some of the participants, but no credible evidence of wrongdoing ever surfaced.

Still, the experience scarred Porter and left him ambivalent about continuing a career in Washington politics. A man with a knack for making friends and organizing public events, Porter left government work at the end of Grant's first term in 1873 for the third chapter of his life: making money. He was hired at a salary of $10,000 a year as the New York–based vice president for the Pullman Company and traveled to Europe in 1877 to try to expand the market for the luxury passenger train cars. He met with limited success. Most of his work, though, centered on New York and the East Coast train routes (he paid one ineffective visit to Chicago during the infamous 1894 Pullman strike, hoping to talk the workers into returning to their jobs). While still working for Pullman, he became involved with other rail businesses—some successful, some not—and his wealth grew.[11]

Porter maintained his position with Pullman until 1896, when the company decided to close down the New York office. By then, Porter had cemented his position among the Manhattan industrialists, capitalists, and high society. Porter had married Sophie McHarg on December 23, 1863, during his Washington, DC, assignment with the Union Army. Their first child, Horace M., was born in October, followed by Clarence in 1871, William in 1878—he died shortly afterward—and Elsie in 1879. The family was part of the Manhattan society circles, and Porter and Sophie were mentioned regularly in newspaper columns, either attending or hosting different luncheons and galas. They bought a summer place in Long Branch, New Jersey, then a popular getaway spot for wealthy Manhattanites. It also became the site of the Porter family burials, and in September 1890 son Horace M. joined his brother, William, in the family plot. Typhoid had stricken the second son just months after his wedding, and less than two years after his graduation from Princeton University. "It was after Horace's funeral," Elsie wrote, "that I noticed gray hairs over my father's temples and lines in his forehead that I had never seen before. Horace was his idol; he represented everything that a proud father could wish for in a son. . . . The day of the death marked the end of a chapter in my father's life. He seemed to age ten years."[12]

Porter returned part-time to writing after the closing of the Pullman office freed him of the time commitments that went with that job. The former general had earlier published a few articles, including one about Lincoln and Grant that appeared in *Century* magazine in October 1885, three months after Grant's death. This was followed by another piece on the end of the Civil War and the now-famous surrender scene at Appomattox Court

House. But then he laid down his pen. After he left Pullman, though, Porter returned with a series of articles that began running in the fall of 1896 in the *Century* recalling his experiences as Grant's aide.

Porter was apparently pleased with the articles: He sent a letter to the magazine setting up gift subscriptions for his wife, his daughter-in-law, his surviving son, his neighbor Cornelius Bliss, his old friend General Edward F. Winslow in Paris, and Mark Hanna's wife in Cleveland.[13] Porter then rewrote and expanded the articles into a book, published in December 1897, *Campaigning with Grant*, best read as both a loyal subordinate's close-up view of Grant in the latter stages of the war and a companion to Grant's own memoirs.

Porter also was active in the growing world of patriotic societies, serving five years as the third president of the national Sons of the American Revolution, which came together in 1889 to mark the centennial of the US Constitution. (Porter was eligible as the grandson of Andrew Porter.) He was a familiar face at gatherings of the New York chapters of the Grand Army of the Republic and the Military Order of the Loyal Legion. He also served as president of the highly influential Union Club of New York and was a member of at least seven other organizations, including the Century Association, the Down Town Association, the Grolier Club, and the University Club.[14]

Porter's oratorical skills kept him in demand as a speaker at formal dinners and Republican Party political functions. In 1892, during the party's presidential nominating convention in Minneapolis, Porter had delivered the second nominating speech backing his friend, New York editor Whitelaw Reid, as President Benjamin Harrison's running mate. (They lost.)

By the summer of 1896, Porter had become deeply involved in the looming presidential campaign. There was even some talk, which quickly went away, of Porter as a possible vice presidential candidate.[15] For Porter, the campaign was partly an effort to help an old friend, McKinley, whom Porter had first met while the two men were soldiers in the Civil War. The summer before, Porter had hosted a dinner for McKinley at his Madison Avenue home, and the guest list included some of the biggest New York City names in the Republican Party: Porter's neighbor and mutual McKinley friend Cornelius Bliss, Elihu Root, Mayor William Strong,

Chauncey Depew, Theodore Roosevelt, and Cornelius Vanderbilt among them. (Thomas Platt, the autocratic head of the New York state Republican machine, was notably not invited.)[16]

Porter also was a loyal party man and eager to see the Republicans' pro-business policies become federal government policies. Porter and Bliss, a dry goods magnate, took over the Auxiliary Committee, which was the finance arm of the Republican National Committee. Beginning in August, they used an intricate scheme of distributing "subscription" books to fellow Republicans prominent in different businesses, who in turn used them to record donations from their colleagues and competitors. This early version of "bundling" was hugely successful. Most of the money was used to create and distribute policy books and pamphlets, as well as humanizing portraits of the taciturn McKinley and his wife, Ida, who suffered from epilepsy. One of the campaign bios emphasized that her frailty emerged following the deaths of her mother and two infant daughters, an effort to counter planted rumors that she was "an English spy, a mulatto, a Catholic, a battered wife, or a lunatic." McKinley similarly was targeted by whisper campaigns that he "was a common drunkard, an agent of the pope, a swindler."[17]

But the driving campaign issues were the economy and American monetary policy.[18] In 1893 the financial system had been staggered by a series of bank failures tied to the collapse of a number of railroad companies following a massive and highly competitive buildup. It was the worst American economic depression prior to the Great Depression, and as in that later decade of hardship, there were few safety nets. When jobs dried up and farm prices plummeted, people starved. Incumbent Democratic president Grover Cleveland was on the losing end of a split within his party over protective tariffs aimed at shoring up American businesses, and for most voters, Cleveland became the face of the depression. After losing 113 seats in the House of Representatives in the 1894 midterm election, the party abandoned Cleveland for William Jennings Bryan, and the rotund president became something of a recluse, rarely leaving the White House, which he had ringed with guards.[19]

In the weeks running up to Election Day, Bryan's campaign began faltering, due in no small part to the funding disparity. The Democrats had raised only about $300,000 for Bryan's campaign, and the candidate often could be seen lugging his own suitcase through train stations. The Republicans, under Hanna's direction and with Porter's work in New York City, raised about $3.4 million. And Porter achieved that despite being outside New York's Republican political machine, controlled by Platt, who had tried to derail McKinley's campaign at the party convention so that he and other powerbrokers could handpick a presumably beholden candidate. But by the final weeks of the campaign, Platt and the internal GOP fighting had faded into irrelevance.

Hoping to drive a final spike into Bryan's campaign, Hanna ordered up a series of parades in different cities for the days before the election. Porter organized the New York City "business men's parade," or "sound money parade," on October 31 as an over-the-top signal of the support by American business for McKinley. Porter pulled strings, called in favors, and micromanaged to a surprising level. Noting that there was construction on Fifth Avenue, he beseeched city officials, from the city streets department all the way to the mayor's office, to get the projects either finished or covered over in time for the parade. "The great howl is over the construction at Fifth Avenue between 30th and 34th Streets," he wrote to Mayor William L. Strong, a single-term mayor whose biggest impact on New York and American politics was appointing Theodore Roosevelt police commissioner.

> Mrs. Hanna and her party and lots of people have engaged every room of the Waldorf, and this will prevent the procession from going past that building. I believe the contractor would be patriotic enough in such an emergency (like the cable car company and all others concerned) to move his stone and earth onto the sidewalk and board over the ditch for the 31st. Won't you please see if this cannot be accomplished, then the parade will go off without a hitch, and we can have the greatest parade that was ever known.[20]

A week later, in a separate letter, Porter sought to put words in the mayor's mouth, suggesting Strong issue this statement: "As the parade on the 31st instant will continue for some hours after night-fall, the occupants of houses along the line of the march are earnestly requested to light as brilliantly as possible the front rooms of their buildings and raise the window shades in order to assist in illuminating the streets along which the parade will pass." Porter told the mayor he could have issued the statement himself "but I think it would be more appropriate to have you take this action," using the tone of a man accustomed to having his way.[21]

The attention to detail paid off. On Halloween, some one hundred thousand people marched for McKinley and "sound money," none of them under overt political banners but as members of different industrial and trade groups. The idea was to portray the parade as an act of nonpartisan solidarity, and the impressive display drew some 750,000 spectators, far exceeding expectations and setting records. "Never before in this nation's history have so many flags been waved as were waved by the army that mustered in the streets of New-York City yesterday," reported the pro-McKinley *New York Times*. "No such political demonstration has ever been seen on the continent. The city kept holiday. Adorned with the red, white, and blue, resounding to the music of patriotic arts, echoing with the cheers of hundreds of thousands of throats, and blessed with the brightest, most genial sunshine, New-York City never before saw such a day."[22]

The credit belonged to Porter. On election night, Porter joined hundreds of fellow Republicans at the Metropolitan Life Insurance Company building on Madison Square to await the returns, which came in fits and spurts via telephone from the national headquarters in Chicago and party boiler rooms in Baltimore, Boston, Des Moines, and other cities. By eight o'clock it was clear McKinley had won enough states to take the Electoral College, and the celebrating began, capped by a dinner for two hundred on the building's tenth floor.[23]

The victory was definitive. McKinley won the general vote by 51 percent to 47 percent and the Electoral College with 271 votes to Bryan's 176 votes. McKinley took a day or two for rest but was already contemplating political appointees and developing plans for the inauguration itself, some four months away. Given the historic heft of the New York "sound money" parade on Halloween, the logical choice of an organizer for the inaugural parade was Porter, a duty the former general shouldered with equanimity. "I have not much liking for the expenditure of time I shall have to put on the preparations for the inaugural ceremonies at Washington, but Governor McKinley invited me to his house in Canton and made the request, and, of course, I had to reply," he wrote to a friend in late December. "If we have good weather, we will have a fine show."[24] Speculation also swirled about a possible role for Porter in the McKinley administration. Given Porter's Civil War record, his work in the Grant administration as a military liaison, and his history of support for fellow veterans, secretary of war was the post most often mentioned.

Porter, though, had had his fill of the hornet's nest of Washington politics during the Grant years. Porter told friends that the widely traveled and well-connected president-elect knew who the best appointees might be and would have his own ideas about who he could count on in his cabinet, a selection "so personal, being a good deal like the selection of a personal staff, that all persons naturally hesitate to make suggestions upon this subject to a president-elect."

Yet Porter didn't hesitate for long. He pushed for his friend, neighbor, and fellow Republican fundraiser Cornelius Bliss—like himself, a figure outside the Platt political machine, which was pressing for some high-level job to go to a New Yorker. "I would really rather see Cornelius Bliss there than anyone else," Porter wrote to a friend.

> He has done splendid work in the campaign, and a high position in Washington would be rather a novelty for him, and perhaps be attractive, whereas I served there as assistant secretary of war and for a short time was acting secretary of war, in charge of the department, so that I have tasted of all the sweets, if there are any in such places. Of course, any citizen would be glad to be identified with Governor McKinley's administration in a prominent capacity, but so far as a Cabinet officer from New York is concerned, I should really, as I have said, rather see Bliss there."[25]

It's unclear when Porter and McKinley first discussed a role for the former general in the new administration, but it was probably during a trip by Porter to Canton in early December to confer on the plans for the inaugural parade. "The Governor has had very full and frank talks with me about all his preparations for the future, Cabinet, etc.," Porter wrote to a friend.

> I told him at the outset that nothing could induce me to camp in Washington and undertake the African slavery of running a Department of the Government; that I was trying to get rest in these days rather than

confining work. He is all adrift as to a secretary of war, but he will no doubt be able to get a good man before the 4th of March. As you say, it is more important than ever that there should be a proper head to the Military Department of the Government, particularly if we should have more domestic insurrections or a foreign war."[26]

Porter was a bit of a Francophile. Over the years, he worked at his French, occasionally hiring a private tutor, and made a near-daily ritual of reading aloud in French. While working for Pullman, he had made at least one trip to Paris and found the city fascinating.

By mid-February, word was circulating that Porter would become McKinley's ambassador to France, speculation that Porter seemed to confirm while trying to be nonresponsive. "I have your letter and note what you say about my going to France," he replied to a friend. "This, as well as some other matters pending, will not take definite shape and be announced until after the 4th of March, and whatever announcement will be made will come from Washington. If the matter takes such shape that it can be announced earlier, I will most gladly communicate with you at once."[27]

McKinley, in fact, worked hard to incorporate his political friends into his new administration, while also trying to shore up support within the party. His pick for secretary of war was a questionable call: Russell A. Alger, a former lumber baron and governor of Michigan, who despite his Civil War experience (more than sixty battles and twice wounded) was an inept planner and leader of military forces. "Alger's appointment is unfavorably received in many quarters," Porter wrote. "I think it will probably be more popular in the West than here. Only future events can tell how successfully he will serve."[28]

McKinley also struggled to find a place for Hanna, who was not an easy man to fit in, given the reputation the Democrats had bestowed on him as a greedy string-puller. McKinley eventually appointed Ohio senator John Sherman—a nephew of General William Tecumseh Sherman—as his secretary of state, despite the aging senator's clear onset of senility. Ohio's governor then appointed Hanna to the vacated US senate seat. Bliss, as Porter had hoped and lobbied, was named secretary of the interior. And Porter, as rumored, was named the new ambassador to France.

So the cabinet and the new administration slowly came together. Before any of it could become official, though, McKinley had to be sworn in as president.

---------- ✿ ----------

McKinley and his small entourage left his home in Canton around 7 PM on March 1 aboard a private train that consisted of a baggage car, a dining car, two Pullmans, and two private cars. The McKinleys traveled in car "No. 38," a rolling piece of luxury with white oak plank walls and floor, a steel ceiling, two "palatial bedrooms" with a connecting bathroom, and, to fight off the chill, a roaring fireplace in the sitting room. The train arrived in Washington around eleven o'clock the next morning, and McKinley and his fellow travelers were ferried by carriage to the Ebbitt House hotel at the corner of F and Fourteenth Streets, where they were to spend the night before McKinley's inauguration.

The president-elect had barely settled in before he left again for a luncheon Cleveland was hosting at the White House, just a couple of blocks away. It was McKinley's first visit as president-elect to his future home and office. Porter and several other political intimates of Cleveland and McKinley, as well as their wives, gathered at the table before the presidents, current and future, split off for a quiet, private conversation. No records detail what was said, but one imagines a discussion of the pressing matters facing the country, from the moribund economy to political pressure on the United States to intervene in Cuba, where insurrectionists were trying to overthrow their Spanish colonial overlords. Neither Cleveland nor McKinley wanted to involve the United States, but Cleveland was growing increasingly certain that war was on the horizon.

The next morning, McKinley returned to the White House in a carriage accompanied by five other men, including his two official ushers, senators James S. Sherman of New York and John L. Mitchell of Wisconsin. The other three men were a detachment from the US Secret Service, a practice begun three years earlier by Cleveland, mindful that two of his predecessors, Lincoln and Garfield, had been killed on the job and that he himself had become a reviled political figure through the 1893 depression.

Two agents rode alongside the carriage while the third sat in the cab with McKinley and scanned the crowd as the carriage rattled along the streets.

At the White House, McKinley and his entourage had to wait a few minutes in the oval-shaped Blue Room as Cleveland signed some last-minute papers in a second-floor office. Around quarter after ten, Cleveland finally descended the stairs, slowed by his weight—some three hundred pounds—and a gouty foot swaddled in a cloth shoe, and hobbled into the Blue Room, using an umbrella as a cane. He greeted the man who was about to succeed him, and in a few minutes, the entourage slowly left the building, climbed into a carriage, and, in a clatter, arrived at the gate. Porter, at the cue, spurred his horse to start the procession down bunting-draped Pennsylvania Avenue to the white-domed Capitol, where members of Congress and the Supreme Court awaited. Supporters who had already

William McKinley and his second vice president, former New York governor and Spanish-American War hero Theodore Roosevelt.
Photo by Fred W. Meyer, courtesy of the Library of Congress, Prints and Photographs Division, reproduction number LC-USZ62-91482

begun gathering for the post-inaugural parade cheered and hollered and waved flags as the carriages passed, Porter prancing at the vanguard. McKinley beamed and waved, an excited display for the usually subdued politician, while Cleveland sat emotionless at his side.[29]

McKinley and Cleveland alit at the Capitol and entered the senate chamber in the north wing, McKinley moving to a chair next to his already seated wife, who was dressed in royal blue velvet accented by a single rose at her breast. They watched McKinley's running mate, Garret Hobart, take the oath as vice president. Then the chamber emptied to the East Portico, where Chief Justice Melville Fuller administered the oath of office to McKinley, their unamplified words whisked away by a brisk northwest wind. (Hanna, the kingmaker, unable to hear from his seat, left early.) Thousands thronged the yard and nearby streets, and some of the more energetic climbed leafless oaks for a better view. Turning to the crowd, the new president acknowledged their cheers, then delivered a brief speech about "prevailing business conditions entailing idleness upon willing labor and loss to useful enterprises" and called for resolution of labor strikes. He also vowed to shore up the value of the dollar and urged Congress to create a commission to revamp federal currency laws.

It was arcane stuff, but the speech got to the crux of the driving domestic issues: the health of the economy and the stability of the currency. McKinley also spoke of governmental austerity in times of economic distress and his desire to rein in federal spending, about business trusts, and about the need to end the lynching of blacks at the hands of whites, a scourge, particularly in the South. He defended the nation's spirit of free thought and speech, free public schools, and fair elections. He invoked the plight of farmers and wage earners during the depression years and underscored the need for improved control over immigration because "grave peril to the Republic would be a citizenship too ignorant to understand or too vicious to appreciate the great value and beneficence of our institutions and laws." And he spoke against those who would slip into the country—he seemed to have anarchists in mind—to oppose its free-market impulses. Citing the growing power of the US Navy, McKinley called for a strengthening of the merchant marine to improve foreign trade. Yet he also sided with international neutrality. "We want no wars of conquest; we must avoid the temptation of territorial aggression," McKinley said. "War should never be entered upon until every agency of peace has failed; peace is preferable to war in almost every contingency." McKinley didn't mention Cuba, but it was clear that was the potential imbroglio he had in mind.[30]

After a brief lunch inside the Capitol—corned beef for the new president—Cleveland and McKinley emerged back out onto the East Portico. Each wore a dark overcoat and a silk top hat, and they walked with linked arms, a show of solidarity, or perhaps a nod to Cleveland's pained gait from his gout-swelled foot. They made for an odd-looking couple. Cleveland stood nearly six feet tall and offered an over-large grandfatherly presence with a ruddy, thick-jowled face and a drooping gray-flecked mustache. McKinley was four inches shorter and fifty pounds lighter—portly in his own right but spry-looking next to the walrus-like Cleveland. McKinley was clean-shaven, his face pale and his hairline receding beneath the top hat. He had the solemn bearing of a small-town parson, except for the thick cigar from which he took the occasional deep drag, a rare public indulgence for a man who valued his high sense of morality and clean living.[31]

The two men, still under watch by the Secret Service detachment, moved to a waiting carriage. The horses stepped briskly to Pennsylvania Avenue then westward to the White House, the parade following along. Porter had come up with the idea that the new president's carriage should be escorted by the sons or grandsons of former presidents Grant, Hays, Garfield, Arthur, and Harrison. So the young men, on horseback, flanked the presidential carriage. Cheers and applause rolled out from a crowd pressed ten deep on each side along the mile-and-a-half parade route, a crowd the police had worked hard to ensure did not include pickpockets and other scammers (photos of known thieves and con men had been passed out to police officers).[32] McKinley's carriage turned in at the White House, where the new president went to his seat of honor in the viewing stand. He remained standing, though, and at a signal, the parade resumed for the official review. McKinley applauded Porter as the Civil War hero and fundraiser pranced past on his horse. Porter dismounted a few blocks beyond the White House to take his seat at the grand marshal's viewing stand, and for the next couple of hours he watched and applauded as military battalions and other parading groups marched past.

That evening, Porter and his wife, Sophie, joined the McKinleys for the inaugural ball at the ornate Pension Office building, where the menu included raw oysters on ice, lobster salad, Smithfield ham, boned turkey, game patties, and varieties of ice cream and cakes. It was a festive and boisterous gathering, a crowd full of self-congratulations but also of confidence.

There were many issues confronting McKinley and his supporters as they sought to direct the nation toward prosperity, with tariffs to protect the American businessman and workers, a gold standard to stabilize the currency, and the unbridled enthusiasm of the small town booster to make it all happen. If McKinley shared the enthusiasm, he was characteristically reserved about it. He greeted old friends and key supporters, thanked backers, and accepted congratulations and well wishes like a groom on his wedding day. For Ida, though, the promenade around the Pension Building atrium was too much, and she took ill partway through. The president, ever solicitous to his frail wife, hurriedly bade everyone a good evening, and the McKinleys left to a rousing round of applause. The party went on without them, both in the Pension Building and along the cobbled streets of the capital. By the time celebratory skyrockets lit up the night sky over the National Mall, the McKinleys were in bed at the White House.

3

McKinley, Grant, and an Ambassadorship

A FEW DAYS AFTER THE inauguration, Porter returned with his wife to their Manhattan row house, a narrow four-story building at 277 Madison Avenue, on the southeast corner of East Fortieth Street. They had little time to rest, though. Porter began spreading word among his friends and business contacts that he was looking for someone to rent the house while the family was in France, and he began scouting around for a place to live in Paris. "I would like to get up in the vicinity of the Arc," he wrote to his friend in Paris, General Winslow, seeking suggestions. "I would prefer a hotel to an apartment, but would rather have a fine commodious compartment than a hotel not so good or not so well located." Porter had some trepidations, too, about the condition of the city itself, based on reports by friends. "They tell me dreadful tales about the odors and sickness that prevail in parts of Paris, caused by the decay of wood pavements, and some have said that the only healthy part of the city is where asphalt pavements exist. Won't you turn this over in your mind when considering the best hotel in which to take up my temporary lodgings?"[1]

Yet Porter had more pressing matters to contend with. In just six weeks, he would witness—and deliver the eulogy at—the dedication of Grant's Tomb, which without his efforts would have been a much more modest monument to his old friend and former boss, the man largely credited with saving the Union three decades earlier. The new ambassador owed his position to McKinley, but he owed a much deeper debt to the earlier president who had plucked him from the ranks and carried him along to the national stage. Had it not been for Grant's patronage, Porter's life, and success, would have taken a much different cast.

Grant had died of throat cancer on the morning of July 23, 1885, just days after finishing his memoirs, which would raise more than $450,000 for his widow and a significant slice for his publisher, Charles L. Webster and Co., co-owned by Grant's friend Mark Twain. Grant had long resisted writing his memoirs, but his faith in others had recently cost him a fortune. Ferdinand Ward, a preacher's son from Rochester, New York, had perfected the technique of taking new investors' checks to make promised payoffs to earlier investors. (It would be years before another con man gave this ruse a name: a Ponzi scheme.) To make the scam work, Ward needed an aura of success and reliability. He drew in as a partner Ulysses S. Grant Jr., known as Buck, and eventually corralled the former president as well. The elder Grant invested nearly his entire fortune in what was touted as the gold-touch investment firm of Grant & Ward.

Porter saw through the scheme and visited Grant's home office in Manhattan, hoping to get his friend to question the returns he supposedly was earning on his money. He discovered Ward was with the president, and so deep was Grant's faith in Ward that Porter went away, his warning never delivered.

In 1884 the nation slid into recession, reducing the influx of new investors as a series of loans came due, and Grant & Ward collapsed in spectacular fashion. A bank closely connected with the firm, Maritime National Bank, also failed, and the scandal led to runs on other banks as well, threatening the foundations of Wall Street's investment business. Ward was quickly arrested and eventually went to prison on fraud charges. Grant was left nearly destitute, with eighty dollars to his name, and another $130 in his wife's name.

Now broke and facing death, Grant wrote an article about his war experiences for the *Century* magazine, which offered to publish the former general's memoirs. Twain intervened and persuaded Grant that he would make much more money if he let Twain's publishing house handle *The Personal Memoirs of Ulysses S. Grant*.[2]

Another friend offered Grant and his family the use of a remote summer home in the Adirondacks, on the slope of Mount McGregor a few miles north of Saratoga Springs. The solitude was perfect for the dying man to finish his memoirs without distractions. As the end of Grant's life neared, old friends made their way to his side, Porter among them, traveling by train from Manhattan. They spent most of the night talking and reminiscing with Grant. But Grant's main focus was the writing, and he finished the memoirs just a few days before the throat cancer finally claimed him.[3]

Grant had left instructions for his family to bury him in one of three locations: the United States Military Academy at West Point; Galena, Illinois, where he and his family lived in the years before the Civil War (Grant had worked in his father's tannery business there); or New York City, a place where he felt welcome after leaving the White House. West Point was quickly eliminated because cemetery rules would have barred the eventual burial of his wife next to him. New York City, in a surprise to no one, won out over Illinois, even as local officials in Washington, DC, and Saint Louis launched last-minute arguments that they should host the former president's grave.

Though the world had known Grant was ailing, his death still came as a shock. Grant's White House years were defined by scandal and corruption, yet his role in leading the Union to military victory over the Confederate Army had sealed his place in the pantheon of American heroes—or at least the heroes of the North. So Grant would receive a hero's send-off. After a funeral at the cabin, which Porter attended, the former president's body was taken to Albany, where it lay in state for three days at the Capitol Building, drawing some eighty thousand mourners. It was then moved by train to Manhattan, where it lay in state again at City Hall as a massive line of the solemn shuffled past for a last glimpse. The plan was to place the body in a temporary crypt on a bluff in Manhattan's Riverside Park overlooking the Hudson River while a larger, more appropriate monument was designed and built nearby, under direction of the Grant Monument Association.

An estimated one million people watched the five-hour, seven-mile procession from City Hall up Broadway, past Central Park, and then finally to Riverside Park. It was the largest peacetime assemblage of military forces in the country's century-long history. "Broadway moved like a river into which many tributaries flowed," the *New York Times* said. People filled windows and balconies, stoops and roofs. Some climbed trees and utility poles, dangerously so, clinging to telegraph wires, and "the statues in the squares were black with climbers." One man fell from a high perch in a tree onto some stones, broke his skull, and died.

It was well after four o'clock when Grant finally reached his temporary tomb, heralded by bugles and steady drumming and, at a signal from a sailor running along the bluff's edge with a flag, cannon salutes from a flotilla of naval ships at anchor in the Hudson River. The temporary tomb was brick-faced and semicircular in shape, like an early version of a Quonset hut or a glassblower's kiln. It backed up to a small rise that crested the bluff overlooking the Hudson. Recent torrential rains—more than eight inches in the previous week—had left the scattered trees looking fresh and the land washed clean, but enough time had passed that the ground was dry and firm.

Words were spoken—unheard by all except those closest to the tomb—and tears were shed, then Grant's body was sealed into place. A polished red-cedar box stood in front of the open vault, and the workers gently placed the coffin inside. They closed the cedar box and slipped it inside a riveted sheet-iron case, which in turn was bolted inside another thick steel case, and then locked behind a wrought-iron gate decorated with a large *G*. It was hard to imagine that someone would try to steal the body, but the planners were taking no chances. Hours later, police were still herding mourners in a fast-moving line past the monument for a glimpse through the closed iron gate. Elsewhere the streets teemed with people, the funeral having turned into a somber citywide party—a fitting tribute for a man known for his love of cigars and a good glass of whisky.

At the time of the burial, the Grant Monument Association had received $37,000 in donations for the permanent tomb. Over the next few days, the amount jumped to nearly $70,000 as New Yorkers responded with a sense of patriotism and nostalgia for its larger-than-life link to the nation's darkest hours. Then life went on; the campaign faltered. A year after Grant's death, the fund for the permanent monument was stalled at $106,000, far short of the $500,000 needed to build the granite-and-marble mausoleum being designed by John H. Duncan. (He would later also design the Soldiers and Sailors Monument in Brooklyn's Prospect Park.) Duncan had a magisterial vision. The monument base was to be ninety feet on each side, with a seventy-foot-wide stairway on the south leading to an entrance sheltered by a portico held up by a double row of six tall, grooved columns. The heart of the building would be a squared room rising more than seventy feet above the ground, topped by a cornice and a parapet that held a pyramid-shaped cupola topping out at 150 feet. Inside the main room would be arches and a paneled dome ceiling, artworks depicting Grant's life, and the tomb itself, sealed shut behind double bronze doors.

Yet it almost didn't happen. In 1891, six years after Grant died, the association decided that, with $150,000 raised, it had enough money to start work. The base, it estimated, would cost $100,000, and if the rest of the money didn't come in to complete the project, the work would stop there. The former president and war hero would be entombed, essentially, inside a massive square. It was a pragmatic solution, but the lagging donations, and the willingness to abandon the original plan, became an embarrassment both to the city and to Grant's friends. Questions were whispered about who might be to blame. A shake-up ensued as the association's top officers resigned.

Porter had been a member of the board of directors, and he became increasingly agitated about the lack of progress and the disorder within the association. He viewed Grant not only as a pivotal figure in American history but also as a personal friend. Porter took control of the Grant Monument Association in the spring of 1892. He re-energized the fundraising, pulling strings with his colleagues at the elite Union League Club, of which he would become president the next year. And he picked up some help from an unexpected quarter: a Chicago wheeler-dealer named Edward F. Cragin.

An active Republican who had opposed Grant's attempt for a third run for the presidency in 1880, Cragin wrote to Porter in February 1893 with an unconventional offer. He would travel to Manhattan at his own cost and undertake to raise the rest of the money for the monument. If he failed, the Grant Monument Association would owe him nothing. If he succeeded, the association could pay him whatever it thought his help was worth. Porter, through his railroad connections (particularly at Pullman, whose executives knew Chicago well) checked into Cragin, decided he wasn't a charlatan—he had been involved in raising money for the World's Columbian Exposition, which was then being built in south Chicago—and figured the association had nothing to lose. A few weeks later, Cragin was in New York.[4]

The fundraising schemes were simple, if labor intensive. Cragin was told not to approach the wealthy patrons who had already been tapped. Porter had recently expanded the association's board of directors to one hundred people, which also expanded the list of those with vested—and reputational—interest in seeing that the money was raised. Cragin, meanwhile, compiled a list of the city's trade associations, then persuaded their leaders to convene membership meetings at which Porter, Cragin, and others would make the case for the monument fund. Porter himself delivered more than one hundred such appeals. As they exhausted the trade associations, Cragin sold limited-edition illustrations of the monument's design, persuaded theaters to host benefits, and placed collection boxes at mass transit stations.

The stalled fund drive caught fire once again, and renewed public interest turned it into a citywide cause. By June, the association had met its goal of $500,000. It paid Cragin $4,000, and he faded into the background.[5] The construction began in earnest, using tons of white granite from a quarry near North Jay, Maine, for the exterior and imported white marble for the inside walls and floor. Still, it wasn't until April 27, 1897, five years after Porter took over and a dozen years after Grant's death and first burial, that the general's body reached its final resting place. The ordeal was, in retrospect, a harbinger.

--------- ✿ ---------

Grant Day dawned with the rawness of early spring. The thermometer was at 41 degrees, and it wouldn't rise much higher than that. Thick, high clouds scudded across the sky, whipped by winds that at the ground level snapped flags and tore at paper bunting. Decorations were shredded, and a cloth roof over the speakers' seats blew away. The wind even stripped the petals from roses woven into decorations on the monument itself. A few hardy people staked out their places for hours against the cold, waiting for the parade to pass. Some held newspapers on the windward sides of their bodies; others pressed horse blankets into service as cloaks. Bars and restaurants hummed as havens for parade watchers who decided to eat and drink in warmth until the parade neared.

President McKinley and his entourage—his family, his vice president, his cabinet, and a retinue of ambassadors—had arrived the afternoon before aboard a special Pennsylvania Railroad train. They spent the night at the opulent, seven-story Windsor Hotel at the corner of East Forty-Seventh Street and Fifth Avenue, where the president's brother, Abner, lived with his family. (The building would burn to the ground two years later, killing forty-five people and leaving forty-one people missing and presumably lost in the rubble; the Abner McKinleys escaped.)

Porter arrived at the Windsor Hotel the next day shortly after 8:30 AM, joined by Mayor Strong. They emerged a half hour later with McKinley and joined him in his open-top, barouche-style carriage for the horse-drawn ride to the monument site. Other carriages followed, and as they traveled north, led by police on horseback, they were joined near Thirty-Second Street by carriages filled with the Grant family and other dignitaries. The gathering crowds cheered as the cavalcade trotted past, and McKinley, Porter, and Strong received particularly loud shouts of support as they clattered past the five-story Union League Club (Porter was the president) at Fifth Avenue and Thirty-Ninth Street. As they neared the Nineties, where the island rises, strengthening winds whipped the top hat from McKinley's head, though he caught it before it could fly away, and the men rode the rest of the way with their heads ducked to the wind, hands ready to snatch their brims.

At the monument, McKinley gave up on the hat, and greeted former president Grover Cleveland and others already in place near the steps. It would be a long day. A nearby tent offered shelter, and the guests of honor lunched there and marked time as the parade, led by a platoon of mounted police, the Governors Island military band, and the Nez Percé chief Joseph, the last of the rebellious tribal chiefs, began the slow march northward up the spine of Manhattan. The parade began at 10:30 AM but didn't reach the monument until after 4:30 PM. The wind was unforgiving, stealing away music sheets from band members and spooking a horse, which fell, severely injuring the soldier who was riding it. Some sixty thousand marchers took part, and an estimated one million people lined the route and filled Riverside Park. The crowd was content to stand; entrepreneurs who invested in building bleachers couldn't fill the seats, despite heavy price discounts the day of the parade, and the half-empty grandstands rose like islands amid the sea of cheering people.

The dedication itself was brief. Grant's body had been moved into the tomb more than a week earlier and the temporary crypt razed, accenting the organizers' desire to hold a celebration, not a funeral. After a prayer by Bishop Newman, Grant's former pastor, McKinley spoke for a few minutes, congratulating New York on the scale and grandeur of the monument. He pointed out that while the Civil War had torn America apart, the nation had come back together. And while the men involved in that brutal convulsion were dying away, many, such as Grant, would be long remembered. "A great life never dies," McKinley said, his words whipped away by the wind as the naval flotilla bobbed at anchor in the white-capped river. "Great deeds are imperishable; great names immortal. . . . With Washington and Lincoln, Grant has an exalted place in history and the affections of the people. Today his memory is held in equal esteem by those whom he led to victory, and by those who accepted his generous terms of peace."

Then Porter spoke, delivering in essence a lengthy eulogy for his friend and former boss.

> There is a source of extreme gratification and a profound significance in the fact that there are in attendance here not only the soldiers who fought under the renowned defender of the Union cause, but the leaders of armies who fought against him, united in testifying to the esteem and respect which he commanded from friend and foe alike. This grateful duty which we discharge this day is not unmixed with

sadness, for the occasion brings vividly to mind the fatal day on which his generous heart ceased to beat, and recalls the grief which fell upon the American people with a sense of pain which was akin to the sorrow of a personal bereavement. And yet it is not an equal occasion for tears, not a time to chant requiems or display the sable draperies of public mourning. He who lies with the portals of yonder tomb is not a dead memory. He is a living reality."

When Porter finished, he formally turned over the monument to Mayor Strong, who spoke for a few minutes; the speakers retired briefly to the food tent before moving on to the parade reviewing stand, and then to a quick meal at the Claremont Restaurant. Afterward, McKinley, Porter, and other dignitaries made their way on foot to West 129th Street and then down steps to a river pier where the presidential yacht, the USS *Dolphin*, was tied up. They steamed out onto the river where they were greeted by cannon salutes from the warships and horn blasts from the working and pleasure craft. The *Dolphin* returned its own volley of a 21-gun salute and began moving south with the current as McKinley reviewed the gathered warships, which included the USS *Maine* and two Spanish warships, the *Infanta Maria Teresa* and the *Infanta Isabel*. Nine months later, the *Maine* would explode and sink in Havana harbor, ushering in the Spanish-American War, which would dominate Porter's first year as ambassador to France. The *Infanta Maria Teresa* would be heavily damaged in the Battle of Santiago de Cuba, and the *Infanta Isabel* would be the only Spanish warship engaged in the hundred-day confrontation to emerge unscathed.

After the tour, the *Dolphin* docked at a pier at West Fifty-Second Street, where McKinley and Porter boarded a carriage back to the Windsor Hotel, arriving a little before seven o'clock, for a short rest. A couple of hours later they arrived together at a gala at the Union League building, which they had passed to such cheers on their way to the monument. As the rich and powerful dined and danced late into the night, bonfires ringed by the less wealthy burned along the bluff at Riverside Park, overlooking the lighted ships twinkling out on the river.

———————— ❖ ————————

The Porters arose early on the morning of May 5 and, after a last-minute flurry of packing, rode by carriage from their Madison Avenue home to the long row of commercial wharfs along Manhattan's West Street, the wide, bricked boulevard hugging the North River, as the lower part of the Hudson was called at the time. The wharfs, which opened under large roofs to the street, were among the newest additions to New York's commercial hub, with local ferries connecting to New Jersey, less than a mile across the river, and large ocean liners linking America to the rest of the world. It was a Wednesday morning, cooled by a steady wind sweeping down from the Hudson River Valley, but with clear skies promising a nice day. The fair weather helped build the crowd, and despite the early hour the piers along West Street were swarming with workers, passengers, and well-wishers seeing friends and relatives off on trips. The Porters' carriage fought its way through crisscrossing traffic of passenger coaches, scurrying pedestrians, and teamsters hauling heavy loads of barrels, crates, and the occasional steel beam.[6]

The Porters alit in front of the American Line dock at Pier 14, at the western foot of Fulton Street. The pier, only five years old, was a massive 125 feet wide. An ornate three-story facade hid a two-story, iron-framed barn of a building extending 720 feet out over the water on thick wooden pilings driven deep in the river bottom. A huge AMERICAN LINE sign ran the length of the roof ridge, easily visible from beyond the Hoboken Ferry dock to the north and the Jersey City Ferry dock to the south. On this morning, though, it was hidden on the south side by the two-year-old steamship *St. Paul*, whose forecastle was about the same height as a six-story building, with fore and aft funnels jutting even higher. As the Porters arrived, the funnels were spewing streams of smoke into morning sky in preparation for the 10 AM departure of one of its biweekly trips to Southampton, England.

The *St. Paul* was one of eight steamships to leave New York that day; another eleven were putting into port.[7] A true luxury liner, the *St. Paul* and its nearly identical sister ship, the *St. Louis*, were the largest US-registered ships on the seas. Built in Philadelphia by William Cramp and Sons, the *St. Louis* launched in October 1894, and the *St. Paul* was pushed into the water six months later. Both were sleek-looking despite their sizes, about 550 feet long and more than 60 feet wide. It took about $3 million and four thousand men to build each ship, with double-bottomed steel hulls, bulk-heads to protect against sinking, and six wood-planked decks over steel beams.

The *St. Paul* was built to move people as much as freight and could hold nearly 1,500 passengers, 320 of them in first-class staterooms on the main deck, 200 in second-class, and 900 in steerage. The first-class salon was large enough to hold all the first-class passengers at once beneath a large, domed ceiling, meant to resemble that of a ballroom in a luxury hotel. And the sister ships were fast. Each had made the crossing between New York and Southampton in six days. It was, at the time, the best ship America had to offer, and fitting for an ambassador's trip to his overseas assignment.[8]

As departure time neared, the hustle and bustle around Pier 14 picked up. Stevedores scurried about the street-level floor to load the last of the freight, luggage, and provisions aboard while, upstairs, passengers checked in then crossed a level gangplank to the ship's main deck. It was an innovation of the relatively new pier "separating passengers from the dust and dirt that accompanied the loading of cargo and provisions."[9] Scores of well-wishers waved passengers aboard, and newspaper reporters buttonholed the best-known of the passengers for some final words to be duly noted in the papers' next editions.

The Porters had their own entourage of friends "who literally carried us on board the boat" and filled the family's deck suite with flowers.[10] The family was traveling in style: the top fare of $750 a head bought a suite with a private bath, toilet, bedroom, and sitting area. Porter's daughter Elsie was caught up in the swirl of excitement. As the privileged child of a wealthy New Yorker, she had traveled by ship to Europe before on a year-long sojourn with her mother. On that trip, she knew she would return to the United States. This was a trip without a set end. For a seventeen-year-old girl, it was to be a grand adventure and would prove to be a critical juncture in her life.

As the family moved about the ship, other passengers called out Porter's name, as did news reporters seeking a last thought from the new ambassador before they were ushered ashore. Porter was likely the best known of the ship's passengers but hardly the only famous face. John K. Gowdy, an Indiana political bigwig who helped deliver the state's electoral votes to McKinley, was aboard en route to Paris, where he would work with Porter as the consul general. The president's cousin and political confidant William McKinley Osborne was sailing for London, where he also would serve as consul general, joining fellow passenger Richard Westacott of Boston, recently appointed vice consul. Colonel William H. Williams, a Treasury Department official, was also heading for Paris as an advance force in looming talks about an international approach to "bimetallism," using both gold and silver to back up national currencies.

Nongovernment people of note were aboard too, including Manton Marble, the owner and editor of the *New York World* newspaper during and after the Civil War. President Lincoln had ordered Marble imprisoned after the pro-slavery editor published an article in spring of 1864 based on a hoax letter that claimed Lincoln wanted to draft four hundred thousand men for the Union Army. (Soldiers occupied the newspaper offices for two days at the peak of the showdown.) In the decades after the war, Marble was an active Democrat, and President Cleveland had sent him on a tour of Europe to measure support for bimetallism. Marble was all but retired now and off to England, where he would live most of the rest of his life with his daughter and her husband.[11] The *St. Paul* also was carrying Henry Dazian, whose family business was creating costumes for Manhattan stage productions. And cast members of the play *Secret Service* by William Gillette, which had just finished a critically acclaimed run at Garrick Theatre on West Thirty-Fifth Street, were settling into cabins on their way for a performance tour of England.[12]

How many of his fellow passengers Porter knew before the voyage is unclear, but he likely was well acquainted with James D. Cameron, who was off to Europe with his wife after stepping down in March as US senator from Pennsylvania. Cameron also had served as President Grant's last war secretary, when Porter was Grant's personal secretary. And while it was barely noted, William S. Cramp and his wife were aboard too. Cramp was head of engineering for his family's shipbuilding firm in Philadelphia, which had built the *St. Paul*.

One of the more intriguing figures aboard was Major General Nelson A. Miles. Like Porter, Miles was a Civil War hero. Where Porter moved into politics, Miles made a career of the military and went on to lead brutal pacification campaigns against Native Americans. Although he was not directly involved and later criticized the action, Miles's troops were responsible for the 1890 massacre of more than 150 Lakota Sioux at Wounded Knee. Miles was born in rural Westminster, Massachusetts, about fifty miles west of Boston, and like many young men he entered the military with the outbreak of the Civil War. He became not only a military leader but also a military student who longed to witness some of the great armies of Europe in battle. That winter, tensions between Greece and Turkey over a Christian uprising in Crete turned into a military scuffle in February when Turkish ships shelled a Cretan village. Confrontations with Greek troops escalated, diplomats were recalled, and on April 17, Turkey declared war. Miles saw his chance, quickly packed his bags, and, accompanied by his aide (and future general) Marion P. Maus, he left Washington, DC, on May 4 to catch the sailing of the *St. Paul* the next day. It was a bit of a gamble, given the amount of time it would take to get to the war zone. He told a reporter as the *St. Paul* prepared to sail that he "would not be surprised to find on arriving in Europe that the Greco-Turkish war is over." At the very least, he said, he could tour European capitals and get a sense of military policies.[13]

So it was a mixed group of passengers settling in as, with a flurry of horn blasts and cheers, a tugboat slowly pulled the *St. Paul* away from Pier 14 and out into the river. Porter was at the deck rail with everyone else, waving a small American flag as the gap between ship and shore slowly widened. The ship eased into the main channel and then turned under its own power and began heading south past Ellis Island, which just five years earlier had become the first landing spot for immigrants arriving in New York. A little farther along the ship passed the Statue of Liberty, fittingly on this morning, a gift from France a decade earlier. From there the ship steamed through the Narrows between Staten Island and Brooklyn and on beyond the spit of land that forms Sandy Hook, New Jersey, and then finally out onto the open ocean.

Over the next eight years, Porter would return to the United States just once. And when he finally sailed home for good, he would return with the body of an American hero.

4

---✶---

Jones: The Scourge of England

N EAR THE END OF its voyage to Europe, when it reached a spot a few
  hundred miles southwest of England, the *St. Paul* steamed across an
invisible line: the course followed more than a century earlier by a small
fleet under the command of John Paul Jones.

Jones and his ships had set forth from the Île de Groix, off the south
coast of Bretagne, France, before dawn on August 14, 1779. The Scottish-
born American naval commander was aboard the warship *Bonhomme Richard*, accompanied by six other American and French ships. It was Jones's
second foray into British waters, and his intent was to seize as many British
ships as he could in the name of the Continental Congress and bring the
violence of the American Revolution to England herself.

As a military maneuver, Jones's efforts didn't have much effect on the
war. The psychological effect, though, was considerable. Jones, in the earlier sortie, had invaded the port of Whitehaven, the first time a foreign
force had attacked a British port since 1667. His men had also raided the

mansion of the Earl of Selkirk, making off with the family silver. So the presence yet again of Jones and a fleet of mismatched warships off the British coast stirred the island with fear. While the excursions would cement Jones's reputation for skill and cunning at sea and help establish him as the father of the US Navy, to the British, Jones was a pirate, and his return to the land of his birth at the helm of an American navy ship was viewed as an act of treason.

Jones was born July 6, 1747, in a worker's cottage on the Arbigland estate near Kirkbean in southwest Scotland, overlooking the Solway Firth, which separated Scotland from England. His name then was the same as that of his father, John Paul (the son would add "Jones" later), a gardener for the Craik family. Jones was the fourth of seven children, though only five survived into adulthood.[1]

The details of his early schooling are murky, but at age twelve Jones moved across the firth to Whitehaven, the port he would later attack, to apprentice himself to merchant John Younger, who handled trade with the American colonies. Dumfries, the market town closest to where Jones was born, was also a major hub for tobacco imports, so the region had a steady and deep relationship with sea trade. Jones's oldest sibling, William, had already followed the trade route to Fredericksburg, Virginia, where he made his fortune as a tailor and local businessman.[2] Jones, though, was as much interested in the way the goods moved as in the trade itself. As a child, he watched ships ply the Solway Firth and later taught himself celestial navigation. He made his first transatlantic crossing at age thirteen aboard one of Younger's ships, but the next year Younger went bankrupt and Jones was cast out on his own. He spent the next few years moving from ship's crew to ship's crew, sailing between England and the West Indies and also several times to Africa on slavers before giving it up for more conventional trade.

In those early days of his sailing life, Jones saw the sea as a means to an end. As he picked up experience, he began to map out a future that did not involve the sea. He hoped to amass enough of a fortune to buy land, maybe near his brother in Virginia, by the time he reached thirty. Given the arc of Jones's career, though, it seems that while he might have yearned for a stable life as a landowner, he gravitated to the sea, and eventually to the salons of powerful men and beautiful women. One suspects that had Jones joined his brother and become a Virginia tobacco grower, he would have died of boredom. And it's hard to tell whether his desire to settle on a farm was a life plan or a dream he ultimately lacked the desire to fully pursue.

Regardless, Jones was adept at playing the hands he was dealt. In July 1768 Jones was in Kingston, Jamaica, and unattached to a ship. He was offered transport back to England as a passenger aboard the *John*, captained by Samuel McAdam, who was from the small port town of Kirkcudbright in the same part of Scotland in which Jones was raised. (He and McAdam likely knew each other.) En route to Liverpool, McAdam and the first mate—the only members of the crew who knew how to navigate—died of illness at sea. Jones, just twenty-one but an accomplished navigator, took command and brought the ship safely to port, earning the gratitude of the owners and two more assignments skippering the *John* to the West Indies.

Jones proved to be a remarkably precocious seaman, though his mercurial personality created troubles. In 1770 the carpenter aboard the *John* got so deeply under Jones's skin that he had the man, Mungo Maxwell, tied to the rigging and flogged. Once moored in Rockley Bay at Tobago, Maxwell went ashore and pressed charges. Jones was cleared by a judge who saw nothing criminal in Maxwell's scars. Maxwell, though, was done with Jones and the *John*. He booked passage back to England via another ship but died en route. When word of the flogging and the apparently unrelated death reached Maxwell's father in Kirkcudbright, he pressed charges. Once the *John* arrived from the West Indies, Jones was imprisoned until he could arrange bail. Still, few in Kirkcudbright gave much weight to the charges, and Jones remained free on bond with the case in limbo. Six months and a trip to Tobago later, Jones obtained copies of the judge's records and the charges in Scotland were dropped.[3]

The realities of life at sea meant that to succeed, a captain had to be tough but fair. Too lenient and he would lose control of the crew. Too strict and a captain might find himself killed or set adrift by a mutinous crew. Over his career, Jones developed a reputation not only for toughness but also for seamanship. He was often disliked by peers because of his arrogance and petulance and by some of his crews for his tempestuous and authoritarian nature. Yet sailors also admired him for his abilities at sea, and his success in trade—the crews received a cut. Still, his arrogance caused him occasional troubles.

In October 1773 Jones was captain of the *Betsy*, in port at Scarborough, Tobago, to sell a cargo of wine and other supplies, intending to reinvest the proceeds in cargo for the return trip to England. He decided to withhold his crew's wages while in port to increase the amount of goods he could buy for the return trip. Many of his crew members, though, were Tobagonians, and they wanted their wages while in their home port. One seaman in particular took umbrage, and after some harsh words, began to steal one of the ship's tenders to take himself ashore. Jones brandished a sword in hopes of intimidating the man. Instead, it drew him out, and the seaman went at his captain with a bludgeon. Jones ran him through with the sword, instantly killing the crewman. In Jones's version of the events, related in a March 1779 letter to Benjamin Franklin, he painted a questionable scene in which the crewman impaled himself on the sword as Jones held it in front of him, a story akin to a child claiming that a purloined piece of candy jumped into his pocket on its own.

Jones turned himself in to the port authorities, viewing the killing as an act of self-defense for which he would be cleared at trial. Acquaintances in port persuaded Jones that the chances of acquittal were not all that strong and that a lynch mob convened by the dead man's friends was not out of the question. That night, after entrusting most of his money and other holdings to a friend, the Scottish captain slipped across the island on horseback, boarded a different ship, and set sail with fifty pounds in his pocket and a new name: John Paul Jones.[4]

Jones disappeared for a few months, eventually surfacing in Virginia around the time that his older brother, the tailor, died. (The estate went to a sister in Scotland, rather than to his estranged wife; Jones was left nothing.) Over the next few months, Jones stayed nearby with a friend, Dr. John K. Read, and courted Dorothea Dandridge, daughter of a wealthy Virginia family. He lost that prize to plantation owner and widower Patrick Henry, soon to become governor of Virginia.

The rebellious mood in the colonies was growing, and tensions with England were increasing. In an effort to isolate the problem, the British barred trade between the colonies and the West Indies, which meant the money Jones had left in trust in Tobago was out of his reach. In April 1775 gun battles broke out between colonists and British soldiers at Concord and Lexington in Massachusetts. In October the Second Continental Congress, meeting in Philadelphia, ordered the creation of a Continental army and a Continental navy.

Jones, low on cash and seeking work, traveled to Philadelphia to offer his services. Though he later wrote that he was moved by the pursuit of liberty, not cash, the words ring a bit hollow given how little Jones had engaged with political thought and debate previously and how energetically he had pursued trade in his quest to retire from the sea by age thirty. It was a large part of his personality to play up the best parts of himself while ignoring the negatives. Failures were the fault of others; successes were his and his alone. Friends such as Benjamin Franklin warned Jones that his petulance, complaints, and transparent grasps for glory were alienating, and not helping his cause with fellow revolutionaries. Jones sought over time to rein himself in and be more magnanimous in doling out credit for victories at sea, but he usually fell short.

Whatever Jones's motives in traveling to revolutionary Philadelphia, on December 3, 1775, he won an early commission as first lieutenant aboard the *Alfred*, and his ambitions for a quiet retirement as part of the Virginia landed gentry rapidly faded.

——————— ✿ ———————

The Continental navy never quite got its sea legs. Between the creation of the navy in October 1775 and the signing of the peace treaty in Paris in 1783, the Continental navy took control of fifty-seven ships through purchase, construction, loan, or seizure. Of those, thirty-five were captured, sunk in battle (some scuttled to avoid capture), or lost at sea.[5] Some of the American captains seized British merchant and warships as prizes, but they did not affect the trajectory of the war, although French warships in 1781 helped George Washington defeat Lord Charles Cornwallis at Yorktown, the last major battle of the Revolution.

Still, the navy gave Jones the chance to shine. The plan for the American sailing force was to hassle the British fleet and interfere with British commerce at sea. Aboard the *Alfred*, Jones served under Captain Dudley Saltonstall, a man Jones intensely disliked. After a foray to the Bahamas with a small fleet of four ships under the command of Commodore John B. Hopkins (they managed to capture some munitions but let a cache of gunpowder slip away and botched an attack on the HMS *Glasgow* on the way back to port), Jones was given command of his own ship, the sloop *Providence*, on May 10, 1776.

His abilities quickly became apparent. Jones's first few trips involved ferrying George Washington's troops or escorting merchant and supply ships. On August 6, 1776, Jones received orders from the Congress's Marine Committee that effectively unleashed him on the seas to wreak whatever havoc he could on British navy and merchant ships. Jones had a crew of about seventy men, which made quarters quite crowded. It was a necessary overpacking, though: Jones needed skilled and trustworthy seamen in reserve to command whatever ships he might capture as prizes and sail them to friendly ports where the spoils would be accounted for. The *Providence* set sail on August 21, and less than a week later it had seized the British whaler *Britannia* and sent it under a prize crew to Philadelphia.

The *Providence* was sleek and nimble, and combined with Jones's shrewd sailing skills, it was able to elude British warships. Over a span of forty-nine days he captured seven ships and scuttled or burned several others, most of them British fishing or trade boats. He had trouble—as did other captains—keeping his crew, though, because the privateers who worked independently of the navy offered more money and a larger split of the spoils from captured ships. Disputes over pay and percentages raged for years—the US Congress would receive bills from descendants of the sailors well into the mid-1800s.

On October 17, 1776, Jones was given the command of the *Alfred*, the ship on which he had served as a lieutenant, and ordered to sail for Canada to rescue captured American sailors pressed into service at a British coal mine. Jones captured several ships on the way and learned from the crew of one of them that the Americans no longer needed rescuing because they had joined the British navy. To add to the failure, the British managed to recapture nearly all of the ships Jones had taken.

Jones spent the winter in Boston as the Continental Congress's Marine Committee rearranged its navy. Despite Jones's seniority—he was the fourth man commissioned—and his skills as one of the force's best and most effective captains, Jones lost out in the politics of the moment. The navy was rushing to build or refit existing ships as warships, and the work was being done at a range of ports. Jones had little history in the United States and only a few friends—political, military, or personal. As the assignments for the enlarged fleet were doled out, Jones found himself ranked eighteenth, which meant someone else would be assigned to the *Alfred* while he was returned to the smaller sloop *Providence*, his first command. Part of the problem was that the Marine Committee sought to pay political favors and so assigned captains in or near the ports where the ships were being built.

Jones took the news poorly, sending off angry letters and denunciations of some of his fellow captains to the Marine Committee and the president of the Continental Congress, as well as his own friends and his two main backers, Robert Morris and Joseph Hewes. Morris was a key figure in the financing of the Revolution and overseer of the Continental navy, and Hewes of North Carolina had a business partner with roots in Kirkcudbright. "I could heartily wish that every commission officer was to be previously examined," Jones wrote bitterly to Morris. "For, to my knowledge, there are persons who have already crept into commission without abilities or fit qualifications."[6]

Ultimately, Jones was saved the ignominy, as he saw it, of being sent back to the ship upon which he began as a captain in the Continental navy, though he never forgot the perceived slight. His friend Morris, with the support of John Hancock and others impressed with Jones's early successes, decided in February 1777 to give the Scotsman command of the *Alfred* and direct him to lead a fleet of four other ships with orders to sail south to harass the British navy in the West Indies and the Gulf of Mexico. That assignment hadn't yet begun when, after some more vacillation, it was rescinded, and Jones was given command of the new twenty-gun sloop of war *Ranger* after its previously assigned captain, John Roche, "a person of doubtful character" in the words of a Congressional resolution, was booted out of the navy for malfeasance.[7] It was the same day the Congress adopted the Stars and Stripes as its new flag, and Jones would long make note that, as biographer Morison phrased it, "the most glorious part of Paul Jones's career in the Navy began on the birthday of the Stars and Stripes."[8]

A shipyard in Portsmouth, New Hampshire, owned by John Langdon, was building the *Ranger*, and Jones traveled there in July to oversee the final construction and to begin outfitting it with supplies and a crew. It was a small town, like most of the colonial villages, and Jones became a familiar figure bargaining with merchants over supplies, discussing the ship's progress with Langdon, and, one presumes, making the rounds of the dinner tables of the city's non-Tories. Jones experienced some frictions with some of the merchants and with Langdon, caused primarily by Jones's exacting standards and his lack of diplomacy when not getting his way. That Langdon was a hard-driving and hard-headed shipbuilder didn't help. They squabbled through the summer over matters both serious—how many cannons to install and the mast configuration—and minor, such as whistles for the boatswains (Langdon thought they should just yell orders).[9]

Jones's orders were to sail the *Ranger* to France and be outfitted there with yet another ship to sail back to America. (After at first balking, so as to avoid an entanglement with the British, France was now beginning to aid the revolutionaries directly.) By November 1, the *Ranger* was ready, and Jones set sail. A month later, after a challenging crossing of the stormy North Atlantic, the ship arrived at the mouth of the Loire. Once in port, Jones discovered that the Dutch-built ship he was expecting to take over was caught up in a diplomatic row between the French and the Dutch. So Jones stayed with the *Ranger*, spending the rest of the winter refitting the ship and waiting for the weather to break. And he received orders that must have gladdened his heart: a blank check from his superiors to engage in whatever sorties he thought would best help the revolutionary cause, whether on sea or land.

In early February, Jones set sail in the *Ranger* along the French coast, acquainting himself with the waterways. He put in at Quiberon, on the south coast of Bretagne, and upon his arrival, Jones exchanged a traditional naval salute with a French ship leading a small squadron of escorts for commercial vessels preparing to leave France. Jones's *Ranger* was flying the new Stars and Stripes, and the exchange of ceremonial fire marked the first time the new flag of the fledgling United States of America was saluted by a foreign power.

On April 10, 1778, Jones finally set sail with his crew on a mission of his own design.

The *Ranger* headed straight for England.

In letters, Jones revealed deep anger at the British over two issues. First, when American sailors were captured, the British treated them not as prisoners of war but as traitors, which Jones viewed as the British intentionally failing to recognize him and his fellow seamen as fighting men. He hoped, in raiding England, to kidnap a high-profile prisoner and force an exchange that would repatriate captured American sailors. The second was the growing British practice of torching civilian ports. Jones aimed "to put an end, by one good fire in England of shipping, to all the burnings in America."[10]

Jones wasn't the first American skipper to try to poach prizes off the coast of England. The previous summer, the *Reprisal,* the *Lexington,* and the *Dolphin,* under the lead of the *Reprisal*'s captain, Lambert Wickes, took twenty-one ships among them in two forays in and near English waters. Jones intended to press further. On April 14, the *Ranger* encountered a different *Dolphin,* a merchant brigantine ferrying flaxseed from Ostend, Belgium, to Wexford, Ireland. He captured the crew, scuttled the ship, and then sailed on. Two days later, the *Ranger* came within sight of the southeast coast of Ireland and then cut north through St. George's Channel into the Irish Sea, where it encountered the 250-ton *Lord Chatham* heading for Dublin with one hundred hogshead of porter, as well as hemp and iron. Jones seized the ship, installed a prize captain and crew, and ordered it to set sail for Brest, France.

On April 18, the *Ranger,* nearing the entry to the Solway Firth—Jones was, in a sense, returning home—encountered the wherry (a small sailing vessel) *Hussar,* which carried a few light guns and tax inspectors. The British ship came alongside and tried to hail the *Ranger*; Jones's crew opened fire with muskets. The *Hussar* fell away and after some quick maneuvers managed to evade the faster *Ranger* by sailing into the shallow waters of Luce Bay, where Jones dared not follow.

Despite these encounters, the *Ranger's* mission remained unknown to most of the ships sailing the waters between England and Ireland, giving Jones the advantage of surprise. Jones took two more vessels and had his eye on the HMS *Drake*, an eighteen-gun sloop of war guarding trade in and out of Belfast, but bad weather interfered, sending Jones back across the sea to shelter the *Ranger* in a lee off the coast of Scotland. Bad weather wasn't his only concern: Jones's crew was becoming increasingly frustrated with—and was complaining about—Jones's focus on causing damage ahead of seizing prize ships. The captain's autocratic impulses were beginning to chafe on the men he most relied upon for the success of the mission—and, indeed, for survival.[11]

Still, Jones pressed on. These were familiar waters for him, and he had been nurturing a plan that he hoped would send a clear message to the British. It would be an audacious act by an audacious man.

By April 22, the bad weather had turned fair, and from the deck of the *Ranger* "the three kingdoms"—Scotland, England, and the independent Isle of Man—"were, as far as the eye could reach, covered with snow." Jones made for Whitehaven, the port city whence he first sailed at age thirteen, though light winds made for slow progress. Around midnight he left the *Ranger* with thirty-one crew members aboard two rowboats and pulled for the pier. Dawn was beginning to seep into the sky as they made landfall. Jones sent one rowboat to the north side of the harbor with orders to set afire the ships moored there. Increasingly concerned that his crew might abandon him, Jones left a trusted seaman to guard the second boat and led the remaining crew to scale the walls of a small fort, where they bound the unarmed sentinels in their guardhouse, and drove spikes into the touch holes of the cannons, rendering them useless. Jones and a crewman named Green then moved along the shore spiking all the cannons they found.

Jones was perplexed by the lack of fire to the north, where the first boat's crew should have already done its damage. When he returned to the landing spot, he found the first crew was already there. Both crews,

PAUL JONES the PIRATE.

Great Britain, and its newspapers, viewed the Scottish-born John Paul Jones as a pirate and a traitor.
Courtesy of the Library of Congress, Prints and Photographs Division, the Harris & Ewing Collection, reproduction number LC-DIG-hec-07972

it turned out, had let their "candles"—smoldering, sulphur-caked canvas torches—go out, so they had nothing with which to torch the ships.

The sky was lightening, but Jones "would by no means retract while any hopes of success remained." He sent a small party to raid nearby homes to find some embers; they returned both with fire and with rousted residents to keep them from sounding the alarm. Jones selected one ship, the *Thompson*, in the midst of "at least 150 others" that had been stranded by the receding tide, and instructed his crew to light it on fire. His men found a barrel of tar and poured it down a hatchway to feed the flames. They reignited the canvas torches and tossed them across the decks of other ships, in hopes of expanding the fire zone.

Yet Jones had an unforeseen problem: one of his crewmen, David Freeman, had snuck away and was pounding on doors, warning residents that raiders were burning the port. Some later speculated that he was a closet Loyalist who had signed on with Jones in order to get a ride back to England. Jones brandished pistols to fend off the gathering unarmed crowd, and once the fire was in full roar, he and his raiders reboarded their rowboats and oared back to the *Ranger*, which had sailed in closer to the port to meet them. Some of the Whitehaven residents ran for their cannons but found them spiked. They managed to scrounge up a few others (Jones speculated later that the guns were aboard some of the ships) and open fire on the retreating raiders, but by then the rowboats were safely out of effective range. Despite the flames and the tar, the damage to the ships in port was minimal. While Jones had lost one turncoat, the raiding party slipped away with three hostages.[12]

But Jones wasn't done. A few hours later, the *Ranger* approached a headland on the north shore of the Solway Firth, and Jones and a detachment went ashore in a raiding party to kidnap the Earl of Selkirk. The lord wasn't home, but his wife and children were. When Jones ordered his men back to the ship, the crew objected; many had signed on because of the promise of prizes. So far, Jones had seized little of value. To defuse their anger, Jones relented and let the crew enter the house, where they terrorized the earl's family but left them unharmed as they made off with 160 pounds of the family silver.

In some ways, the raid was personal. Jones and Lord Selkirk knew each other, at least in passing, and Jones would later buy back a purloined tray and return it to the Selkirk estate. He had chosen Lord Selkirk as his victim because the earl was close to the king, Jones knew the territory, and he saw it as the most efficient way of grabbing a valuable hostage with which to force the release of American sailors. In a post-raid letter to Selkirk's wife, Jones drove home the point that what was good for the British soldiers should be good for the Americans. "Some officers who were with me could not forbear expressing their discontent, observing that, in America, no delicacy was shown by the English, who took away all sorts of moveable property—setting fire not only to town, and to the houses of the rich without distinction, but not even sparing the wretched hamlets and mil[k] cows of the poor and helpless, at the approach of an inclement winter." His raiders, Jones wrote, wanted their spoils and their revenge.[13]

The *Ranger* set sail again. The damage was minor, and England's losses were light, but as word spread across the kingdom, so did fear. The *Morning Post and Daily Advertiser* reported on the raids on April 28 and gave details of the ship and crew provided to investigators by Freeman, the turncoat crew-man: "A number of expresses have been dispatched to all the capital sea-ports in the kingdom where any depredations are likely to occur; all strangers in town are, by order of the magistrate, to be secured and examined; simi-lar notices have been forwarded through the country." Many newspapers included details of the run-in with the *Hussar* and wrote of the ships being sent in pursuit of the *Ranger*, while issuing calls for better fortifications along the coast. The *Morning Chronicle* and *London Advertiser* observed that the raids and the "audacious conduct" of Jones and the men of the *Ranger* "will have this good effect: It will teach our men of war on the coast station, and our cruisers in St. George's channel, to keep a more sharp lookout."

Jones next went in search of the *Drake*, the eighteen-gun warship sta-tioned off Belfast. This time the weather was better, and after an hour of intense and close-quarters battle, the *Ranger* gained the advantage. A musket shot to the head killed the *Drake*'s captain, and another grievous wound left his second in command on the verge of death. Cannon and grape shot—an artillery version of a shotgun shell—had wounded men on both ships and shredded the sails and rigging on the *Drake*, leaving it all but dead in the water. Leaderless, the crew quit the fight and gave up the *Drake* to Jones. The *Ranger* lost three men. As the British sent more ships to the channel in search of Jones, the American captain had his crew quickly refit the *Drake* with basic rigging and sails, and sent the two ships sailing north and then west around Ireland, eluding the searching warships. They arrived in Brest on May 8, 1778.

If Jones's goal were to agitate the British navy and citizenry, then it would have been a good trip. But his goal was different, and he fell short of his three main objectives: capturing a notable hostage to force the release of imprisoned American sailors, burning villages in revenge for British atrocities in America, and amassing plunder for his crew. The lack of spoils proved to be the biggest problem. In the hours before the attack on the *Drake*, the *Ranger*'s crew huddled below deck so the *Drake* spyglasses wouldn't spot them. Talk of mutiny over the lack of loot arose, fanned by Lieutenant Thomas Simpson, and the crew's mood worsened at sea when a communi-cation failure led to mixed signals and a botched attempt to seize another ship. Simpson, in charge of the *Drake*, thought Jones had signaled him to continue on to Brest, when in fact Jones had ordered him to sail with the *Ranger* as it chased the other ship, which slipped away. When the *Ranger* and *Drake* reunited, Jones, presuming his subordinate had intentionally spurned his order, had Simpson put in chains; the crew, though, faulted Jones. It was a surly and resentful band of seamen that finally put into Brest. Jones eventually paroled Simpson so that he could sail the *Ranger* home after other unspecified plans emerged for Jones, much "to the joy and satisfaction of the whole ship's company."[14]

Other than the success against the *Drake*, Jones's trip was a mixed bag. The *Ranger* seized several ships, but they sold for less money than Jones and, more important, his crew had hoped. The port of Whitehaven had barely been scorched. And though Jones had failed to kidnap Lord Selkirk, he did manage to sweep up the crew of the *Drake*—some 133 strong—and other hostages, who were eventually part of a trade through which the British released 228 American sailors held as pirates and traitors.

The biggest success, though, was one of perception. Jones's reputation soared as one of the fledgling American navy's savviest captains.

--------------------❖--------------------

It would take ten months idling in France before another ship could be arranged for Jones, and six more months before it was outfitted and ready to sail. The ship was an East India trader named *Duc de Duras*, which Jones—with an eye toward keeping one of his patrons, Benjamin Franklin, happy—renamed *Bonhomme Richard*, after the French translation of Franklin's *Poor Richard's Almanac*. Jones also freshened his crew, sifting through the unattached sailors in port, including a number of American sailors released by their British captors during prisoner exchanges. One of them, Nathaniel Fanning, met Jones, who lied and said that the *Richard*, once she was outfitted, would sail directly to America and Fanning could get passage as a midshipman. Other officers told Fanning that Jones's true destination would be the waters off Great Britain; Fanning, lacking any other options, signed on anyway.[15]

When Jones and his fleet of seven ships left Île de Groix on August 14, 1779, they were to be an ancillary part of a broad military plan hatched by the French to invade southern England: the ill-fated Armada of 1779. With Spanish allies, they planned for a fleet with sixty-four ships of the line carrying 4,774 cannons, and scores of lighter craft arrayed against a depleted British navy, which had sent most of its ships to the colonies. The French part of the armada, which included forty thousand soldiers to serve as an invasion force, set sail in early June to rendezvous with the Spanish, who were slow in arriving. By then, smallpox and other diseases had swept through the French fleet. The ultimate goal was to land the fighting men somewhere in Plymouth as the start of an invasion, but with thousands of men dead or dying from illness, and food and water running low, the invasion was called off, and the ships limped back to their home ports.

Jones, meanwhile, had set out for his part of the plan, which was to sail around the western side of Ireland, over the top of Scotland and into the North Sea. He knew nothing of the failed invasion, and two of his ships—both privateers—quit the mission before the fleet reached its northward turn. Weather—fog, followed by a gale—separated many of the rest of the ships. Seven of his crew, all Irish seamen, slipped away in a small tender and made for shore; loyal crew members in a second tender who were sent to capture the runaways were themselves taken captive, news that quickly reached the newspapers. The *London Evening Post* reported "the country was in an uproar" and that the escaping Irish sailors warned "that Jones's intention was to scour the coast, and burn as many places as he could."

It wasn't. The *Bonhomme Richard* continued north and then east and south—taking prizes or burning merchant ships as they sailed—and by mid-September the fleet of now four ships was off Dunbar, the southern entrance to the Firth of Forth, with Edinburgh a reachable target. Jones toyed with invading the Scottish seaport to draw British forces away from the south coast, where he presumed the invasion was underway. He hatched a plan to occupy the port of Leith and demand a ransom—under the threat of burning it to the ground. He had trouble persuading the French captains in his fleet, and by the time they came around, a gale blew up that led Jones to delay acting. One of his prize ships sank during the storm, and he released another for ransom rather than see it sink too. By the time the winds died down, Jones's ships had been spotted, the alarm raised, and the element of surprise destroyed. So Jones turned his ships and headed south, collecting prizes as he went, though ships that got away continued to sound the alert. Rumors spiraled over the islands and were repeated in the newspapers that Jones had been sighted in several places—warships were still looking for him off Ireland. On the east coast of Scotland, where Jones had indeed been sighted, the fear reached near frenzy level.

Jones might have had more success if his fellow captains and their crews had shown as much fear of him. Throughout the voyage, Jones wrestled with insubordination from the other ships. Captain Pierre Landais, the French skipper of the *Alliance*, was a particular problem, refusing even to board the *Bonhomme Richard* to discuss attack plans and greeting an emissary from Jones's ship with an oath-laden denunciation of the man himself.

Still, Jones had a much better relationship with the crew of the *Bonhomme Richard* than the one he had maintained with the *Ranger*'s crew. Jones selected most of the men himself. With plenty of time in port while the ship was readied, Jones was able to train with the men, shaping them into a loyal and effective fighting force. Still autocratic and prone to angry outbursts, Jones had earned the men's loyalty "like a temperamental orchestra leader who enrages almost every musician under him, yet produces a magnificent ensemble."[16] Yet he also treated them, in anger, to the tantrums of a spoiled child. After losing the chase for one ship, Jones crowned members of his staff with his "trumpet," or megaphone. In another instance, after an argument with one of his lieutenants, Jones ordered the man to the brig and kicked at his back as the man descended below deck.[17]

With the ships once again separated after the storm, Jones made for the water off Flamborough Head, near Hull, which he had prearranged as a rendezvous point. As dawn broke on September 23, the *Bonhomme Richard*, the *Alliance* (with the unreliable Landais in charge), the *Pallas*, and the small cutter *Vengeance* were all together again, cruising off the headland looking for prize ships. Around two in the afternoon, they spotted an invigorating sight—more than forty sails from a convoy of trade ships en route from the Baltic under escort by the forty-four-gun British *Serapis*, and the twenty-gun sloop of war *Countess of Scarborough*. The captain of the *Serapis*, Richard Pearson, had been warned by a boat sent out from Hull that Jones was in the area, and as the convoy cut closer to shore the *Serapis* and the *Countess of*

Scarborough faced off against Jones and his ships. The *Serapis* was far better equipped (it had a double deck of cannons) and was more seaworthy than the *Bonhomme Richard*, which would help it survive the battle to come. But the *Serapis* would then sail away with Jones in charge.

The battle remains a classic encounter of the sailing era. Just after sunset on a moonlit night, Jones, his *Bonhomme Richard* flying a British flag, sailed to within hailing distance of the *Serapis*. The vessel's suspicious captain—he thought it was Jones but wasn't yet sure—hollered out for Jones to identify his ship. A crew member, at Jones's order, shouted back a lie, and Pearson asked again for the ship's captain to identify himself. At that, Jones ordered that the British colors be struck and replaced by the new American insignia as both captains ordered their gunners to fire. At that close range, the power of the shots was incredible, but the biggest damage to the *Bonhomme Richard* came when two of its own cannons exploded, heavily damaging the ship and killing or maiming a large number of the crew.

The captains sailed their ships in a slow-motion dance, each trying to angle his ship such that his men could fire across the other vessel's deck, with cannonballs and grape shot shredding flesh, wood, and rigging. Jones, realizing that he was outgunned and likely to lose in a battle of broadsides, quickly changed strategy. Gliding to within feet of the *Serapis*'s starboard quarter—the back right of the ship—he attempted to board her. As gunfire from the *Serapis* mowed down the men trying to cross over, Jones veered off. Pearson countered by trying to cut across the front of the *Bonhomme Richard*, where his gunners could fire blasts along the length of the deck, front to back. He miscalculated time and speed, however, and the bow of the *Bonhomme Richard* struck the *Serapis*'s stern.

The most famous words of Jones's life never came from his mouth, but they are part of the lore anyway. Pearson asked Jones if he was ready to strike his colors—to surrender. Years later, one of his crew members would say that Jones replied, "I have not yet begun to fight." According to biographer Morison, the true words were closer to "I have not yet thought of it, but I am determined to make you strike!" A memoir by the midshipman Fanning offered a different version: "Ay, ay, we'll do that when we can fight no longer, but we shall see yours come down first. For you must know, that Yankees do not haul down their colors till they are fairly beaten."[18]

Whatever his actual words, Jones was not ready to quit, even though the *Bonhomme Richard* had taken several cannon shots below the water line and was leaking badly, with many of her guns no longer working. The ships separated, and Pearson ordered several of his sails struck to reduce speed, letting the *Bonhomme Richard* come up alongside her where the British cannons blasted yet again as the American ship sailed past. Jones steered his ship to starboard—the right—as it cleared the *Serapis*, cutting across her path and getting the British bowsprit (the mast jutting forward from the front of the ship) caught up in the sails at the back of his ship. Jones kept steering to the right, using the *Serapis*'s spar as a pivot point, and came alongside so close that "the muzzles of our guns touched each other's sides," Pearson said later.[19] Jones ordered his men to tie the ship to the *Serapis*, which significantly reduced the cannon advantage the British enjoyed.

The crews battled for two hours under the near full moon. Each kept trying to board the other's ship, only to be repelled by lead and sword. The fighting was gory, the decks covered with bodies and limbs and blood as flames licked at the timbers. The Americans won the battle of the upper masts, with Fanning and others firing muskets and blunderbusses directly across at the men aloft above the deck of the *Serapis*. When the last of those British sailors fell, the Americans moved across and turned their weapons to the deck, peppering it like snipers.[20]

The *Alliance* had stayed out of the engagement (as had the *Vengeance*). In an act of treachery, its captain, Landais, now sailed around the bound ships and poured cannon fire to try to sink the *Bonhomme Richard*, hoping to claim the *Serapis* for himself. Cannon blasts did significant damage to the ship, disabled several of the *Richard*'s cannons, and killed a number of crew members. Then Landais sailed off to watch the end of the death struggle between the *Serapis* and the *Bonhomme Richard*.

The wind had died down, turning the sea to glass, and a current was carrying the two ships closer to shore. Pearson ordered an anchor dropped, hoping that if the grappling lines could be severed, the *Richard* would float free of his ship and give the *Serapis* enough space to finish her off with cannon fire. The effort failed and the ships remained tethered, a bond made faster after the Americans strapped their yardarms to those on the *Serapis*. The gunfire from above by Fanning and his men kept the British on the lower gun decks, where they continued to blast holes in the *Bonhomme Richard*'s hull—above the water line and on levels in which no American sailors remained—with eighteen-pound and twelve-pound cannons. More than a dozen fires broke out on the *Serapis* alone, from below deck to the sails and rigging, which meant sailors had to fight both fires and the enemy seamen. Pearson again ordered some of his men to cut the binds that held the two ships together, but they couldn't get past Fanning and his men in the rigging. Lashed together, Jones stood a chance; if the ships separated, and the *Serapis* could again use her cannons, the *Bonhomme Richard* would be lost.

As it was, the American ship was grievously damaged. The *Serapis* was holding together better, but around 9:30 PM one of Jones's men inched along a yardarm over the deck of the *Serapis* and began dropping grenades, one of which plummeted through an open hatch to the lower gun deck strewn with gunpowder cartridges. The grenade did its work; the blast and flash fire killed about twenty British fighters and badly burned many others.

A short time later, the *Bonhomme Richard* fell quiet. A rumor ran through the British command that the Americans had "asked for quarter" and "struck," that is, surrendered. Pearson yelled to Jones for confirmation but received no reply. Pearson ordered his crew to board the other ship, but once the sailors were on deck and exposed, Jones's men, carrying sharp pikes, emerged from hiding spots and swung away, killing several and forcing the rest to scamper back to the *Serapis*. Amid the renewed fighting, Jones's men kept firing small cannonballs at the *Serapis*'s main mast, which began to creak and crack. A short time later, his ship ablaze and his cannons useless, Pearson—believing incorrectly that the *Alliance* was also trying to sink his ship—surrendered.

Jones had won the battle, but he lost his ship and a greater portion of his men as well. Efforts to save the *Bonhomme Richard* failed, and she sank into the North Sea. Jones reported 150 of his 322 men dead or wounded; Pearson, who had about 325 men, lost 49, with another 68 wounded. More would die over the next few weeks from their wounds or infections. And while Pearson lost the naval battle and two ships (the *Pallas* had taken the *Countess of Scarborough*), the convoy he was assigned to protect escaped unscathed.

Jones and his small fleet arrived at a port on the small Dutch island of Texel on October 3, 1779, four days after the battle. The British quickly learned of his presence and blockaded the harbor; they pressed the Dutch, who were neutral in the war, to return their ships and captured crewmen and order Jones to sail from Texel and, presumably, into their waiting blockade. The French intervened, arguing that Jones's squadron consisted of French ships, and suggested that turning them over to the British would insult the French king, a not-so-veiled threat of retaliation. As the diplomats wrangled, Jones's crew worked to get the ships seaworthy; Jones himself traveled to Amsterdam, where he was feted as a hero. Landais went on to Paris, where Benjamin Franklin had already received reports from Jones and crew members of both the *Bonhomme Richard* and the *Alliance* of his treachery at sea, and Landais was eventually bounced from the navy.

Jones, though, was hailed as a hero, and as word spread of the unlikely victory of the outgunned *Bonhomme Richard* against the *Serapis*, Jones's reputation grew.

5

The Ambassador Arrives

I**T TOOK THE *ST. PAUL*** a week to reach England, and Porter, who had turned sixty just a month earlier, spent a lot of the crossing thinking about his upcoming role as the US ambassador to France. Thinking, in fact, about what the proper role of an ambassador should be.[1] It was a fairly new job in the American diplomatic corps. In the years after the Civil War, being an American emissary was little more than a patronage scheme, a place for the well connected and the adventurous to enrich themselves in the name of the US government.

In 1893, the State Department was reorganized as the United States began paying more attention to foreign relations and to its place in the world. Until then, the highest possible rank available to an American emissary was minister, which in the world of international protocol was a rung down the ladder from an ambassador, who traditionally represented royal courts. By now declaring their top diplomats ambassadors, the US government put its representatives on equal footing in foreign capitals with emissaries from the great nations of Europe and around the globe. It was as though the upstarts from the New World were inviting themselves to the adult table.

President Cleveland opened the first American embassies in England, Germany, Italy, and France, where the United States had stationed a representative ever since Benjamin Franklin arrived to persuade Louis XVI to side with the colonial rebels against France's recurring enemy, Britain. The first representative to hold the new rank of ambassador was Thomas F. Bayard, whom President Cleveland sent to London just a few weeks before he appointed James B. Eustis—the man Porter was replacing—to France. Porter understood the significance of the job he was undertaking. He would be the connection between the US government and that of France, the nation's oldest ally, as well as a link between old Europe and new America. He also saw his role as representing American industry and pursuing policies and lobbying efforts that would improve trade between US businesses and France, as well as the rest of Europe. And he had to act and live accordingly.[2]

The *St. Paul* arrived in Southampton, England, on the afternoon of May 12, 1897. Porter's wife, Sophie, and daughter, Elsie, went on to London, where they planned to spend a month touring and visiting friends while Porter settled into his office in Paris. The ambassador spent the evening at the port, then boarded a midnight steamship from Southampton to Havre, where he transferred to a train and arrived in Paris late in the morning on May 13. It's unclear whether John Gowdy, who also sailed on the *St. Paul* to assume his post as consul general, was on the same train, but he arrived in Paris around the same day.

Porter was met on the platform by a small party of fellow Americans led by Eustis, the departing ambassador, who was a Confederate war veteran and former US senator from Louisiana.[3] The welcoming party also included two other Confederate veterans: the embassy's first secretary, Henry Vignaud, another Louisianan who first went to Paris in 1862 as an aide to the Confederate minister to France, and Arthur Bailly-Blanchard, a New Orleans native who did occasional work for the embassy. A smattering of other embassy officials and Americans living or working in Paris at the time were there too, including former Union army general Edward Winslow, an old friend of Porter's who had agreed to host the new ambassador while he searched for a home of his own. And that would prove to be no easy task.

The American embassy occupied part of a five-story building at 59 Rue Galilée, a narrow cross street a few blocks southeast of where the Arc de Triomphe anchored the western end of the Champs-Élysées. The embassy was all offices, with no living quarters for the ambassador, a function of the US government's policy to not provide housing for its emissaries. And it was much too small for the staff. Weeks before Porter stepped aboard the *St. Paul* to sail to Europe, Vignaud, the embassy's first secretary, had written him about the need for more space. Porter agreed. "When I last saw the office rooms they did not appear to be in keeping with the dignity of the Embassy," Porter had replied. "I appreciate the importance of moving promptly in the matter, and I have no doubt with your intimate knowledge of all the requirements you will be able to select eligible new quarters. I should think that they ought not to be a great distance from the present location, as Americans have been accustomed to finding the Embassy in that part of the city."[4]

Vignaud eventually found larger space in a five-story building at 18 Avenue Kleber, some five hundred yards west of the existing embassy and still near the Arc de Triomphe. Porter quickly approved Vignaud's selection and made the pitch to the secretary of state, John Sherman, in Washington. "The new quarters will consist of a suite of rooms on the ground floor and a very large apartment on the second floor in a house," which he described as being on "one of the finest streets in this part of Paris." In addition, he declared that it was "by far the best quarters to be found for anything like the price of 8,000 francs per year. The present quarters were not fit for a legation and are totally inadequate for an Embassy. There is not even space for the archives and the rooms do not rise to the dignity of the 'shabby genteel.' The new location will be a matter of congratulation to all who have had to visit the present offices." Sherman wired back that he approved, though he told Porter that regulations barred leases longer than two years.[5]

Porter also decided that the US ambassador's residence needed to be grand, an emblem of wealth and success, and large enough to host receptions and other diplomatic social obligations. So his first efforts after arriving in Paris were focused less on representing the United States than on meeting with brokers, inspecting buildings, and trying to fight off the inflated prices he was quoted once it was learned the potential renter was the new American ambassador.

It took more than a month, but Porter eventually found the right spot, a mansion at 33 Rue de Villejust, a short street linking Avenue Victor Hugo and Avenue Bois de Boulogne just three blocks southwest of the Arc de Triomphe. Porter thought the space was perfect for what he wanted: big and roomy, it exuded a sense of contemporary wealth, with enough trappings of old Europe to give visitors a sense that this was the home of a serious man. Porter was leery of European prejudices against Americans, who were seen as brash, uncouth, money-hungry upstarts. Porter sought to project an image of modernity and business competence, but also of long-term stability. And he paid for it out of his own pocket, an annual rate about equal to his ambassadorial salary of $17,500—which meant the wealthy one-time railroad executive and former presidential aide was essentially working for free.

The mansion was in the heart of the upper-class sixteenth arrondissement, which was the anchor of the expatriate American colony and home to a few notable French as well. Impressionist painter Berthe Morisot and her husband, Eugène Manet, younger brother to painter Édouard Manet, had lived up the street until their deaths a few years earlier. The place "suits me to a T," Porter wrote. "The reception floor is as large as the entire second floor of Union League Club and with the garden etc. it enables me to receive any number of people."[6] The building and grounds had been owned and renovated by art dealer Frederic Spitzer, who died in 1890 after amassing one of France's premier private collections of art and medieval relics (and restoring many objects—with subsequent controversy over whether some of the items he sold were forgeries). A portion of the collection was still in the mansion and included in the rental agreement. "I raked this city with a fine-toothed comb to find a house into which I would not be ashamed to take the folks when they come to see me. . . . It is in the best quarter of the city, has no end of rooms for receptions, is filled with old tapestries, interesting old art objects, etc., so that I am very fortunate in a matter really so important in this Capital."[7]

The Porters moved into the Spitzer mansion in time to host a formal reception on the eve of the American Fourth of July celebration, relatively meaningless to the French but significant for the expatriate community in Paris. In a sense, it was a coming-out party for the new ambassador. Following the directions of the French protocol office, Porter invited top French officials as well as all the ambassadors in residence in Paris and their families. Porter, to send a message of independence, also broke with protocol and invited another two hundred expatriate American families, bringing the top businessmen into close contact not only with French officials but also with the top delegates from other countries represented in France. Some 1,500 people ultimately were invited, and they streamed into the mansion, the most notable couples pausing to be announced by "a tall, pompous man in black, with knee-breeches, a silver chain around his neck, a rod in his hand and a voice like a megaphone."[8] Porter and his wife waited on a landing of the sweeping staircase to greet each arriving guest as they passed through the large *salle d'armes* and then on up to the main ballroom on the second floor. Porter wore a deep-black suit; Sophie was in a white satin dress with silver accents, wearing "diamonds around her neck and in her hair." They made for an impressive-looking couple.

Two days later, the Porters hosted a second, less formal reception celebrating American independence, to which, via newspaper ads, they invited every American living in Paris at the time. "His house is splendid—the finest any of our representatives have ever had here, and the American colony is tickled to death," William S. Sims, the embassy's naval attaché, wrote to his mother. "General Porter saws wood [note: Sims used the expression to mean "works hard"] and doesn't bother anybody. Mrs. Porter is very nice. The daughter is a 'kid' of 17 and a right good-looking girl. None of them speak French well, unfortunately, but you needn't say I said so."[9] More than two thousand people streamed through the Porters' new residence and small grounds that day. "They all had something to eat and drink and wound up with a dance and were set ahead about ten years in their patriotism," the ambassador later bragged to Hanna.[10] The Porters had indeed arrived.

And Paris was teeming with Americans, drawn by an endless fascination with the city. The Paris Commune was of particular interest, even though it didn't last very long and the socialistic underpinning of the occupation was diametrically opposed to the predominant American procapitalism ethos. The Commune arose in the aftermath of a losing war with Prussia, when socialists and workers seized political control of Paris in the spring of 1871 and self-organized into the Paris Commune. They elected workers, professionals, radicals, and small businessmen to an eighty-one-member Commune council and began pushing a worker-centric set of reforms, including free education and the right of workers to take over closed businesses.

It was a short-lived workers' paradise. In May, the national army attacked the city. It was a rout, with more than twenty thousand Communards killed, compared with about one thousand army fatalities. The fighting was marked by atrocities on both sides, including the killing of hostages and the torching of key government buildings by the Communards. The army was by far the worst of the transgressors, however, conducting summary executions. They chased the last few remaining Communards into the Père Lachaise cemetery, where they captured 147 of the rebels, lined them up against the southeast wall, and shot them. The bodies were tossed into mass grave pits that quickly filled with other Communard bodies dragged in from all quarters of the city. A week after the battle for Paris began, the Commune was lost.[11]

By the 1890s, popular books revisiting the Commune, from children's adventure tales to historical romances, adult novels, and memoirs, had become a genre of their own, leading one unidentified literary critic to write, "We have had the Commune from the point of view of the novelist *ad nauseam.*"[12] Paris held a romantic fascination across the classes; wealthy tourists used Paris as a hub for visits to other parts of Europe, while bohemian artists sought inspiration among the living French painters and in the museums.

George Dyer, the US naval attaché to Madrid, spent several weeks in Paris with his family, including daughter Susan, renting rooms on Rue de Clichy, a few blocks northeast of the Gare Saint-Lazare train station. "It is a great house built around a court with the front doors inside, and is more like a hotel than a boarding house," the daughter wrote in her diary, an evocative view by a teenage girl of those days in Paris.[13] As her father tended to business, Susan and her mother joined the throngs of American tourists visiting museums and shops, which she found more interesting than those in New York City, but just as expensive. She spent each late afternoon, weather permitting, strolling through the city streets, picking a different area to visit with each walk. In early December, the Christmas displays filled shop windows along Rue de la Paix, just north of the Tuileries and the Louvre, where "the street is lined with jewelers' stores, as it was dark and everything was lighted up it made a brilliant display. We stopped and chose things out of every window and were just as contented as if we had them in reality." Evenings out centered on the opera and ballet performances, but also the Folies Bergère, where the young Miss Dyer "saw the best variety show of my life," though "I could have dispensed with . . . the 'ballet' (so-called). It was too suggestive and Frenchy—I looked at the ceiling most of the time. A woman all but undressed on the stage. Such a thing would not be allowed at Keith's or Proctor's in New York."[14]

Ambassador Porter took in some of the sights, but his focus was primarily on promoting American business and trade through social connections, in effect recreating his life in New York. His approach differed from the embassy's standard practice, and Porter fought something like a cultural intransigence. "He wants to work the society racket, so they say, but he is in hard luck with his staff," Sims wrote. "His first secretary and the military attaché are men who don't 'go out' at all, and you know how much use the naval attaché is in that line."[15] Porter had to go it alone. He issued and accepted an endless stream of dinner invitations and quickly got to know the French leaders, particularly President Félix Faure, with whom he struck up a fast friendship. Faure regularly invited Porter and his wife to his private box at the opera, as well as garden parties and days at the racetrack, a favorite of the diminutive president.

Porter used that friendship to impress visiting Americans, such as Chauncey Depew, president of the New York Central Railroad and future US senator from New York, who "went away the most tickled man you ever saw. I made a special request of the president to invite D[epew] to a little theatrical entertainment he was to give at the palace in honor of the Prince and Princess of Bulgaria. This was granted and I took Chauncey with me, presented him to the President, Mrs. Faure and their daughter, and a number of ministers and he 'underwent' no end of delight. I did not hear any sore-head talk from him while here."[16]

Porter regarded Faure as "a man of distinguished presence, extremely courteous in manner, possessed of real tact, unpretentious but not lacking in dignity, and understands the French people thoroughly." In reality, Faure was something of an accidental leader, having won the presidency during a fractured convention. He was elected primarily because he offended no specific interests in French political society. Porter might well have seen a bit of himself in the French president. They shared military backgrounds—Faure had been minister of the French navy—and they both had become wealthy through industry, Faure as a leather merchant and Porter in railroads. But there they split. Where Porter embraced a sense of personal conservatism—he'd wear an overcoat until it all but fell apart—Faure "was passionate and expansive" with great appetites for good food, fine clothing, and compliant women. Yet he was a moderate when it came to political affairs, which at the time in France were decidedly unsettled.[17]

The late 1890s coincided with the third decade of what would be a seven-decade run for the French Third Republic. (It would collapse under the onslaught from Nazi Germany.) Porter's arrival came as the nation was struggling with searing and divisive issues, from the role of the Roman Catholic Church in an increasingly secularized society and government to simmering class divisions that had led to the insurrection and then brutal suppression of the Paris Commune uprising just twenty-five years earlier. Violent anarchists continued to agitate for reforms and revolution, which made for a murderous time. French president Marie François Sadi Carnot was assassinated in Lyon in June 1894 by Italian anarchist Santo Caserio, part of a spree of killings and assaults by the radicals that swept through Europe. Faure himself was the target of botched assassination attempts on July 14, 1896, when a gunman opened fire but missed as Faure's carriage rolled through Bois de Boulogne, and on June 13, 1897, when a pipe bomb was detonated as his carriage rolled past a thicket, again in Bois de Boulogne en route to the Longchamp racecourse for the Grand Prix horse race. Both would-be assassins were captured and deemed insane, rather than anarchists, though the latter is what they seemed to have been.

Internationally, the European powers—including France—were near the end of the race to colonize the African continent even as they struggled to maintain a military balance in Europe itself. France had declared war on Prussia in 1870 in hopes of maintaining its dominance over Europe. Instead, it suffered a humiliating defeat and saw its power and influence fall as the German states united. By 1897 France was still struggling for power and position, and tensions among the major powers ebbed and flowed as they sought the upper hand in backwaters and byways in the heart of Africa. King Leopold of Belgium was setting a high bar for inhumane acts through his brutal exploitation of the Congo.[18]

Porter, though, focused on little of that. He was a man of business more than diplomacy; updates on French tariff legislation and a looming meeting in Paris on bimetallism dominated his communications with Sherman, his boss back in Washington. McKinley had appointed a three-member bimetallism commission to represent the United States' view that the nation would pin the value of its currency to both gold and silver if the European powers did the same. The commission arrived in Paris around the same time as Porter and waited for his credentials to be presented formally to the French before beginning its work. Porter also regularly met with Americans touring Europe. "I cannot feel lonesome as I spend half of every day receiving Americans at the Embassy; still I miss the folks at home, and wait with eagerness for American news."[19]

---------------------- ✿ ----------------------

For all the whirl of social Paris that Porter encountered, high society was in a state of deep depression in the late spring and early summer of 1897. Each spring since 1885, wives of the city's most prominent men had come together for the annual Bazar de la Charité, in which they staffed booths selling a range of fashionable products to raise money for dozens of Catholic charitable organizations working in Paris. Over time, the event had evolved into a sprawling temporary enclave of stitched-together booths and stalls under a massive roof. It was also an affirmation of the social and political power of the Catholic aristocracy, a vibrant symbol of old France even as the new France, in the form of the occasionally anticlerical Third Republic, looked ahead to the next millennium.[20]

The 1897 incarnation of the Bazar was modeled after a medieval Parisian street and built on an open lot, measuring 300 feet by 150 feet, just off Rue Jean-Goujon on the Right Bank near the Grand Palais. While open at the street, the lot was surrounded on the other three sides by adjoining walls, rising as high as fifteen feet, and multistory buildings. Into that was nestled the temporary superstructure, measuring some 240 feet along the road and about 40 feet deep. The walls were wooden tongue-and-groove panels pieced together beneath a glassed skylight that ran along the ridge of the slightly angled roof, the rest of which was covered with tar paper. A ceiling of suspended canvas hid the trusses from view within the rooms. There were two side-by-side doors in the middle of the structure at the sidewalk, and four other doors at the back, though they were hidden from the view of people inside the building. Wooden planks laid across wooden beams flat on the ground formed the floor. Each charity booth was elaborately decorated with paper and other highly flammable objects—all in all, a recipe for disaster.

And the disaster came. On the afternoon of May 4, some 1,200 members of mostly Catholic Parisian society—given the time of day, nearly all were women and children—milled through the Bazar. It was a place to be seen, so the women dressed in their finest, long frilly gowns of multiple layers, and bonnets or hats. It was spring, so many wore cloaks which they checked at a booth near the door where they entered, setting something of a mental marker for where to find an exit in a hurry. One of the displays featured a cinematograph, an early movie projector, in a closed room near the main entrance. The lamp was placed too close to a container of oil, and the heat ignited the flammable liquid. Panic broke out in the full theater as the fire, fueled by a strong breeze coursing through the loose construction, quickly consumed wood and paper and frilly decorations and chased moviegoers into the main hallway. Flames sprinted along the underside of the roof and blew out some of the skylights, creating a chimney for the conflagration—and fueling its terrifying growth. Flaming joists and tar paper rained down on the crowd of screaming women and children in their loose and flammable finery, a mass of humanity unable to find the exits.

"There is no doubt that many of the visitors practically died where they stood at the time of the outbreak, being enveloped almost immediately in the burning canvas which fell from above," British fire inspector Edwin O. Sachs wrote after reviewing the fire. "Of the others who succumbed, many were entrapped either by being cut off from the exit; by finding these blocked when they reached them, or by not knowing their exact position. Of those who escaped by the principal exits, a large number were injured by the crush at the doors."[21]

Some 130 people, the vast majority of them women and children, were killed; a high percentage of them burned to death. More than 450 others suffered injuries ranging from slight to critical, with scores deeply scarred both physically and emotionally. Many of the dead were charred beyond recognition and had to be identified by partially melted jewelry as their blackened and shrunken bodies were laid out side by side in the nearby Palais de l'Industrie, pressed into service as a makeshift morgue.

The fire broke out the day before the Porters boarded their ship for Paris. By the time they arrived, the first shock of the catastrophe had given way to angry finger-pointing—three organizers eventually would be tried for negligence in the design and operation of the bazaar—but the city was dominated primarily by deep, profound sadness. Given the intermarriage of the city's elite, few families were untouched by the tragedy, and the social fabric of the aristocracy was shredded as families were suddenly motherless and a number of new widowers also found themselves without one or more of their children.

It was into this muted Parisian high society that the Porters sought to insert themselves, focusing their social attentions at first on fellow expatriate Americans at embassy-hosted dinners. Their daughter, Elsie, was deemed too young at age seventeen to play a role, and was sent off to the Convent of the Assumption on Rue de Lübeck—just a few blocks from the Porters' rented home at the Spitzer mansion—where she hoped to improve her French language skills.

Elsie stayed at the convent in a private room separate from the dormitories that housed the other young women. She returned home at noon on Saturdays and arrived back at school by 9:30 AM on Mondays. In her diaries, Elsie said she had asked to attend the school, though once she was enrolled, she referred to the convent as "this blessed hole." Dinners were taken from benches at common tables and eaten in silence; afterward the young women passed by the mother superior in pairs for a visual inspection.

Raised a Protestant, Elsie was uncomfortable with the Catholic icons. "Christ is too holy, it seems to me, to be carved for ten cents on a cross all dripping with gore and in the most awful agonies." Yet she was equally harsh in her view of the social responsibilities of an ambassador's daughter, which meant spending Sunday with her mother visiting society ladies. "It is very nice, I suppose, being in society, especially when you have a great name and position, but as far as I can see, it consists of standing for hours at the dressmaker and invariably having your clothes tight . . . or cackling to a lot of freaks you don't care anything about."[22]

Yet Elsie would be spending more time than she anticipated fulfilling social obligations as her mother's health began to flag. The issue, never detailed publicly, was a weakened heart, and Sophie Porter found the mountain air in Switzerland better for her health than the pollution—and stress—of Paris. Over the next few years, she would be absent from her husband's side for months at a time, and her daughter would stand in.

<hr />

Porter had only been at work a few weeks when a special dispatch from the secretary of state, John Sherman, landed on his desk. Sent to both Porter and John Hay, the US ambassador to England, Sherman's message advised that Stewart Woodford, the newly appointed ambassador to Spain, would be arriving in late July. Weeks earlier, President McKinley had settled on Woodford for the delicate post after several other men turned down the appointment. Woodford's marching orders were to negotiate an end to the Cuban crisis; McKinley was becoming increasingly worried that the United States would be drawn inexorably into a military intervention.

Woodford's first step would be to stop in Paris to meet with Porter, as well as the American ambassadors to England and Germany, to discuss the growing tensions with Spain and the mood of America's European allies. There was a lot to discuss. The Spanish colonial empire had been dwindling since its peak in the 1600s, when it dominated the Americas, and it now consisted of Spanish Sahara and a few other small outposts in Africa; the Philippines and other islands in the East Indies; and Cuba. Insurrectionists had been active in both the Philippines and Cuba, but it was the latter, just ninety miles off the coast of Florida, that had seized the attention of the American public, many of whom saw parallels to the American colonies' fight for independence from Great Britain—the fight that made John Paul Jones an American icon.[23]

The trouble in Cuba had surged and ebbed numerous times during the 1800s, with native-born Cubans chafing under Spanish rule. A violent insurrection broke out in 1868, and lasted a decade before it burned itself out. In 1895 rebellion began anew when José Martí's Cuban Revolutionary Party organized military landings and uprisings in three places in Cuba. (The plans were crippled by the US government, which seized two ships planning to move weapons and revolutionaries from Fernandina Beach, Florida, to Cuba.) Martí was killed in one of the early skirmishes, but the rebels battled on with a scorched-earth policy seeking to destroy the sugar industry, believing that the resulting economic crisis would so destabilize Spanish interests that they would grant independence rather than spend the money to quell the rebellion. It was effective, at least in disrupting the sugar cash crops. Cuba produced about $65 million in sugar exports in 1895, the year the rebellion began in earnest. In 1896 the value of the sugar crop dropped to $13 million. At the same time, two insurrectionist fronts were opened up in western Cuba, which led to media accounts that overstated the strength of the revolutionary forces. That helped increase the sense of instability in Cuba and raised questions about Spain's ability to maintain control.[24]

American media accounts over the years, often embellished and romanticized, pushed political pressure for US intervention, though neither President Cleveland nor President McKinley wanted to lead the nation to war. Since its founding, the United States had largely pursued a policy of isolation. In June 1895 Cleveland had issued a statement of neutrality on Cuba that was read as a de facto recognition of the insurrection. The American public was split between those who favored American support for the revolutionaries and those who wanted to aid Spain in putting down the rebellion. But the revolutionaries found support in Congress, leading to a vote on April 6, 1896, urging Cleveland to recognize the rebellion and offer support.

Cleveland was unmoved, and he privately informed Spain that the United States would be willing to mediate negotiations with the rebels. Spain took two months to consider the offer then rejected it. McKinley, both during the campaign and once in office, wanted neither military intervention nor a pledge of US support for either side. He seemed to be wishing the problem would just go away so he could concentrate on reviving the still-moribund US economy.

In April 1896 Spanish prime minister Antonio Cánovas replaced the general in Cuba, Arsenio Martínez de Campos, with the more aggressive General Valeriano Weyler. Weyler immediately ordered all rural Cubans in areas where the insurgents were most successful to move to villages and towns, in the belief that this would undercut the rebels' access to supplies and support. Many of the forcibly displaced were collected in unsanitary camps, and the focus on civilians in what was ostensibly a military conflict drew sharp international condemnation, particularly among Americans backing Cuban independence.

President Cleveland, in his final address to Congress in December 1896, implied that the US government saw little difference between the insurgents and the government. Where Spain had once sought to preserve private property during the course of quelling the rebellion, it

> has now apparently abandoned it and is acting upon the same theory as the insurgents, namely, that the exigencies of the contest require the wholesale annihilation of property that it may not prove of use and advantage to the enemy. It is to the same end that, in pursuance of general orders, Spanish garrisons are now being withdrawn from plantations and the rural population required to concentrate itself in the towns. The sure result would seem to be that the industrial value of the island is fast diminishing and that unless there is a speedy and radical change in existing conditions it will soon disappear altogether. The spectacle of the utter ruin of an adjoining country, by nature one of the most fertile and charming on the globe, would engage the serious attention of the Government and people of the United States in any circumstances.

Cleveland seemed to be laying the ground for eventual US intervention. Americans had invested upward of $50 million in Cuban enterprises, and trade between the two countries had hovered around $100 million a year before the insurrection broke out.

Complicating the issue was the fact that many of the insurrectionists had both raised money and plotted strategy in the United States—some assuming American citizenship—before returning to the island. Stretches of the US coast were being monitored to intercept those going to join or arm the fight. Cleveland dismissed calls for the United States to side with the rebels as counter to American interests and instead suggested that granting autonomy to Cuba would both take the steam out of the rebellion and allow Spain to retain its financial and historical interests. But he also warned that American patience was not limitless:

> A time may arrive when a correct policy and care for our interests, as well as a regard for the interests of other nations and their citizens, joined by considerations of humanity and a desire to see a rich and fertile country intimately related to us saved from complete devastation, will constrain our Government to such action as will subserve the interests thus involved and at the same time promise to Cuba and its inhabitants an opportunity to enjoy the blessings of peace.

That time was coming sooner than Cleveland anticipated. And it would lead, surprisingly, to a resurgence of American interest in a long-forgotten sea warrior, John Paul Jones.

6

Of War and Heroes

IT TOOK AMBASSADOR PORTER nearly a week to respond to the letter from his boss, Secretary Sherman, but on July 13 he wrote back that he would welcome meeting with Woodford and his fellow ambassadors to England and Germany. He also reported that he had "already been taking measures to acquaint myself as to the views of influential persons in France, statesmen, financiers, etc., in reference to the Cuban question, and can soon ascertain pretty clearly the drift of opinion."[1]

French leaders were sympathetic to Spain for several reasons, including neighborliness—with a shared border, it made sense to pick disputes judiciously—and a recognition that with its own colonial possessions France had little moral authority to tell another country how it should deal with uprisings. More significant was that French investors held some $400 million in Spanish bonds and railroad investments, a significant portion of Spain's $2 billion national debt. Without the trade revenue from colonial plantations, the financiers feared those bonds could become worthless.

"I think it will be found that these considerations would not induce [France] to take any hostile steps towards us as a nation in case we should be obliged to resort to vigorous action in reference to the deplorable condition of things in Cuba," Porter advised Sherman. Many of the financiers, he said, recognized that if the rebellion in Cuba continued its course, the bonds would lose their value anyway. There also was a counteranalysis that "if Spain lets Cuba go, stops the enormous expenditure of men and money . . . and devotes her energies to developing her resources at home and her possessions in Africa, there will be a prospect for the creditors to get a better price for the securities which they hold."

Woodford arrived in Paris in late July and spent a couple of weeks consulting with Porter and others. Porter, whose military experience had been forged in the direct confrontations of the Civil War, saw in the persistence of the Cuban rebels signs that they ultimately would succeed. "If we ever get this infernal Cuban question settled we will have some peace and quiet," he wrote to his old friend and neighbor Cornelius Bliss, McKinley's secretary of the interior. "It is perfectly absurd that Spain with 200,000 regular troops cannot handle 30,000 insurgents and it is the best proof that Cuba will some day be free in spite of everything. The administration has shown great patience, which is wise."[2]

Despite his own military history, or perhaps because of it, Porter was among those who would welcome war with Spain—and maybe even with Great Britain, if it came to it. While Woodford was in Paris, Porter arranged a series of private dinners for American diplomatic figures, as well as military attachés. The Cuban crisis was never far from their minds during those gatherings, but the conversations roamed far. Woodford's naval attaché, George Leland Dyer, was bouncing around European ports to assess both military strength and happenings in those cities. Yet he was at the ambassador's elbow during most of those Paris meetings and discussions, as well as at the less formal dinners. Dyer found Porter an odd figure. Over a meal of sweetbreads, duck, and champagne on the evening of August 17, Dyer listened to Porter in all his patriotic fervor. Woodford was the focal point of the dinner, and in addition to Dyer, he was accompanied by his army attaché, Tasker H. Bliss, and the new first secretary to the embassy in Madrid, John R. MacArthur. Andrew D. White, the ambassador to England, was also at the table.[3]

Porter, Dyer later reported in a letter home to his wife, "did most of the talking and the rest of us, notably Bliss, MacArthur and I, did most of the listening. It was real good American jingo talk" by Porter, who repeatedly made himself the center of the stories he told, stories in which he inevitably "twisted the lion's tail." In one of Porter's stories, he told of a conversation with "an Englishman of note and standing" who had asked Porter why Americans hated Great Britain. Porter launched into a monologue that began with British atrocities in the Revolutionary War, some of the same acts that had so incensed John Paul Jones. "He made out an indictment which took him a half hour to repeat" and that finished with detailing British military presences "from Halifax through Bermuda, the West Indies around to Belize, just for the purpose of watching us." Porter told the group the United States should prepare itself for eventual war with Great Britain to ensure that the Americans maintained supremacy in the Western Hemisphere. The dinner dragged on until well past 10 PM, when Dyer and Bliss "left to give the high muckety-mucks a chance to talk together."

Summer in Spain, as in France, was a popular time for vacations, and there was no sense of urgency to the timing of Woodford's arrival there. He needed to learn as much as he could about the general mood of the European powers before dealing directly with Spain. War against Spain would be one thing; war against Spain and a range of powerful European military allies would be something else entirely.

A crisis within Spain itself added to Woodford's delay. Prime Minister Cánovas and his wife left Madrid in July for a vacation at the Santa Águeda spa in Mondragón. Cánovas was standing in a hallway on August 8 waiting for his wife to emerge from the baths so they could go to lunch. An Italian anarchist named Michele Angiolillo, who had been following Cánovas for a day or two, stepped into the hallway and fired three shots from a pistol, one hitting Cánovas in the chest and the other two striking him in the head. Cánovas lingered for two hours before succumbing to the wounds.[4] Angiolillo was himself executed two weeks later.

Those three pulls of an anarchist's trigger helped propel Spain and the United States to war. The killing of Cánovas, which was believed to have been in retaliation for his brutal repression of anarchists, upended the political balance in Spain as Cánovas was replaced as prime minister by liberal leader Práxedes Sagasta y Escolar, who favored limited autonomy for Cuba. In the midst of the confusion, Woodford delayed his arrival in Spain, fearing his sudden presence could give a rallying point for those in Spain who wanted to continue the current policies in Cuba. He finally moved on to Madrid in September to present his appointment papers to the queen regent, Maria Cristina.

Porter reported to Sherman that before Cánovas's assassination, Spanish diplomats had been working quietly to organize support for its position among the European powers, but with little effect. Their task became even harder after the murder of Cánovas, whom Porter described as "the only statesman Spain possessed. . . . There is never much disposition on the part of a nation to entangle itself with the affairs of a country which has neither statesmen nor money." Thus France, he said, was unlikely to respond should the United States act to "put a stop to the disastrous Cuban war" between Spanish forces and the Cuban rebels.[5]

In November Sagasta's new Spanish government issued a series of decrees granting more autonomy to Cuba and Puerto Rico, which was read by the United States as an attempt to both defuse the violence and to meet US demands that McKinley had delivered to the Spanish ambassador in Washington, Enrique Dupuy de Lôme. The president told the ambassador that he wanted Spain to withdraw General Valeriano Weyler, who was forcibly moving civilians from the countryside and small towns into cities; to take other unspecified steps to end the violence on the island; to adopt policies to relieve the suffering of the Cuban people; and to move toward some sort of home rule for Cuba, which inherently meant a lessening of Spanish control of the colony. Those communications were made quietly, through diplomatic channels. But McKinley would soon push the issue publicly.[6]

McKinley delivered his first presidential address to Congress on December 6, 1897, just weeks after the new Spanish proclamations, and he put the Cuban crisis at the top of the nation's international affairs. The insurrection, McKinley said, was a testimony to Cubans' drive to determine their own destiny, and the violence on the island was of concern to the United States. "The existing conditions cannot but fill this government and the American people with the gravest apprehension," McKinley said. "There is no desire on the part of our people to profit by the misfortunes of Spain. We have only the desire to see the Cubans prosperous and contented, enjoying that measure of self-control which is the inalienable right of man, protected in their right to reap the benefit of the exhaustless treasures of their country." McKinley condemned Spain's policy of reconcentration as "not civilized warfare. It was extermination." Still, the president rejected calls for American intervention and urged patience to see how the new Sagasta policies might change conditions in Cuba, particularly after Sagasta recalled the hated General Weyler. "It is honestly due to Spain and to our friendly relations with Spain that she [Cuba] should be given a reasonable chance to realize her expectations and to prove the asserted efficacy of the new order of things to which she stands irrevocably committed," McKinley said.

Mixed in with this message of a clear desire to remain uninvolved in Cuba, McKinley added what could be read as an ultimatum to Spain, pressing the Europeans to effect meaningful change:

> The near future will demonstrate whether the indispensable condition of a righteous peace, just alike to the Cubans and to Spain as well as equitable to all our interests so intimately involved in the welfare of Cuba, is likely to be attained. If not, the exigency of further and other action by the United States will remain to be taken. When that time comes that action will be determined in the line of indisputable right and duty. It will be faced, without misgiving or hesitancy.

Spain's move toward more autonomy for Cuba backfired; the rebels saw it as affirmation that the rebellion was working, which hardened their resolve for full freedom. At the same time, McKinley ignored a request from Spain's queen regent that the United States move against New York–based supporters of the rebellion, fearing that such action would be read as a tacit acknowledgement that the rebels were working from American soil. Yet he also renewed the American policy of courtesy visits by US warships to Cuba as a gesture of goodwill, in part to ensure the United States had a presence in case violence threatened American interests and civilians on the island. One of the US Navy's newest ships, the twenty-four-gun battleship *Maine* under Captain Charles D. Sigsbee, was dispatched from Key West and anchored in Havana harbor on January 25, 1898. Sigsbee played the role of diplomat-without-portfolio, calling on local Spanish dignitaries and accepting social invitations in the capital.

In February the subtleties of diplomacy disappeared in smoke. Cuban sympathizers got hold of a letter from Spanish ambassador Lôme, in Washington, to a friend in Havana. The letter included a rather undiplomatic passage about McKinley: "Besides the natural and inevitable coarseness with which he repeats all that the press and public opinion of Spain has said of Weyler, it shows once more what McKinley is: weak and catering to the rabble, and, besides, a low politician, who desires to leave a door open to me and to stand well with the jingoes of his party."

The letter was shared privately with US government officials, who were outraged and determined to demand Spain recall Lôme. Before they could act, William Randolph Hearst's *New York Journal* published a translation of the letter, leading to a surge of anti-Spanish public opinion. In Madrid, a special guard was added to the house where Ambassador Woodford was staying.

Six days later, a massive explosion ripped through the *Maine* as it lay at anchor off Havana, killing 266 men out of 354 aboard and within minutes sending the ship to the bottom of the harbor. Sigsbee suspected a mine; other naval officials thought it might have been caused by the *Maine*'s own magazine of explosives. The American public, spurred by sensationalized reports in the newspapers of Hearst and Joseph Pulitzer, believed the ship had been attacked by Spanish forces. The demands for war reached a fever pitch, and the passions stretched all the way to Paris.

Horace Porter didn't leave diaries or a deep trail of intimate letters, but his daughter, Elsie, kept her own record of those days in Paris, a diary full of youthful innocence as it details the mood of the capital and of her father. Shock and suspicion dominated. "It seems a dreadful thing, not only the uselessness of wasting [so] many lives, but also that it should have occurred in the port held by Spain, who at present is quite hostile," she wrote on February 21. A boiler explosion seemed unlikely, as did sabotage, and "it is very unlikely the Spaniards would dare do such a thing as blow up a United States vessel. But somehow in my mind I am afraid of foul play."[7]

Many Americans, both in the United States and in Paris, similarly suspected the Spanish, and as the diplomatic corps—including Spanish ambassador Fernando Leon y Castillo—delivered notes of condolence, tensions in Paris ratcheted up. Porter encountered a Spaniard at a reception who warned that "Spain won't stand it" if America blamed the explosion on them. Porter demurred, saying that Spain and the United States remained on good terms. "We have 300,000 men in our prisons who would be glad to be let out to fight America," the man said. "They would just go over and take New York in a twinkling and pillage and plunder it." Stepping around the arguments of logistics—how would Spain move that many men unimpeded?—and the unlikelihood that prisoners would be so willing to fight for the regime that had imprisoned them, Porter told the man that the New York police would be sufficient to keep the city safe.

As the public furor over the *Maine* grew, Elsie noted in her diary that her father feared the Spanish were behind it and that war was possible. "Things look worse and worse," she wrote. "Nothing has been decided [on the cause] but a great deal points to treachery." Much of the pointing was being done by pro-war elected officials and in the yellow papers of Hearst and Pulitzer. For two years Hearst's *Journal* and Pulitzer's *World* had been publishing sensationalized stories of the rebellion in Cuba, and in the aftermath of the tragedy in Havana, they competed to see who could publish the most inflammatory stories. The *Journal*'s first-day headline read DESTRUCTION OF THE WAR SHIP MAINE WAS THE WORK OF AN ENEMY. The *World* had *MAINE* EXPLOSION CAUSED BY BOMB OR TORPEDO? McKinley sought to dampen the outrage while naval officials sorted out what had happened, but there was no controlling the yellow press—or public sentiment.[8]

In the midst of the march to war, Elsie Porter underwent her own personal transition. With her mother sick more often than not and regularly gone to the Swiss Alps for recovery, Elsie left the convent and ended her studies. "I am not sorry," she wrote in her diary. "I am much happier than stuffing my head till it aches and being with girls I care very little about. I learned to jabber French at the convent, to find out I wasn't any worse than most people."

For the daughter of a diplomat, Elsie was, as her father told her, "something of a snob," and her derision toward French women, and toward

Catholics, is jarring, even if they are the private words of a teenager. She wrote that the young French women studying at the convent were uninterested in education and sought primarily to marry well. "If they were brought up on wholesome ideas, good books, a free out-of-door life, wouldn't there be nobler, better women in France? . . . When will they learn that the greatest education lies in observation of everything around you, the study of people, traveling and reading, and above all cleanliness and open air."[9]

With the convent behind her, Elsie became her father's diplomatic companion, joining him on visits to other embassies, for dinners in the family residence, and at formal dinners given across Paris. She listened to the war talk. She had young male friends who were either in the military or likely to sign up should war come, which she—and many others—began to see as inevitable. And Elsie feared that if it did break out, she would miss it. "I know war is a very dreadful thing but I should be tremendously put out if war recurred in America and I wasn't there to see 'the wheels go round,'" she wrote. "And besides, it makes me mad to hear Mother say, 'Oh, my dear child, you don't know what war is. If you only knew how frightful the slaughter was at Chickamauga.'" Elsie wrote that she understood how bloody war was, yet still ached to touch it, writing with a jingoistic and romanticized fervor. "I like my own glorious country . . . and a war rouses patriotism, and just a short one, of course, [would be] very exciting, very emotional, very sad, and very glorious."[10]

———————— ✿ ————————

A US Navy court of inquiry determined in late March that the battleship *Maine* had been blown up by a Spanish mine, a determination that history has cast in doubt, but one that set the stage for war. With the yellow press clamoring for a military intervention in Cuba, Congress urging recognition of the rebel forces, and American business leaders shifting from isolationism to recognizing the market gains to be had from annexing Cuba and the Philippines, President McKinley found himself swept up in a surge of pro-war sentiment.

The navy had already been exploring different scenarios for war, plans that included fighting in Cuba and the Philippines. Strategists like Alfred

T. Mahan, whose 1890 book *Influence of Sea Power upon History, 1660–1783* undergirded the argument for a robust US Navy to expand American political and economic power, and such political leaders as Henry Cabot Lodge, a powerful Republican senator from Massachusetts, were urging the United States to seize a larger role on the international stage. Behind the scenes, Theodore Roosevelt, an assistant secretary in the Department of the Navy, agitated for more focused preparations, including bolstering the American fleet.[11]

Negotiations and gamesmanship continued as McKinley demanded that Spain withdraw from Cuba, though the president simultaneously refused to recognize the rebel forces. He prepared a message to Congress seeking permission to intervene in Cuba, which Congress approved on April 19, 1898. The message called for Cuban independence and the immediate withdrawal of Spanish forces, with American military intervention as the final step. Spain responded by withdrawing its ambassador to the United States and, on April 23, declaring war. McKinley quickly ordered naval ships to blockade Cuba and, as the nation geared for battle, accepted the resignation of Secretary Sherman—two weeks shy of his seventy-fifth birthday—and replaced him with fellow Ohioan William R. Day, who had been brought into the administration to handle the Spanish-Cuban crisis.

The focus of most Americans was on Cuba, but in February—ten days after the sinking of the *Maine*—Roosevelt had sent a telegram ordering Commodore George Dewey, stationed in Nagasaki, to sail for Hong Kong to be in closer proximity to the Spanish-held Philippines in the event war broke out. The idea, developed in a War College scenario the previous year, was that a US naval attack on the Philippines would force Spain to spread its naval forces more thinly, giving the United States an advantage in Cuba. Dewey, though, had already set sail, deciding on his own that Hong Kong, seven hundred miles from Manila, was a better anchorage than Nagasaki, some 1,400 miles away.

Dewey was new on the job: he had taken command of the Asiatic Squadron, as it was known, in January. Calling it a "squadron" was a bit grandiose: Dewey's command consisted of his flagship, the *Olympia*, under Captain Charles V. Gridley; a small cruiser, the *Boston*; the gunboat *Petrel*; the *Concord*, a supply ship; and the *Monocacy*, a rather worthless paddle steamer. In Hong Kong, Dewey bought two more supply ships, and after Roosevelt's order, the squadron was buttressed by three other ships, though its ammunition supply was about 60 percent of its capacity.

Dewey agreed with the War College assessment that the best place to attack the Spanish forces would be at Manila Bay, despite heavy land fortifications that could make entering the bay treacherous. Even blockading Manila—there was one entrance to the harbor—would effectively isolate the Philippines. Dewey was already rolling around different approaches when the British administrator for Hong King notified him on April 23 that since war had broken out between the United States and Spain, the US naval squadron would have to leave British waters at Hong Kong.

Dewey sailed the fleet the next day to Mirs Bay, a Chinese anchorage just northeast of Hong Kong, and awaited orders. They were quick in coming; McKinley made the decision that day to attack, and Dewey set sail two days later after receiving intelligence that the Spanish ships were planning to defend the Philippines at Subic Bay, near Manila.

As thin as Dewey's squadron was, the Spanish fleet was even weaker, and while Dewey had few details about the strength of the enemy, the Spanish commander knew all too well his forces would not be able to mount a very vigorous defense. Admiral Patricio Montojo y Pasarón, like Dewey, had been contemplating a fight for Manila and was uncertain about how to defend the city. He dismissed an open sea engagement as suicidal given the superior American guns. He didn't have enough mines and ammunition to defend the bay at its opening to the sea and was distressed to learn that land-based battlements at Subic Bay, north of Manila Bay, had not been upgraded to war readiness. Defending Manila itself would invite a disastrous shelling of civilians. Montojo ultimately decided to position his fleet off Cavite in Manila Bay, nearer the straits to the ocean and where his ships could receive some artillery protection from a land battery.

Dewey's squadron arrived at Subic Bay on April 30 and found it empty of Spanish ships. Dewey presumed that meant Montojo had retreated to Manila Bay. Islands and shoals narrowed the navigable entrance to the bay to a width of about three miles, a passage that should have been easily defended. Dewey worried that Spanish cannons on the bluffs could reach his ships as they passed into the bay, and he gambled that a night attack would give him the best chance of success. So around midnight on April 30, with lights darkened, his ships began moving through the straits, cruising at full speed and hoping the gunners' aim would be bad in the dark. Dewey was surprised to draw only a smattering of ineffective fire; the guns, it turned out, were lightly manned because the Spaniards didn't think Dewey would hazard a nighttime attack. And what Dewey also didn't know was that Montojo and his chain of command were viewing the coming battle with a sense of doom, assuming they didn't stand a chance of victory. In fact, one of the factors in Montojo's decision—defending Manila not in open water but from such close proximity to the city and the shore—was to enable his crews to swim to safety when their ships were sunk.

About quarter after five on the morning of May 1, Montojo's ships and the land batteries near Manila opened fire at the approaching squadron, but most of the shells fell harmlessly into the sea. Dewey arrayed his ships in a straight line at intervals of up to four hundred yards, making them even more difficult to hit. When the *Olympia* reached within five thousand yards of the Spanish fleet, Dewey issued his famous order to the ship's captain, "You may fire when you are ready, Gridley."

And fire they did. The squadron made five passes by the Spanish fleet, using guns from starboard and then port side in alternating patterns as they cruised in an elliptical path past the immobile Spanish ships. The Americans' marksmanship was weak but good enough, and shells blistered the Spanish ships, whose gunners were even less effective than the Americans. After several passes, Montojo sallied forth on his flagship, the *Reina Cristina*, to engage the *Olympia*, hoping to change the course of the fight. But the *Reina Cristina* was much slower than the *Olympia*, and by moving to engage the Americans, Montojo exposed his flagship to the waiting guns of the American squadron. After suffering crushing damage, Montojo ordered the *Reina Cristina* back to the fleet—it would sink a short time later—and moved his flag and command to the *Isla de Cuba*. Little good it did.

Dewey halted the action for a short time and had breakfast while he awaited an accounting of his remaining ammunition, concerned that his gunners had done little damage to the Spanish ships while draining his supply of ordnance. As reports came in, though, Dewey learned that he had more ammunition than he thought and that the Spanish ships had indeed been heavily damaged. As Montojo took advantage of the lull to maneuver the remainder of the Spanish fleet closer to shore, Dewey sent word to Don Basilio Augustin, the Spanish governor general in Manila: if the shore batteries did not cease firing, he would shell the city. The batteries went silent, and Dewey's squadron moved in for the final battle against Montojo. It began about 11:15 AM; an hour later, the white flag went up over Cavite.

The tally was remarkable. Three of Montojo's ships sank during the battle; Dewey's men burned six others to ensure they couldn't be brought back into action. Montojo lost 161 men, mostly from his *Reina Cristina*, and another 210 were wounded. Dewey, remarkably, lost no ships and no men, with only a handful of men wounded. Spanish forces still held the island and Manila itself, but Dewey's victory sealed them off; American ground forces arrived by August, just as the war was winding down, and the Americans took military control of the islands.

Before the battle of Manila Bay, the Philippines were a minor part of the American consciousness. When people thought of Spain and the possibility of war, the focus turned to Cuba. And few Americans had ever heard of Dewey, who before taking command of the Asiatic fleet had been president of the navy's little-known Board of Inspection and Survey. Yet within days, Manila Bay was part of everyday conversation, as was Dewey, who was feted as a hero in an orgy of nationalistic pride. He was immediately vaulted into the upper echelon of the nation's military and, more directly, naval heroes, despite the reality that Dewey's victory had as much to do with the weakness of the Spanish defenses as it did with Dewey's military seamanship.

"Commodore Dewey's victory is one of the greatest naval triumphs of modern times and will rank in history with the achievements of John Paul Jones, Nelson, Perry, Farragut, and other heroes," President McKinley told a visiting congressman on May 2. "It's true that our ships were superior to those of Spain, but it must be remembered that Commodore Dewey engaged not only the opposing fleet, but the Spanish forts. The battle was a hard-fought one, and the fact that Commodore Dewey was able to win it shows that he's a hero." McKinley also said he planned to promote Dewey from commodore to rear admiral.[12]

Not to be outdone, members of Congress fell over each other to heap praise on Dewey and the US Navy. "It was a glorious victory," said

Representative James R. Mann of Chicago. "The American officers and men are the best in the world. Commodore Dewey can have anything he asks for at our hands, and if we should be so unfortunate as to lose a man of his caliber in battle, the same consideration will be shown to his widow." Another congressman, Charles B. Landis of Indiana, was similarly taken with Dewey's feat. "Commodore Dewey's victory adds another bright page to our naval history, which is resplendent with heroic deeds," Landis said.

> The American people do not now appreciate the magnitude of this victory and the splendid courage and daring of Dewey and those who were with him. Way off from his base of supplies in the Asiatic sea he and his brave companions deliberately and fearlessly grappled with a fleet practically equal to their own, and, nestling under the guns of a strong fortress, ran the risk of floating and submarine mines, and in a few hours wiped the enemy from the sea. To the names of Jones, Decatur and Farragut must be added that of Dewey. God bless him—he is a dandy.[13]

Jones, of course, was the naval hero of the Revolutionary War. Stephen Decatur won his spot in naval history with battles against the French during the French and Indian War and against the pirates of the Barbary Coast in 1804. Decatur sailed again for the United States during the War of 1812, ending up as a prisoner when his ship was heavily damaged by British warships. After the war, Decatur went to Washington as a naval commissioner, but died young, at age forty-one, from a wound suffered in a pistol duel with former Commodore James Barron, who had accused Decatur of damaging his reputation and career. Decatur's body was interred near Washington but was reburied in 1844 near his parents' graves in the St. Peter's Church cemetery in Philadelphia, beneath a tall Corinthian column topped by a stone eagle with wings spread.

David Farragut, the last of the trio of naval heroes invoked by Congressman Landis and other Dewey admirers, won his fame in the Civil War, where his exploits at the Battle of Mobile Bay ("Damn the torpedoes. Full speed ahead!") and in seizing the city of New Orleans led to his appointment as the US Navy's first admiral. Unlike Jones and Decatur, Farragut lived to a relatively ripe old age of sixty-nine before dying in 1879 in Portsmouth, New Hampshire. He was buried in Woodlawn Cemetery in the Bronx, the family plot marked by a tall marble replica of a mast adorned with a carved stone flag; belaying pins, ship cable, sextant, and other sailing tools; bas reliefs of two forts (probably Forts Jackson and St. Philip, which Farragut took during the Battle of New Orleans); and several shields. The monument, erected by Farragut's family, was carved by Casoni and Isola, among the best-known nineteenth-century stone artists in New York.[14]

It was august company into which Dewey was propelled. But he also found fame among everyday Americans as Deweymania grew amid the jingoistic fervor of war. Street vendors ordered up buttons bearing Dewey's face, and cities renamed streets for the war hero even as the fighting raged on in Cuba. Enterprising restaurateurs changed Spanish omelets to "scrambled eggs à la Dewey," and in Chicago, a theater troupe hastily put together a revival of the play *Paul Jones*, then tacked on a reenactment of the Battle of Manila Bay as an added feature.

Newspapers filled their front pages and features sections with stories about Dewey, and as the details of the Battle of Manila Bay were explored, so too did the newspapers revisit the past successes of Farragut, Decatur, and Jones. As the nation's first American naval hero, Jones received an inordinate amount of the attention. Newspapers and magazines retold the dramatic story of Jones's "David versus Goliath" battle against the *Serapis*; others ran short biographies of the diminutive, long-dead Scotsman.

The comparisons of Dewey with Jones echoed long after the end of the war itself, and with the comparisons came questions about monuments to heroes. Decatur's body was in Philadelphia. Farragut was buried in New York. But where was Jones's body? Tucked away in a forgotten grave somewhere in Paris? Mixed in with the countless skeletons in the famous Catacombs below the city itself? Spirited away to Scotland?

Exactly where were Jones's bones?

7

Jones: The Fall

JOHN PAUL JONES AND his crew spent the rest of the fall and early winter of 1779 holed up in the Texel harbor, working to refit their ships while a British naval squadron waited offshore for the Americans to put back to sea. The Dutch were neutral in the war between the colonies and Britain, so the British did not pursue Jones into the port itself. They made regular demands for the Dutch to turn over the *Serapis* and the *Scarborough*— demands the Dutch resisted.

While the diplomatic drama played out, Jones's crewmen fumed at being stranded without money in a port town that offered little in the way of diversions. It made for a long and boring stay, one in which small frictions could quickly escalate into confrontations and fights. And Jones himself bristled at being in command of a small fleet but not of his own fate.

In early November, the British changed diplomatic tactics and began demanding that the Dutch expel Jones. Of course, sending Jones out to sea would mean directing him into the guns of the waiting British warships.

The French stepped in, arguing that Jones had set sail from Lorient, on the south coast of Bretagne, and was under French protection and thus not to be touched for fear of insulting Louis XVI. The Dutch seemed to fear the British more than the French and began wavering. As winter settled in, they ordered Jones to leave. The French ordered him to stay. Significantly, Jones had no orders from Franklin in Paris or from the Continental Congress.

Jones, for his part, kept crews working on getting the ships seaworthy after the intense battle off Flamborough Head. He was losing patience with the French as protectors, particularly after they asked him to accept a letter designating him a French privateer, a maneuver he found insulting. He saw himself as a captain in the US Navy and not some pirate or floating opportunist. Jones had no intention of hiding behind a French letter, turning himself over to the British, or making a suicidal run against the blockade. He could be a patient man, and sometimes the weather rewarded those who waited.

Jones's hand was played for him in mid-November when the French told him they were taking control of all the ships except the *Alliance*, part of a maneuver rooted in diplomacy. The French were trying to forestall a rift between the Dutch and British, which occurred a short time later anyway, leading to war. For the moment, though, the French preferred that the Dutch remain neutral, as that made it easier to move and trade goods. Jones obeyed the order, transferring his flag and crew from the *Serapis* to the *Alliance*, and continued refitting the ship, which Landais—called to Paris by Franklin over his actions during the battle with the *Serapis*—had left a mess, including a rat infestation of seemingly biblical proportions.

For much of November and into early December, Jones couldn't have left port if he had wanted to. Persistent westerly winds made it nearly impossible to sail out of Texel. Jones knew his moment would come, however, and it finally arrived in the form of a stiff gale from the east, which drove the British blockade some miles off their line. On December 27, on the strength of the fresh wind, the *Alliance* slipped out of port and, hugging the coast, sailed southwest, shadowed by a couple of British warships that several times looked as though they were ready to attack but then veered away. In detailing those encounters, Nathaniel Fanning wrote that Jones and the crew presumed the ships were uncertain of starting a fight they feared they would lose to the captain who, from the deck of his own sinking ship, had forced the surrender of the *Serapis*. And the British ships could not match the *Alliance* for speed; it zipped along at an average of ten knots per hour for much of the run along the British coast, past the cliffs of Dover and at least two anchored British squadrons, which could only watch helplessly as the ship sped by at a distance. Jones had made his escape.[1]

According to Samuel Eliot Morison, the *Alliance* was not "a happy ship." Landais was a poor captain and had countenanced a fractious crew. Many of his men remained aboard, augmented now by Jones's surviving *Bonhomme Richard* crew—the same crew that had been fired upon by the duplicitous Landais and his men. It made for a tense voyage, marked by spats and the occasional fistfight among the crew, and a threatened duel or two among the officers from the two ships. The *Alliance* took a couple of minor prizes and then put in at Coruña, Spain, for fresh water and other supplies.

After a couple of weeks, Jones ordered the crew to get ready to set out once again, but the men balked, angry over their lack of pay and the lack of proper clothing for winter sailing in the North Atlantic—most had lost their possessions when the *Bonhomme Richard* went down. Jones, with the support of his lieutenants, finally persuaded the men to return to work so they could head for Lorient. Once at sea, the tensions between Jones and the crew increased when word flitted around the ship that, rather than making straight for Lorient and a payday, Jones intended to cruise for three weeks looking for more prizes.

After some two weeks of fruitless cruising, the *Alliance* encountered a British warship, and Jones ordered the crew to get ready to take her. "But our crew swore they would not fight, although if we had been united we might have taken her with a great deal of ease," Fanning wrote. When Jones was told of the rank-and-file insubordination, he gave in. "Our courses were dropped, and we in our turn ran from her, and made all the sail we could, by his order. All this time he appeared much agitated, and bit his lips often, and walked the quarter-deck muttering something to himself." Three days later, on February 13, the *Alliance* anchored at Lorient.[2]

The *Serapis* and other prizes taken by Jones's crew were already in port, sailed there from Texel under the French flag. Jones received orders from

Paris—presumably, from Franklin—to ready the *Alliance* for a transatlantic voyage to carry crucial communications from Europe to the Continental Congress. The *Alliance* was in miserable condition despite the refitting at Texel. Part of the issue was an oddly imagined placement of ballast—ordered by Landais—that made it hard to control the ship as tightly as Jones liked, a crucial lack of flexibility given the likelihood of more sea battles. Jones had the crew and port carpenters set to work, on the United States government's bill, to ready the ship, a project that would take several months.

But the captain managed to squeeze in some fun too. One afternoon the American agent at work in Lorient, James Moylan, boarded the ship to conduct some business with the ship's purser; Jones went ashore leaving strict orders that no one was to leave the ship—including Moylan, an Irish-born man nearly sixty years old—until Jones returned. Moylan was "very rude in his manners . . . and he was what people commonly call a homely man, but rich in the good things of this world. His present wife was only about seventeen years of age, very handsome, and a little given to coquetry."[3] According to Fanning, Moylan had caught Jones in compromising positions with his wife before. This time, there would be no interrupting: Jones went straight to Moylan's home, where he spent the afternoon and evening with Moylan's young wife. The crew, meanwhile, got Moylan drunk and poured him into a berth, where he spent the night. The next day, gossip about Jones's "gallantry," as Fanning described it, swept through the port. On another occasion, Jones swept up the wife of a Lorient man and kept her in his cabin during a short cruise of a couple of weeks.

In mid-April, Jones traveled to Paris, where he was received as a hero and presented at the royal court. Louis XVI gave him a gold-and-jewel sword. Jones also attended the opera with Marie Antoinette and was the guest of honor at a series of dinners and parties, despite his inability to speak or understand much French. (He would later gain some fluency.) Jones saw Franklin regularly, as well as a steady stream of women. The king also recommended that the French legislature bestow upon Jones the Cross of Military Merit, a first for a non-Frenchman. This would eventually lead to Jones being recognized as a chevalier, a title Jones clenched as though it was his key to the palace door. The Freemasons swore him into the elite Lodge of the Nine Sisters and then commissioned Jean Antoine Houdon, the premier sculptor of the day, to carve a bust of the naval hero. Jones trimmed his long hair by eighteen inches and sat for the artist, and once the bust was completed, contemporaries declared it an exact likeness. Jones was so pleased he ordered extra copies sent to George Washington, who kept it on display at Mount Vernon; Thomas Jefferson; and his friend Robert Morris in Philadelphia. Eventually he distributed about sixteen of the statues.[4]

The trip to Paris wasn't all pleasure, though. Jones was trying to pressure the French to sell the *Serapis* and other prizes so he could collect the money needed to pay his crew members, who were becoming mutinous again as they heard "of Jones's gay doings in Paris. . . . While the Commodore was making love to countesses and sleeping with scented courtesans, they hadn't enough money to buy a drink or command the services of such poor trollops as a seaport provided for enlisted men."[5] Jones was also pushing plans for a joint American-French naval attack on British waters.

Jones was frustrated on both fronts, and by late May was back at Lorient empty-handed and overseeing the final reconditioning of the *Alliance*.

Houdon bust of John Paul Jones, one of which was used to preliminarily identify his body in Paris.
Courtesy of the Library of Congress, Prints and Photographs Division, reproduction number HABS MD,2-ANNA,65/1--24

Landais surfaced in the port town by early June, though he largely stayed away from the wharf and out of sight, according to Fanning. He had booked passage to America, where he was to stand court martial, but he was hardly a chastened man and in fact was making plans for yet another act of duplicity. On the afternoon of June 23, Jones was ashore for a social call, and his officers were below deck eating, when they heard shouts from above. Scrambling topside, they found their ship freshly manned, and Landais striding back and forth. As soon as Jones's officers were assembled, Landais claimed that his commission by the Continental Congress gave him command of the *Alliance*, and neither Franklin, in Paris, nor Jones could countermand that. He was taking control of the ship and would sail it to America. And, he said, if any officer aboard could not accept his captaincy, the officer was to go ashore immediately. The crew was given no option. All but one of the officers left the *Alliance*.

Jones was livid and set off for Paris to consult with Franklin and French naval officials, but by the time he returned, Landais had moved the *Alliance* to an offshore anchorage. The entry to the port was a well-protected narrows, and at Jones's request the French dropped a boom across the mouth to preclude the *Alliance* from leaving. As violent confrontation loomed, Jones backed off, striking a diplomatic pose by saying that French cannons firing on a French captain sailing an American ship would benefit only the British. He let the *Alliance* leave for America. Morison, Jones's insightful biographer, suspected Jones let the ship go because he didn't like sailing it and wanted to be rid of Landais, whose acts of treachery would catch up with him. As the *Alliance* neared Philadelphia, Landais's officers seized control and steered for Boston, where Landais was called before a court of inquiry and, after a hearing, kicked out of the navy.

Shipless, Jones returned to Paris for a short stay and presumably discussed the events at Lorient with Franklin. He was lobbying hard to be given the *Serapis*, but the French refused to give her up. In July, Jones was back at Lorient and had a fresh ship to command—the twenty-four-gun *Ariel*, which the French had captured from the British. Jones once again oversaw a refitting, and on October 7, 1780, the *Ariel* set out as part of a convoy of fourteen America-bound ships. They almost immediately encountered a massive tempest with "mountain seas," as Fanning described the waves, which the *Ariel* barely survived. It was an epic storm; the French coast was littered with ships blown aground. After the storm passed, the *Ariel* limped back into port for another full refitting—the masts and sails were all but gone.

By now, Jones's celebrity in Lorient was waning, in part because of his own sexual escapades, viewed as scandalous by many of the local residents, not to mention the cuckolded husbands. Jones added to his troubles with an odd set of actions, as recounted by Fanning. He had persuaded an Irish-born passenger named Sullivan to stay on the ship for several days after it made its way back to port to oversee a contingent of marines aboard ship. As Jones kept extending his need of Sullivan, the man eventually demanded to be let ashore. Jones instead ordered him thrown in chains and held below. Sullivan won his release through the intercession of friends in Lorient and then stalked Jones to a room the captain was renting in port and beat him savagely with a cane. Several days later, Jones was again beaten by a member of the military garrison after refusing a challenge to a duel.[6] Twice battered, Fanning reports, Jones rarely left the ship again until it set out again for America, but only after further straining local relations when he rounded out his crew by pressing into service—essentially, kidnapping—a number of American sailors at port in Lorient.[7]

Jones set sail around December 12. With his guns reduced and his hold full of military supplies (not to mention volatile gunpowder) and other cargo for America, he chose a southern route in hopes of avoiding a battle. He almost succeeded. Near the end of the voyage, a loyalist privateer far faster than the *Ariel* approached. Jones ordered the *Ariel*'s deck cleared, the gun ports closed, and a detachment of French marines to stay ready below deck. Hoisting a British flag, Jones struck a pose as a British captain and demanded that the privateer, the *Triumph*, account for itself. After a shouted exchange, he ordered *Triumph*'s captain to present his papers aboard the *Ariel*; the captain refused. Jones ordered the Stars and Stripes hoisted and directed his men to fire; they did, strafing the deck of the *Triumph*. The gambit caught the *Triumph* by surprise, and after a weak attempt at defense, the captain, John Pindar, surrendered.

Yet Jones wasn't the only commander capable of a ruse. As Jones was distracted issuing orders to seal the victory and assemble a crew to sail the

Triumph to the United States as a prize, Pindar suddenly ordered his men to unfurl the sails. The ship sprinted away before Jones could maneuver the *Ariel* into a position in which it could use its cannons. The duplicitous Jones had been outmaneuvered. There was nothing left to do but set out again for Philadelphia. En route Jones caught wind of a mutiny plot and headed it off; the *Ariel* sailed into port with twenty crew members in irons but its cargo of military supplies, French soldiers, and letters from Franklin and the French government to the Continental Congress intact.

The voyage of the *Ariel* was Jones's last sailing command for the US Navy. The *Ariel* was returned to the French, who sailed it back to Europe. Jones sat through a board of inquiry to satisfy lingering questions about the Landais affair. Jones was cleared, but his volatile personality and reputation had long ago soured his peers in the navy. Jones desperately wanted to be named admiral and be placed in charge of the entire US Navy, but he was much less savvy on the battlefield of politics than at sea. Backroom communications by fellow captains—Captain James Nicholson prime among them—with members of Congress raised the specter of high-level dissent should Jones be made admiral. So Congress did what it has done ever since: it failed to act. Jones didn't get his promotion, but his friend Robert Morris, who was overseeing naval operations, arranged a consolation prize. He gave Jones command of the *America*, which was under construction in Portsmouth and would be the largest fighting ship in the small and ineffectual American fleet.

Jones arrived in Portsmouth on August 31, 1781, his first visit to the city in the four years since he had overseen the fitting-out of the *Ranger*. Jones found many old friends waiting to greet him; old frictions had been smoothed by time and his growing fame.

One relationship, though, picked up right where it left off. John Langdon, the wealthy and irascible builder of the *Ranger*, was also building the *America*. Jones discovered the ship had barely progressed beyond the framing-out stage, and Langdon was unwilling to assign more than three or four workers at a time to the project. Jones and Langdon's antagonistic relationship renewed to the point that they weren't speaking and instead communicated through an intermediary—Morris in Philadelphia. This meant decisions that could have been made in minutes now took weeks. And Jones's professional life was about to get more complicated.

In July 1782 a French squadron arrived at Boston harbor and, after taking on an American pilot to guide them into port, three of its ships went aground. Two were refloated, but the third broke apart on the rocks. To recompense the French, the Continental Congress turned over the *America* to its European allies, robbing Jones of his command. He stayed with the project until the ship launched, and then the chevalier watched as the French took command of it.

Jones was again without a ship, and by now the Revolutionary War was in its final stages. The French navy had driven the British out of Chesapeake Bay the previous fall, and Lord Cornwallis had surrendered his troops at Yorktown. In November 1782 the Americans and the British signed the initial articles of peace.

Seeing the end in sight and seeking a better understanding of—and contacts within—the French navy, Jones secured permission to sail the Caribbean with a French fleet to study its operations. The tropics were not kind to the native Scotsman: he came down with a persistent fever, probably malaria, which laid him low. He was slow to recuperate and, once back in Philadelphia, still felt the effects of the illness. In May 1783 Jones went to a sanitarium in Bethlehem, Pennsylvania, for the summer and finally regained his health.

And, it should be noted, his ambitions.

With the war over, Jones was anxious to create a future for himself. He contemplated settling down as a farmer, but a plan to buy land in New Jersey fell through. He wrote letters and advised his friend Morris that if the United States was to survive, it would need a true navy and not a hodgepodge of hastily drawn together privateers and merchant seamen—an institution that trained young sailors for sea and young leaders for commands. It was likely the first vision for what would become the United States Naval Academy at Annapolis.

None of those ideas sparked a new life for Jones. Finally, though, he hatched a plan that took root. Jones and his crews were still owed tens of thousands of dollars from prizes they had seized during the war and sent to Danish and French ports. Jones persuaded Congress to deputize him to go to Paris to pursue settlement of those claims. It took some three years for the accounts to be settled (and decades more for the heirs of Jones and his crew to get their shares), a frustrating marathon of claims, counterclaims, and French royal bureaucracy. By the time the work ended, Jones was hungry for a next step. He dallied in the merchant world, concocting then aborting a scheme to trade otter pelts from the Pacific Northwest with Far East merchants, and losing money on a short-lived project to import American goods to Lorient. A sailor and fighter he might have been; a merchant he was not.

In Paris, Jones kept up his romances and his social life. But he pined to lead a navy. In 1786, he wrote a memoir of his life at sea for an audience of one: Louis XVI. The work reads like an immense job application. But the French king had no need of his services. Jones sailed for Denmark, hoping to recoup more prize money, but then, running low on cash, he decamped for the United States.

Jones spent the summer of 1787 in New York City, staying with his friend Robert Hyslop as he waited for the new Congress gathered at Philadelphia—which would sign the new Constitution—to approve his settlements for the prize money he was owed. By December, he was back in Paris, where good news awaited him. Jefferson, then the US representative to France, told him that the Russian ambassador to Louis XVI's court had asked if Jones might be available for service under the czarina, Catherine the Great, who was heading to another war against the Ottoman Empire in the Black Sea.

Jones, it seemed, was about to get the fleet command he so hungered for.

———————————— ✦ ————————————

Jones was still trying to wrest a settlement out of Denmark for three British ships he had captured and sent to the Norwegian coastal city of Bergen, bounty that the Danes—who then controlled the city—turned back over to the British in what the United States considered a violation of international law. To push the issue, Jones traveled by carriage from Paris to Copenhagen. The late-winter trek took several days, during which time Jones caught a chill; he fell ill when he arrived on March 4, 1788. Following a few days of convalescence, Jones was presented to Danish officials, who, after some vacillation, told him that he had no authority to negotiate the issue and that it must be done in Paris by Jefferson.

Jones was flummoxed, but not particularly upset, for in Copenhagen he wasn't talking only to the Danes. He met several times with Baron Krudner, the Russian envoy to Denmark, and through him cemented the deal that would give him a command in the Imperial Navy. It was a delicate situation, and Jones went to pains to clear the assignment first with Jefferson, saying that while he was an American citizen, his services were not needed by the United States and he wished to sail for the czarina unless the United States saw a conflict. There was none.

Catherine II was one of the most powerful women to ever engage in international relations. She was a minor German princess by birth, betrothed to the inept Peter III when both were teenagers. She supplanted him in 1762 in a bloodless coup (he was quietly strangled shortly afterward by members of her inner circle) and, through a masterful grasp of politics and manipulation, quickly assumed tight and ambitious control. As empress, Catherine added to the empire in significant ways, pushing westward into Europe and eastward as far as Alaska. Most significantly for Jones, she also pushed southward and engaged in a series of wars and skirmishes with the Ottoman Empire. In the winter of 1788, the Ottomans were fighting to regain territory in the Crimea lost in the war of 1768–74. And while some of the fighting was land based, a key battleground was the Black Sea, which was why Catherine was looking to add Jones to her stable of naval commanders.

Jones signed on, after some negotiations, as rear admiral. In a confirming letter from Krudner, Jones was told to proceed to Russia "as soon as your affairs permit, the intention of her imperial majesty being to give you a command in the Black Sea, and under the orders of Prince Potemkin," who was not only Catherine's lover for a time but also her most trusted advisor.[8] Jones apparently presumed that he was being offered the command of the Black Sea fleet; he would soon learn this was not the case.

The court of Catherine the Great was as much a snake pit as any other royal court, and if Jones had reservations about serving a royal court in which two of the previous four leaders had emerged from coups, he never gave voice to it. The pay was about twice what he made as an American captain, and while he was antsy to get back into battle, the prime draw was the rank. He had long coveted what is known as a "flag rank," which was unavailable to him in the United States—there was no longer even a US Navy—and here Catherine was making him a rear admiral. It was, Jones believed, the crowning achievement in an up-and-down career. He was anxious to get to Saint Petersburg to receive his commission and get to work, so he set off in mid-April from Copenhagen for Stockholm and then Grisslehamn, a coastal Swedish town to the northeast. Jones planned to hop on a packet ship there to cross to Finland, but the Gulf of Bothnia was still packed with winter ice and packet ships weren't moving.

Jones feared delay. So he hired an open-deck thirty-foot boat with several oarsmen and a smaller craft to be towed behind, which he could, if needed, drag across an ice field and then drop back into open water. He didn't tell the crew where he was going. He had the men pull to the south, along the Swedish coast, and as they reached the end of the ice pack, he brandished a pistol and ordered the men to steer eastward. It took four mostly sleepless days of frozen spray and cutting wind—they lost the small boat in heavy seas—to get to Tallinn, in Estonia, where Jones paid off the crew and then bought some horses and continued overland for Saint Petersburg, arriving May 4. He wasted no time in getting to the Hermitage to present himself to his new employer. Catherine was satisfied, writing to her friend and confidante, Friedrich Melchior, the Baron von Grimm, that "I think he will suit our purpose admirably."

Jones was similarly pleased. "I was entirely captivated and put myself into her hands without making any stipulation for my personal advantage," he wrote. "I demanded but one favor: That she should never condemn me without hearing me," meaning he exacted a pledge that Catherine would always give him a chance to tell his side of a story. That he sought such an assurance suggests he was either sensitive to the palace intrigues of the royal court or anticipated problems in the war zone or with his crews. Or perhaps both. Regardless, the promise was worthless.[9]

Jones left immediately for Crimea and was stunned to discover when he arrived twelve days later that he would be but one of four rear admirals fighting the Empress's sea battles and answering to Potemkin. The other three were Charles, prince of Nassau-Siegen, the heir to a worthless German principality who had known Jones in Paris; Marko Vojnovic, a veteran of the first Russo-Turkish War; and Nicolay Mordvinov, who was in charge of the arsenal.[10] The existing admirals had no interest in sharing command with Jones, and he quickly realized that he "had entered on a delicate and disagreeable service," as he later wrote. Jones was assigned to lead a small squadron consisting of his flagship, eight dodgy frigates, and four other small boats deployed in an estuary of the Dnieper River, whose shallows made it difficult to maneuver a fleet in battle. Nassau-Siegen, assigned a small yacht for his flagship, commanded a more practical fleet of agile, oar-propelled fighting ships that could navigate shallow water and would not have to rely on the shifting winds.

The estuary, called the Liman, ran roughly thirty miles east-west at the northwest extension of the Black Sea east of Odessa. The Turks manned a significant fort on the north shore of the mouth of the estuary, at Ochakov Point, and the Russians were hurriedly trying to establish a countering bat-tery—Jones's suggestion—two miles across the water on the sandy spit of land that marked the southern edge of the mouth, near the Russian Fort Kinburn. The Russians hoped to use their fleet to provide cover for land forces to take the Turkish fort; the Turks hoped to keep the Liman clear of Russian ships so they could help defend and resupply their troops at Ocha-kov. Just to the east of the fort was the mouth of the Bug River, another stra-tegic asset the Russians wanted to keep out of Turkish hands—in large part because Russian land forces would have to cross that river to get to the fort.

When Jones arrived, he found there was no coherent plan for attack. Given the politics of tsarist Russia, Potemkin stayed aloof from the com-mand decisions so as not to be stained in the event of failure, while main-taining his ability to claim credit for success. Jones had an aide row him out into the Liman to get a look at the Turkish forces, which he found con-siderable. The ships were large, numerous, and well armed with powerful cannons. The Russians would stand little chance in a head-to-head confron-tation. So Jones hatched a plan in which he would maneuver his squadron at an angle running from the southwest to the northeast and Nassau-Siegen would place his detachment of smaller ships along the northern edge of the estuary to attack the Turkish flank.

On the morning of June 7, the massive Turkish fleet of fifty-seven ships sailed into the Liman, drawing fire from Nassau-Siegen's ships; the return fire sent the small Russian boats scurrying in retreat, which Jones anticipated would embolden the Turks to press forward. They did, and with a favorable wind Jones's ships shifted their line into a *V* and let loose with a withering series of cannon blasts. Hollow, perforated shells filled with incendiary material were launched from mortars, and the flaming missiles were devastating to the wooden Turkish ships with their tar caulking and cloth sails. The Turks quickly retreated, losing two ships.

In reports submitted to Potemkin, Jones sought to spread around the credit for the victory, likely mindful that his ego in the past had caused problems with his peers. Jones overstated Nassau-Siegen's role and actions, while Nassau-Siegen, who was better at politics than fighting, savaged Jones in his reports and took all the credit. Jones learned of the other commander's reports and stifled his outrage, but his further communications with Potemkin took on a veiled edge. The poison was in the well.

The next battle took more than a week to come together. In the dark hours of June 16, the Turks again sailed into the Liman, this time holding nothing back. Some one hundred ships moved eastward, flags fluttering in the breeze and crews screaming and banging on drums and other items to create a ferocious—and intimidating—din. The Russian ships were anchored inside the estuary, which meant the Turks had to navigate tricky shallows that caused a series of groundings—including that of the flagship of the *capitan pasha*, or fleet commander. As the Turks stalled to free the flagship and others, and to regroup, Jones embarked on the kind of foray of which legends are made.

He wanted to take some depth soundings of the estuary near the anchored Turkish fleet, and selected a Russian named Ivak, who later wrote of the experience, to row him. They slipped along the shore on the northern edge of the estuary, Jones taking the measurements. They drew no interest from the anchored ships so ventured closer. And closer. Soon they were among the enemy ships themselves. Jones had Ivak pretend to be a vendor selling salt and strike up a conversation with Russian-speaking crew members on one of the large warships. As they conversed, Jones used a piece of chalk to write a message in French on the stern: "To be burned. Paul Jones."[11]

Back at the Russian fleet, Jones met with the other commanders on Nassau-Siegen's yacht to pass along the soundings. As they spoke, they heard cannon fire in the distance. Some of the Turkish fleet had tried to use the cover of darkness to sail back into the Black Sea, but the Russians at the fort Jones had recommended they build on the south spit caught sight of the sails and let loose. The ships were damaged and driven aground, setting the stage for Nassau-Siegen to again wander off to collect grounded prizes. Nassau-Siegen was intent on burning the Turkish ships, a tactic Jones deplored; better, he believed, to seize the ships and add them to the Russian fleet. The two admirals quarreled, and an already sour relationship was destroyed.

Jones had seen the array of Turkish ships and decided the best counter would be to reestablish the pincer array of ships that had worked so efficiently in the space in the previous battle, and to surprise the Turks by attacking first. Under cover of darkness, the Russian ships moved westward, and at daybreak they filled their sails and began the assault. The Turks, already disorganized, began to panic, cutting anchor cables and turning into the wind. Jones was aboard the *Vladimir* and was within pistol range of the *capitan pasha*'s command ship when his advantage was quickly wasted. The captain of the *Vladimir* dropped anchor, saying later that he was saving the ship from running aground on a sandbar (which may or may not have been a real possibility). The *capitan pasha*'s ship was again aground, as was another, and Jones was eyeing the prizes when Nassau-Siegen, who had held back during the attack, suddenly surged forward to claim them. The *capitan pasha* himself had already escaped to another ship, and his fleet regained some composure and began firing on the Russian ships, including raking the *Vladimir*'s decks. Jones slipped into a small boat and was rowed to Nassau-Siegen's ship, where he vainly asked his colleague to leave the prizes and help repel the fleet. Jones finally persuaded several of the Russian captains individually to join the attack. By dusk, the Turkish ships had retreated westward to the protection of the fort's cannons.

At dawn, Nassau-Siegen sailed off, leaving Jones with light protection in the event the Turkish fleet decided to attack, a strategic error that, fortunately for Jones, wasn't pressed by the Turks. But a different slaughter ensued. Nassau-Siegen was taking no prisoners and offered no quarter. His ships bombarded the grounded but still manned Turkish ships with flaming missiles. The Turkish-oared galleys were propelled by slaves and prisoners chained to the vessels they rowed. Their panicked, then dying, screams echoed across the estuary.

Over the next several weeks, there were more skirmishes as Potemkin took his time moving the army into position, first crossing the Bug River and then preparing to lay siege to the fort. There were more internecine squabbles, too, and Jones, who had started out seeking to be gracious, returned to character. Potemkin was a capricious and autocratic commander, and he issued a series of senseless orders to Jones—including risking Russian men and ships to remove a single cannon from a Turkish ship that Potemkin deemed a threat. They were impossible and ill-considered assignments; still, Jones obeyed orders. Each failure, though, was a black mark. (One wonders if Potemkin, rather than being capricious, was hoping to get his American charge killed.) In one final exchange, Potemkin wrote Jones to confront the Turks "courageously" or face a charge of negligence.

If Potemkin was looking for the right button to push, he found it. Jones sent back a puckish response, including a gibe at Nassau-Siegen, telling Potemkin that "since I did not come here as an adventurer, or as a charlatan to mend a broken fortune, I hope in the future to suffer no further humiliation."

Potemkin sent for Jones, and they quarreled, Jones telling his commander that Nassau-Siegen had duped Potemkin, Potemkin taking offense at the notion that he could be manipulated. Jones was relieved of his duties and offered a command in the Baltic Fleet, which he took as a meaningless gesture. Jones returned to Saint Petersburg hoping to make his case before Catherine and thinking that the promise he had exacted to be heard had indeed been sincere. In the midst of the turmoil, Jones learned that none of the correspondence he had sent to his American peers had made it out of Russia; Catherine's secret police had intercepted it all. Reports from Potemkin, Nassau-Siegen, and others had reached the empress, however, and she had already written Jones off as a bad decision.

Jones continued to try to hatch plans, including proposing a US-Russian naval alliance. His extended stay in Saint Petersburg, though, only exposed him to more intrigue. In what was apparently a scheme engineered by Nassau-Siegen, a young girl selling butter went to Jones's apartment and then claimed that the commodore raped her. The girl's story eventually fell apart, and a new version, featuring an ill-described man in a uniform who had paid her to play the role, emerged. Jones faced no criminal charges, but his reputation was left in tatters.

As the Russian summer faded, Jones left Saint Petersburg and floated around Europe for a year or so, still trying to come up with a fresh plan. Physically, though, he had been battered by both the Liman campaign and the court intrigues. His schemes found few listeners, and in May 1790 he was back in Paris. It was a far different city than he remembered, with the smell of revolution in the air and the aristocracy under siege. His health was failing and he was at loose ends. He became a bore to his friends, and his plans for resurrection seemed to miss the obvious politics of the moment. The French royal family was barely able to help itself let alone Jones, as Paris slid further into turmoil.

Jones still struggled to find fresh relevance for himself in the world. Jefferson was one of the few who envisioned a role for the former commodore, a role that Jones would have relished. Jones had suggested the United States join up with European powers to send a fleet into the Mediterranean to confront the audacious Barbary pirates, who were extorting European powers for safe passage and seizing American merchant ships for refusing to pay protection. The Americans weren't looking to forge any such alliances, but they did need to confront the piracy. Jones, Jefferson thought, would be the perfect American agent to deal with the pirates, and on June 1, 1792, Jefferson and Washington, as secretary of state and president, respectively, appointed Jones a special commissioner to negotiate with the Barbary pirates for the release of enslaved American sailors. Washington also appointed Jones a special consul to Algiers. The hope was that Jones's reputation as a sea warrior would strengthen his hand against the seafaring Barbary states.

But by the time the documents reached Paris, Jones was dead.

--------------------- ✿ ---------------------

Three weeks after Jones was buried in his lead coffin, Paris erupted in violence. Anti-royal mobs stormed the Tuileries, and the Swiss Guards protecting the royal family were no match. A slaughter ensued. Louis XVI was deposed and taken prisoner, and the bodies of the dead Protestant soldiers were heaved into carts and hauled off, many of them to the Saint Louis Cemetery. It was still the only place in Catholic Paris that could receive

Protestant dead, though it's unclear how much the revolutionaries were hewing to religious doctrine and protocol. Deep trenches were dug in the cemetery, a few yards from where Jones was buried, and the dead men were stacked in like cordwood then covered over with dirt.

The cemetery continued to receive Protestant dead for a few more weeks, but was then closed and eventually sold off, its location, and its best-known body, quickly forgotten amid the turmoil. Five months later, the king who had decorated Jones and presented him with a golden sword was executed on the guillotine in the middle of la Place de la Révolution, which until recently had been la Place de Louis XV, named for the freshly killed king's predecessor and grandfather.

The day after Jones died, his friend Jean-Baptiste Beaupoil, former aide to Lafayette, wrote a letter to Jones's sisters informing them that he had died, where the will was filed, and that his possessions had been sealed up in his apartment on Rue de Tournon. He also wrote that Samuel Blackden, another Jones friend, was heading to England and could be reached at No. 18 Great Titchfield Street in London. Janet Taylor, one of the sisters, wrote to Blackden there, and on August 8, Blackden replied with details on Jones's final days and his burial.

Taylor traveled to Paris in October to collect her brother's belongings and money owed him by the French. She found the city in violent uproar. She checked into the Hôtel Anglais on le Passage des Petits-Pères, where Beaupoil lived, a few blocks from the Tuileries, and then went to the Rue de Tournon apartment to collect her brother's papers and possessions. She also linked up with an unidentified friend and an Irish-born Parisian *valet de place*—something of a tour guide for people seeking to navigate the local bureaucracy—to petition the French National Assembly for payments Jones had felt he was due. [12]

Paris, though, was coming apart. A few weeks before Taylor arrived, the Republic had been declared, and roving mobs attacked prisons, executing some 1,400 inmates. Other revolutionary gangs invaded the homes of royalists, priests, and observant Catholics, or others not perceived to be aligned with the masses; others were simply the victims of score-settling under the guise of revolution. Revolutionaries roamed the streets, and Taylor quickly perceived that it would not be safe for her to linger. She fled before the Assembly could consider her request, a decision that may have saved her life. Three days later, the proprietor of her hotel was arrested and his assets seized. The Irishman and *valet de place* were also swept up and quickly lost their heads to the guillotine.

Interestingly, for all of Jones's naval battles in the name of freedom from the rule of the British king, in France he was aligned with the king against those who sought their freedom. Had he not died of his illnesses, he could well have lost his head on the guillotine, too, a reminder—much like Jones's role in the American Revolution—that often one man's hero is another man's pirate.

8

War in Cuba, Peace in Paris

FROM PARIS, THE AMERICAN war with Spain was a distant affair, though it permeated life in the diplomatic community. Ambassador Porter's daughter, Elsie, filled her diary with the light social events of the day as well as details from a trip to Germany with her father. She also tracked the early progress of the war, noting with nationalistic pride when American ships took Spanish ships. "The torpedo boat *Porter* captured a Spanish vessel yesterday, which makes me quite proud of the family name sake," she wrote on April 25. (The ship was named after David Porter, no relation, a former navy officer and diplomat.) She fretted that while the official French diplomatic position was neutrality, the French people and institutions seemed to side with Spain.[1]

The war was moving quickly. The first battle, for which Dewey received so much praise, came at Manila Bay on May 1, 1898. At the same time, US warships half a world away were establishing a blockade outside Cuban port cities. In early June, American ground troops landed at Guantanamo

Bay on Cuba's southeast coast, and then at nearby Daiquiri and Santiago de Cuba. With American forces—including Teddy Roosevelt's Rough Riders—seizing Cuban towns at the start of July, a half-dozen Spanish navy ships under Admiral Pascual Cervera tried to break through the blockade and leave the Santiago de Cuba harbor. A US naval squadron under Rear Admiral Winfield Scott Schley, with the USS *Brooklyn* as his flagship, cut them off and destroyed all six ships, including the *Infanta María Teresa*, which had been part of the 1897 Hudson River flotilla marking the dedication of Grant's Tomb in Manhattan. The death toll was high: some 350 Spanish sailors were killed, with another 160 wounded and more than 1,700 men captured. As at Manila Bay, the US losses at Santiago de Cuba were minimal. Aboard Schley's *Brooklyn*, which was hit by some twenty-five Spanish shells, one sailor was killed and one was wounded. Those were the only casualties on the American side, though two other ships were damaged in the fighting.

Horace Porter received a wire in Paris with skeletal details about the destruction of the Spanish fleet at Santiago de Cuba. "Father, when he received the telegram, rushed into my room, took me in his arms and whirled me about, to the destruction of my hair, but what did I care when I heard him exclaiming with tears in his eyes that 'It's all gone, all destroyed, the fleet, Cervera's I mean,' this between whirls and kisses." Later, during the open house party, "Father read it aloud, while the people cheered and shouted and the band played *The Star-Spangled Banner.*"

Despite the war, the ambassadorial dinner parties went on. And Sophie Porter's health worsened. As the mother took to her bed or off to the Alps for rest, Elsie spent more time as her father's hostess, making a quick transition from teenage girl to young woman. Given the health problems and the war, Elsie's social "coming out" dinner was a small affair hosted by a family friend instead of the grand ball one might expect for the daughter of a wealthy diplomat. "I was rather glad [the grand event] with a great ball, brass bands and trumpets at street corners [that was originally planned was canceled]," Elsie wrote. "It was a terrible nuisance, so Mrs. Winslow [the wife of Porter's friend, General Winslow] gave me a beautiful dinner and dance and I managed to kill time in a most agreeable manner." She also described in great detail the gown she wore that evening, the dancing, and the French suitor who came calling, the extent of her descriptions suggesting she really would have preferred the grand party.

For Elsie, the war was shrouded in romance. She noted in her diary two men—suitors, actually—who were heading for battle. "Captain Horton[2] is going, I wonder if he will ever come home again. His letters are studiously respectful and yet whenever he can he sends me presents. I mean little remembrances. I don't see why he should care for me, I am certainly not very attractive because I'm such a young volcano." Another man identified only as Elliott was also headed to the battlefields, and Elsie struck a tone of longing to taste battle herself. "How I wish I were there, yes, right in the war. It's very dreadful, I know, but I want to see it all. I am not satisfied to read about it or to hear Father tell stories. I want to see it myself, the defeat and victory and all the awfulness of war. I want to feel all the sufferings and joys of life, the good and the bad. I don't mean such things as dreadful suffering—but if it's got to come, let it come. I always have such longings for all sorts of excitements and passions."

Elsie received letters sporadically from Horton, and it's clear she began to develop some affection for him. He wrote little of himself in those letters but instead offered observations of others and some details of the battles he had been through. "When he writes of the most trivial things," Elsie noted, "he is deep, deeper than I thought, and what a spirit. Passion and love are buried down in a noble heart." When there was a gap of several weeks, she fretted to her father, who "scornfully replied" to her that she was being silly: "A man in as important position as he is, and in an exciting campaign, has not time to write letters to girls. He has other things to do and think about." Elsie bet her father that "he will write me, and write me from the battlefield, if he isn't ill or wounded."

Elsie knew her captain better than Porter did. Horton was writing, he just wasn't mailing, and a packet of letters eventually arrived, including one written as his outfit was engaged in the battle of Santiago. He offered a few details of the campaign and confessed that he had indeed been ailing with malaria. Enclosed in the packet was a swath of the Spanish flag he told her had been cut down as the Stars and Stripes was hoisted above the Cuban city. But there the communications and the burgeoning romance ended, at least as recorded in Elsie's diaries, until an enigmatic mention around her twenty-first birthday in December 1899, in which she wrote that she had treated him coldly despite her romantic interest in him and that distance seemed to have weakened the attraction. "My soldier boy is in the Philippines dead or alive, I don't know. . . . It seems so long now since he has loved me. . . . It seems like my real life only began two years ago when on that never-forgotten Fourth of July, 1898, I woke up to the fact that he was all the world to me and a good deal more besides. . . . If he lives to [come] back from the Philippines and claims me as he says he will, how good I will be to him. These and nothing else, love to a man and thankfulness to God, are my birthday thoughts." Records indicate Horton eventually returned to the States, not Paris, and married a woman from New Orleans.

While the French government was toeing a neutral line, many of the top French newspapers were in full-throated support of Spain, something that US State Department officials worried about, fearing that a steady barrage of anti-American articles could build pressure on the French government to pick a side. Secretary Day wrote Porter asking whether the ambassador could find some way to counter or at least quell the voices. Porter replied that public opinion and the French press were volatile and hard to measure "because the conditions change rapidly even from day to day and it is difficult to write a circumstantial account which would be up to date when it reached Washington."

At the start of the war, Porter had made the rounds of top French government officials and "received assurances that everything would be done to preserve in all respects a strict and impartial neutrality," even as he delivered a clear threat "that the action of certain elements here adverse to the United States" could affect trade between the two nations and leave the United States "fostering an alliance with their hereditary enemy, Great Britain." The message to the French was clear: remain neutral or risk a diplomatic and financial backlash.[3]

The French government had little sway with the French newspapers, a separation between government and the Fourth Estate that both the United States and France embraced. "They say with truth that the Paris press does not represent the government nor the mass of people," Porter wrote, before dissecting the mood of the various French factions. Backing Spain were conservative aristocrats who "dislike the Republican Government of

France and look with horror upon another Republic in Cuba" and who, in many cases, still pined for the days of the French monarchy. French bankers with investments in Spanish bonds opposed US intervention, fearing that a free Cuba would leave them with worthless investments. "The radical clericals make common cause to a large extent with Spain, the most prominent of Roman Catholic countries." Porter assured Day that France had a silent majority of US sympathizers who couldn't be heard over the din of the opposition that set the tone for public discourse. "These elements have a voice, while the great mass of the French people who are friendly, or at least not unfriendly to the United States, have no means of giving public expression to their feelings." Porter said he was working to wedge pro-American viewpoints into the large papers and had been lobbying US newspaper correspondents "not to exaggerate the state of things and widen the breach, and they are now reporting that there is a change here for the better." He also intimated that some of the pro-Spanish newspapers were being paid off by Spain; Porter said he did not have the budget for similar investments but arranged a pool of $5,000 to commission pro-American articles by French journalists.

Porter was vigilant about defending the American line in France. In early June he learned of a cadet in the French school for the Infanterie de la Marine, "a corps corresponding to our Marines," who pushed through a student body resolution "expressing their sympathy for Spain in the present war and sent it to Madrid." Porter, peeved that future military men were contravening France's official position of neutrality, complained to the French foreign affairs office and asked "that the cadets be disciplined. . . . The minister of foreign affairs, however, took the initiative of informing me that he had taken official notice of the incident and would see that the Cadets were properly reprimanded. He now informs me that this has been done. It was not much more than a boyish prank, but I deemed it worthy of some attention."[4]

Porter seemed to be itching to play a larger diplomatic role in the war. Before American troops began moving through Cuba, Porter had long, informal talks with Gabriel Hanotaux, France's foreign minister and a noted historian, in which the French diplomat asked Porter to pass along to Washington his readiness to serve as an intermediary in talks with Spain aimed at ending the fighting. "His relations are very close with the Spanish Ambassador here, who is a man of ability, has always been desirous of peace, and possesses the confidence of his government," Porter wrote to Washington on June 7. "Mr. Hanotaux is, I feel certain, the person whom Spain would trust rather than any other statesman in Europe to bring about negotiations for peace. His relations with me are so intimate that he talks with the utmost frankness upon every phase of the question."[5] It didn't seem to occur to Porter that such intimacy was less a mark of personal cordiality than it was a practiced diplomat's way of sending out feelers.

Hanotaux's concerns—and those of the French government he represented—came through clearly. He feared the war "might possibly start a conflict among the European nations. He sees that a continuance of hostilities will further depress Spanish bonds held by Frenchmen who have already lost enormously." Money was a concern to the Spanish too. Government finance officials were making the rounds of European capitals and banks seeking to borrow 250 million francs, using as collateral Spain's state tobacco company, which relied on the Cuban crops for much of its business. Porter and other American diplomats leaned on their counterparts in the European capitals to not invest in the company. "The Rothschilds have refused to take part in it, and it is very difficult to come to terms with any of the bankers," Porter reported to Washington. "There is a rumor that an effort will now be made to obtain the money in Brussels. It is thought that eventually a part of the sum named may be obtained but upon ruinous terms. Active steps are being taken to show to bankers the insufficient and uncertain character of the security offered and the risks to which lenders would be liable." In a mark of the delicacy of the diplomacy over Spain, French officials approached Porter wondering if the United States would object to the French national mint contracting with Spain to mint coins. A couple of days later Porter cabled to Washington that France had turned down the Spanish contract and that the coins would likely be minted at a private facility in Belgium.[6]

After the long and frustrating run-up to the war, the United States wasn't ready to talk peace. Hanotaux's overture went nowhere as the American blockade of Cuba tightened and the troop count increased there and in the Philippines. Two weeks after that first offering, Hanotaux met with

Porter again, this time as a private citizen—the Faure cabinet had resigned June 15 in a political shakeup sparked in part by the infamous Dreyfus affair, in which anti-Semitic French military officials had framed Jewish captain Alfred Dreyfus for espionage. Dreyfus was eventually exonerated, but not until he had served nearly five years of a life sentence in the notorious Devil's Island prison; the case exposed deep undercurrents of anti-Semitism in French society and government and in some ways presaged the collaboration between the Vichy government and the Nazis during the World War II German occupation of France.

It's unclear why Hanotaux continued to involve himself in diplomacy around the showdown between the Spanish and the Americans, especially since he was "tired of office," in the eyes of *New York Times* London correspondent Harold Frederic. "He wants to write history, and instead is grinding at the thankless task of making it." And while Hanotaux was a respected political figure and writer, he had lost credibility—along with the rest of the French government—over the handling of the Dreyfus affair. "His position has been rendered very unpleasant in the past two years by the fact that the entire diplomatic corps at Paris possesses complete knowledge of Dreyfus's innocence," Frederic wrote. "Hanotaux also knows he is innocent, but he must keep his lips sealed on the subject, with the result that diplomatic intercourse at the capital of the republic has been stiffened and embarrassed to a distressing extent."[7]

Still, Hanotaux called on Porter to convey a message from the Spanish ambassador in Paris that "he wishes to meet [with Porter] on the part of his government for the purpose of opening negotiations looking to a declaration of peace." The Spanish ambassador, Leon y Castillo, had recently returned from Madrid, where the newspapers reported political gossip that Castillo was being considered for a larger role as Spain's foreign minister. With the war progressing badly and with Spanish pride on the line, there was growing political pressure within Spain to make peace with the United States. The Spanish government decided that France would be the best place for any peace talks that might occur—and that Castillo would be Spain's best representative at the table.

Porter listened to Hanotaux's message, but he demurred from signaling any intent on behalf of his government. He told Hanotaux that as an ambassador to a neutral country he felt it was outside his portfolio to meet with Spanish representatives. He told Hanotaux he would pass along to his superiors any formal overtures Spain wished to make through the French diplomat. "I hardly expect anything to come about very suddenly," Porter wrote to Secretary Day after the meeting, "but it would seem the idea of peace is gaining ground in Spain."[8]

While Porter was listening to Hanotaux and reporting the French official's overtures to Day back in Washington, President McKinley was quietly sending messages to Spain via Ambassador Hay in London. In early June, McKinley set the conditions for peace: Spain must give up Cuba and Puerto Rico but could retain the Philippines, though the United States would maintain control of an unspecified port, presumably to aid in its desires for a stronger presence with Asian trading markets. And he demanded Spain cede a port in the Marianas Islands as a coaling station, again to foster US trade with the Far East.

The Spanish government balked, and the United States pressed forward, intent now on military victory rather than diplomacy. More American troops arrived in Cuba, where they fought in concert with Cuban rebels, as other American forces made their way to the Philippines, which was experiencing its own independence movement, led by Emilio Aguinaldo (who would soon become an enemy of the United States).

Some two months after Dewey's triumph, the Spanish were all but done, their troops surrendering across the war zones—including Puerto Rico and Guam—as Spanish diplomats asked the French to serve as intermediaries in negotiating the peace. McKinley amended his demands slightly, broadening the Philippines component to allow a future role for the insurgents led by Aguinaldo. Spain continued to drag out the process, offering counterarguments and proposals. McKinley, losing patience, sent word that he was done negotiating, and in early August the terms of the ceasefire were agreed to through the French ambassador in Washington, Jules Cambon. By mid-August, the "splendid little war," as Ambassador Hay so famously described it, was over. Paris was set as the site for the formal peace conference, with the future of the Philippines hanging in the balance.[9]

The negotiators began filtering into the City of Light in late September. The American delegation was led by Day, who had stepped down as secretary of state to direct the American negotiating team himself. Ambassador Hay was recalled from London to become McKinley's new secretary of state. Porter was pleased with the shift, writing in a private letter to McKinley that "you remember in one of our conversations in Canton I advocated his original appointment to that place and I am very happy personally and officially to see that he is now to take the portfolio."[10] The rest of the American delegation included three US senators—William P. Frye of Maine, Cushman Kellogg Davis of Minnesota, and George Gray of Delaware—and the expansionist editor of the *New York Tribune* Whitelaw Reid, whom Porter had endorsed as the Republican's 1892 vice presidential candidate. Porter and other embassy officials met the delegates at the train station as they arrived.

The United States might have won the war, but they had yet to win the hearts of the French press, which intensified its cultural and political criticism of the Americans. "The French and Spanish papers, because they don't dare say anything against our system of carrying out a war, are attacking our peace commissioners, saying they looked like Cooks Tourists" in town to visit the sites, Elsie Porter wrote in her diary on October 2. The commissioners did look like they were on holiday, with wives and entourages in tow as they checked into suites in the Continental, Paris's premier hotel. The delegation, numbering thirty people in all, also rented out three connecting rooms for office space. "Our commissioners came in grand style with the secretaries and attaches," Elsie wrote. "Each gentleman and family had his parlor and rooms, the ladies of course with maids."

Horace Porter played the host, getting some of the Spanish and American negotiators together for occasional informal breakfasts and setting them up with French president Faure to attend the opera as his guests in the president's private box. On October 18, Porter hosted a dinner for the negotiators, American and Spanish alike. More than forty people dined at a long link of tables in the grand room, which ran the length of one floor of

Porter's rented mansion. Antique weapons and armor hung on the walls, along with medieval tapestries and modern oil portraits. Stained-glass windows filled one end wall, and at the other end, the room opened into a round conservatory similarly windowed with stained glass. The table was decorated with baskets of fruit and roses, with small electric lights tucked in among the displays. A small group of musicians hidden in the conservatory played softly, their music flowing through the banquet room. "It was a brilliant scene when the music played, the hundreds of lights sparkled, and the ladies in their rich dresses leaned forward to talk, and in turning their heads the little lights seemed to reflect the glitter of their jewels a thousand fold," Elsie recorded in her diary.

Four days after the Americans celebrated Thanksgiving, the Spanish delegation accepted the terms for peace, giving up Cuba, Guam, Puerto Rico, and the Philippines in return for $20 million from the United States. The treaty was signed a couple of weeks later, and even before the US Senate ratified it, McKinley issued orders to the US military to use force if necessary to extend American sovereignty over the archipelago, setting the stage for the next American war—this one against Aguinaldo's insurgency, a brutal exercise in repression that would display to the world that the United States was no more benevolent a colonial power than its European peers.

In the midst of the war, John Paul Jones remained a touchstone for those seeking to amplify the reputation of America's military history, which was rooted in the early days of the nation—from the Revolution through the War of 1812—and in the Civil War. There had been other battles, from the border-setting war with Mexico to the relentless campaigns to subdue the resistant Native American tribes as they were pushed westward or onto pockets of land set aside as reservations.

In July and August 1898, *Scribner's Magazine* published a two-part military biography of Jones by Alfred T. Mahan, one of the most respected naval strategists of his time, who pushed the influential theory that whatever countries dominated the seas would also dominate the world. Mahan's biography of Jones was thin and made only passing references to Jones's personal shortcomings, but was highly laudatory of Jones's intellect and seamanship. "It would give a very imperfect idea of John Paul Jones, however, were the impression allowed to remain, uncorrected, that he was distinguished merely by extraordinary energy, valor, and endurance," Mahan wrote. "On the contrary, he belongs to that class of true sea-kings, whose claim to the title lies in the qualities of his head as well as of the heart. . . . Jones possessed considerable originality of ideas, resultant upon his insight into conditions round him and his appreciation of their relative value; and this quick natural perception received direction and development from habits of steady observation and ordered thought."[11]

The articles were mentioned in several other magazines and newspapers—going viral in a pre-viral media era—which added to the attention already focused on Jones after Dewey's win at Manila Bay.

In Indiana, Republican congressman Charles B. Landis had closely followed the trajectory of the war. He was among those who had lauded Dewey as a hero within hours of the victory at Manila Bay and compared the new American hero with Jones. As a former newspaper publisher, he knew a good story when he saw it. That Jones's final burial place was unknown struck him as both an embarrassment and, potentially, a cause. Landis was an old friend of John Gowdy, the American consul in Paris, and though the war was essentially over, John Paul Jones remained on Landis's mind. So the congressman wrote to Gowdy asking whether it might be possible, after all those years, to poke around Paris and find the burial spot of America's first naval war hero.[12]

Landis didn't have much hope the grave could be found. Still, given Dewey's success at Manila and the way the victory had stirred national pride in the US Navy, it seemed a shame to not try.

9

The Missing Grave

In late November 1898, Americans in Paris carved out a little piece of home by celebrating Thanksgiving with private dinners and a handful of public functions. In the most high-profile celebration, Consul General Gowdy presided over a banquet at the ornate Hotel Continental, where the American peace delegation was housed, midway between the Tuileries gardens and la Place de Vendôme. The toasts and speeches went late into the night. Horace Porter, a West Point graduate, gave one of the addresses, speaking of the American universities that had spawned leaders "who have won distinguished positions not only in war, but in the Cabinet and on the bench, whose renown has extended to the uttermost parts of the earth." Other celebrations stretched into the weekend, including a gathering of expatriate art students in "club rooms" along the Quai de Conti, a party that seems likely to have been much livelier than the speeches delivered at the Continental.[1]

A few days after Thanksgiving, Congressman Landis's letter, in which he wondered about the location of Jones's body, arrived at Gowdy's desk.

The letter itself has disappeared, but given the men's relationship back in Indiana, the tone was likely a personal overture from one friend to another rather than a congressman's formal request for assistance.

Gowdy seems to have made a perfunctory search and replied in early January that he agreed with Landis that the United States had been remiss in not trying to find Jones's body and in not according him an appropriate memorial. "It does seem strange that we have not identified ourselves in gratitude to him who fought our battles at sea in our struggle for independence," Gowdy wrote. "Every thoughtful American citizen can not but feel the deepest regret that we have shown no interest in his resting place" while "other heroes of the Revolution have been marked, and honor paid. . . . He certainly deserves a fitting memorial as the great hero that he was, and as the founder of our American navy."[2] Still, Gowdy couldn't be particularly encouraging. "I very much fear that the remains of John Paul Jones lie in the Catacombs," the vast network of old quarries and tunnels beneath Paris that hold the unidentifiable remains of some six million people that had been moved there over the decades from old Parisian cemeteries. "I am still trying to get some information, if possible, and if I succeed will write you at once."

The truth was, it seemed no one knew where Jones's body might be, in part because of the confusion sown by the French Revolution and in part because, as the legend of John Paul Jones grew, so too did erroneous details of his life and death. Public interest in the mercurial war hero had surged and ebbed. In the early 1800s, while the United States was still finding its place in the world, letters between Jones and some of the Revolutionary-era heroes were reprinted in pamphlets, newspapers, and magazines, the first wave of image-buffing.

Books also emerged, beginning with a translation of Jones's private memoir of his role in the American Revolution, which he had written for the French king Louis XVI. The book was published in Paris in 1798 as *Memoires de Paul Jones* by "Citoyen Andre," Benoit Andre, Jones's secretary. Eight years later, a first-person memoir of the *Bonhomme Richard*'s fight with the *Serapis* came out in the United States. Called *Narrative of the Adventures of an American Navy Officer*, the book was published anonymously because of its scandalous details about Jones, from his treatment of his men to his ego and his rather full love life in bordellos and in the boudoirs of married women. The author was identified in subsequent printings as Captain Nathaniel Fanning, the midshipman who had directed the rigging-level battle against the *Serapis*. After Fanning died of yellow fever on September 30, 1805, in Charleston, South Carolina, his brother, Edmund, a writer, published the book to raise money for Fanning's widow.[3]

That book is most interesting for the details Fanning included about the battle with the *Serapis*. Published well before other books that began to romanticize Jones and the famous sea fight off Flamborough Head, Fanning described four hours of blood-soaked confusion, with cannons blasting through timbers and limbs, cutlasses gashing deeply into flesh, and flaming decks slick with gore. Fanning wrote that at one point, as word circulated that Jones and his top lieutenants were dead, three of his crewmen called out a surrender and began lowering the *Bonhomme Richard*'s flag as a signal that they had given up. A very much alive Jones shouted out, "What damned rascals are them! Shoot them! Kill them!" Then the commander threw his unloaded pistols at the men, cracking the skull of one of them and knocking him unconscious. The flag remained aloft, and the fighting raged on. When the battle ended, its cost was clear: "I now took a full view of the mangled carcasses of the slain on board of our ship; especially between decks, where the bloody scene was enough to appall the stoutest heart. To see the dead lying in heaps—to hear the groans of the wounded and dying—the entrails of the dead scattered promiscuously around, the blood (American, too) over ones shoes, was enough to move pity from the most hardened and callous breast."[4]

Most of the books about Jones, though, ignored the brutality of the battles in which he fought and the occasional petulance of his character, preferring instead to frame him as the embodiment of what many supposed a great naval leader should be: smart, brave, and daring, with a touch of insouciance thrown in. And they served to rehabilitate a reputation that during Jones's lifetime had been dragged down by his personality, his womanizing, and the scandalous circumstances of his departure from Russia. While admired for his seamanship, bravery, creativity (attacking Whitehaven might have failed militarily, but it had had a significant psychological effect on the British), and ferocity in battle, Jones's peers simultaneously disparaged him for his ego and boorishness. Naked ambition and a need for public recognition aren't very endearing qualities, and, in the words of James Fenimore Cooper, they engendered "a species of indefinite distrust [that] clouded his reputation even in America, until the industry of his biographers" began reconstructing his public persona.[5]

Yet Cooper was part of that reconstruction himself. He helped popularize Jones with his novel *The Pilot*, published in 1823—just after *The Pioneers*, which established Cooper as the nation's preeminent novelist. *The Pilot* was based on Jones's raids on the British coast. A former navy midshipman himself, Cooper wrote the book in part as a response to earlier sea tales by Sir Walter Scott, which Cooper thought had failed to capture the spirit of life at sea, because Scott was not a sailor himself. "Paul Jones is the real hero of the novel," one review said. "Its principal design is to delineate his skill and courage in the most desperate enterprises." The review then left Cooper's book behind and offered a lengthy biography of Jones. Like other articles of the period, the spotlight was focused on Jones's bravery and contributions to the Revolution, while the more sordid details of his life fell into the shadows.[6] Yet Cooper himself was ambivalent about Jones's character, and a close reading of *The Pilot* suggests Cooper viewed him as a consummate sailor and commander but also a man nursing resentment against the aristocratic class for not granting him the recognition he so craved.[7]

With the newfound interest in Jones, newspapers and magazines reprinted even more letters between Jones and figures in the Revolution, some of whom, like Thomas Jefferson and James Madison, were still alive. This helped cement Jones's public image as a hero of the Revolution while the young nation faced growing tensions over slavery, nagging economic crises, and political turmoil between the Whigs, who favored a more powerful Congress, and Jacksonian Democrats, who simultaneously championed the voice of the common man and sought a stronger presidency. They were divisive, distracting times, and one gets the sense that readers of *The Pilot* and the reprinted Jones letters were looking for the comfort of nostalgia and a time when the political options seemed simpler: freedom or colonial subjugation.

Jones himself, despite his lack of formal education, was a prodigious letter writer. In the latter years of his life and career, he kept copies of many of the letters he sent as well as those he received, leaving behind a significant paper trail. Or rather, many trails, for after his death the letters scattered to the winds. When Jones left for Europe at the end of the Revolutionary War to try to recover the prize money from the ships he and his crews had captured, he put his logbooks and other papers in the hands of his friend Robert Morris in Philadelphia. The rest, mostly letters, he took with him, and they were part of the estate bequeathed to his two sisters when he died.

The estate also included claims to war prizes, and the sisters and their heirs spent years petitioning Congress to make good on debts owed—primarily, three ships and cargo Jones had captured and sent to Bergen in Norway, then under Denmark's rule. Denmark, to appease the British, seized the ships and returned them to England, creating a diplomatic rift with the United States. The heirs believed the issue was between the US government and Denmark; in the interim, the US government owed them their prizes. Jones's heirs hired Robert Hyslop, a lawyer and family friend in New York (Jones had stayed with him in the summer of 1787), to handle the estate's American claims, including petitioning the young House of Representatives "for compensation of services rendered, or property to be secured and recovered in this country."[8] It would be decades before that claim was settled.

While the family members seemed to be hungry for their due under Jones's will, some were also cognizant of their connection with history. At the sisters' direction, Hyslop obtained the papers that Jones had left with Morris in Philadelphia. There were some rustlings about getting them published, but nothing materialized. In late March 1820, Janette Taylor, Janet Taylor's daughter[9] and Jones's niece in Edinburgh, Scotland, wrote to Hyslop that she possessed a large—though incomplete—collection of Jones's letters, many of them to or from Thomas Jefferson, Benjamin Franklin, John Adams, the Marquis de Lafayette, and other key players from those tumultuous years. Taylor had contemplated publishing the papers in England but feared Jones's anti-British comments would be suppressed.

The family wanted to publish the letters at a profit, yes, but not at the expense of history. "I apprehend the suppression would have essentially injured the work," the niece wrote, adding that she hoped the letters would "exhibit my uncle's character in a just point of view." She asked Hyslop to show the letters around and "let me know if there is any bookseller in New York, who would undertake to publish them, and what I may expect for them. There is one thing however, must be insisted upon, which is, that they are not to be garbled, but are to be given to the world just as they are, without either adding or diminishing." She acknowledged it was impossible to get an estimate since Hyslop did not have all of the letters, but "you may perhaps, after enquiry, have it in your power to give me a hint of what it is probable that I might receive. If you will have the goodness to assist me in this affair, the papers shall be sent to you, addressed as you shall direct, and to be disposed of as you think best; with only this one provision—that they must be published as they are."[10]

It's unclear how many of Jones's letters Taylor sent along, but it was only a taste of the collection. Hyslop approached the New-York Historical Society, whose members saw the value of the letters, but a book project there fell through. Hyslop died, and the letters passed into the possession of his brother, John Hyslop, who owned a bakery in New York, and from there to a man named George A. Ward, who turned them over to John H. Sherburne, register of the US Navy.

Sherburne was already at work on what he hoped would be a biography of Jones. He advertised in newspapers that he was seeking letters and other details on the war hero's life, and he approached the Taylors for whatever documents they might have. Jones's heirs refused to share any letters, likely because they were planning their own book. Sherburne, though, gathered letters from other sources, including John Adams and Thomas Jefferson. He had asked Jefferson for his memories of Jones, but Jefferson, then eighty-two years old, demurred. "My memory is so decayed that from that source I can furnish you nothing worth a place in his history," Jefferson replied. "I believe I cannot better comply with your request than by sending you all the papers relating to him in my presence."[11]

Sherburne published his book, *Life and Character of the Chevalier John Paul Jones*, in 1825 to scathing reviews. Sherburne did little with the material, simply stitching together excerpts of the letters he collected, with transitions of over-the-top accolades for the Scottish captain. The *New-York Review and Atheneum Magazine* dismissed the book as a money-grubbing exercise by Sherburne that fell far short of the project he had advertised at the start in hopes of gaining public subscriptions. (It was common at the time to publish a book based on preorders by readers.) "We do not hesitate to declare it our opinion that Mr. Sherburne has unfairly disappointed the expectations he had so industriously excited," the magazine wrote. The work indicates "an ignorance of history, and a crudeness of style, only pardonable in a work of the most moderate pretensions. The want of method and discrimination manifest in the selection of the letters, induces us to believe, that they were taken blindfold[ed] from the mass to complete the complement of pages. . . . In short, it is very palpably, a money-making concern, and Mr. Sherburne, the editor, and Mr. Van Zandt, the compiler [publisher], are probably the only persons not disappointed."[12] Another critic writing the foreword to a later biography incorporating the Taylors' letters dismissed Sherburne's work as having been presided over by "some singularly capricious demon, wonderfully ingenious in producing puzzling and painful disorder."[13]

Still, the book helped fan interest in Jones. In 1830, the Taylor collection was finally published in New York. A year later, an American naval lieutenant named Alexander B. Pinkham took a year's leave to travel to the British Isles to seek out the haunts of some of his favorite authors, such as poet Robert Burns and novelist Sir Walter Scott, who was still living. He also wanted to visit the birthplace of Jones, "whose memory he venerated to the point of idolatry, not only as a brother sailor and adopted citizen of America, but above all as the first man who dared to hoist the flag of independence on the gigantic waters of the new world."[14]

Pinkham, the son of an American whaling captain and a Scottish mother, was a powerfully built, heavyset man, gentle in demeanor despite his prizefighter physique, with a face reddened and worn by years of sea, sun, and wind. He landed at Cork in southwest Ireland with a small stash of cash, a single faded blue suit, and a knapsack "containing a change of linen, materials for writing, and a few books and mathematical instruments." After wandering Ireland for a few weeks, Pinkham shipped out from Dublin across the Irish Sea to Liverpool and then headed north to Dumfries, where he spent a few days resting up and visiting with the editor of the local newspaper. From there, Pinkham journeyed some fourteen miles west to Jones's boyhood home at Arbigland, where he was saddened to the point of tears to find the cottage a roofless wreck. He sketched the ruins in his notebook and continued on his travels.

Pinkham wandered western Scotland for a few weeks, then crossed to the east and tried to visit Scott, who refused to see him. (Scott had recently suffered from a stroke and would die the next year.) Pinkham was disappointed but did manage to have breakfast with poet James Hogg, a friend of Scott. He then spent several days in Edinburgh.

Yet Pinkham was haunted by the condition of Jones's childhood home. So he reversed course and returned to Dumfries with a plan. Working through the local editor he had befriended when he first arrived, Pinkham approached the owner of the estate, D. H. Craik, and gained his permission to have the cottage reroofed and made habitable. Pinkham left twenty-five gold sovereigns with his editor friend to cover the cost. The amount, though substantial for a wandering seaman, was insufficient for the project; Craik made up the difference, and the cottage was restored the next spring. The renovated building, with its white walls visible from the bay, became a local sailing landmark. Its first tenant was the widow of a local fisherman who had drowned at sea. It stills stands as a summer tourist destination.

Over the next twenty years, Jones's legacy made recurring appearances in official Washington and in popular culture in the United States as well as Europe. In Washington, Congress voted in 1834 to honor the commodore by naming a frigate after him, though the plans were never carried out.

In Paris, Alexandre Dumas père wrote the play *Paul Jones: A Drama in Five Acts* in 1838 and then converted it into a serialized novel, *Le Capitaine Paul*. Though viewed as something of a sequel to Cooper's *The Pilot*, Dumas's work made Jones a French captain and staged most of the scenes in Brittany, apparently several years after Dumas had visited Lorient, the home port for Jones's real-life forays to England. The play was largely ignored, but Dumas's serialized novel sold well, and several London-based houses published English translations that were also sold in the United States.

In 1841, US Navy captain Alexander Slidell Mackenzie—a writer as well as a career navy man—published another biography, *Life of John Paul Jones*, which received wide attention and sales. Novelist James Fenimore Cooper was not a fan of Mackenzie or his work, however. "Mackenzie, I have discovered, is authority for nothing," Cooper wrote to fellow author William Gilmore Simms in January 1844. "I do not accuse him of intentional departures from the truth, but he has an obliquity of mind, and an obtuseness of morals that are almost as bad."[15]

Part of Cooper's dislike for Mackenzie was rooted in a moment of high drama at sea. In November 1842, the year after his Jones biography appeared, Mackenzie ordered that three crewmen be executed after hearing rumors of a possible mutiny aboard the *Somers*, which was under his command as a training ship for young navy men. The plot purportedly included killing Mackenzie and his officers and converting the ship to piracy. The thin evidence was a conversation between the alleged ringleader and a crewman he supposedly sought to enlist in the conspiracy. Even more troubling was the nature of the *Somers*'s mission. It was a training ship crewed primarily by teenage midshipmen to test them for careers at sea. The alleged plot, and Mackenzie's reaction to it, was akin to a school headmaster inflicting capital punishment, and it sparked an uproar, as well as questions about how the US Navy was training young seamen. When the *Somers* reached port, Mackenzie faced a court martial that was closely followed by the public because one of the dead mutineers, Midshipman Philip Spencer, was the son of a political appointee: John C. Spencer, secretary of war. But the military appeared to take care of its own, clearing Mackenzie of any wrongdoing in a process many dismissed as a whitewash. Cooper was outraged. He conducted his own review of the inquiry based on the transcript, resulting in the 1844 publication of a scathing indictment of the scandal and of the navy's failure to deliver justice for the three young men against whom Cooper saw little evidence of culpability.

Cooper, whose novels made him one of the century's most recognized American writers, had returned to Jones and his life story in 1843, publishing a two-part biography in *Graham's Lady's and Gentleman's Magazine* as part of a series of profiles destined to be collected in a book. Near the end of the piece, Cooper wrote that Jones's body had been buried in Paris's famous Père Lachaise cemetery. Taylor, Jones's niece, was living then in New York City; she read the articles and sent Cooper a lengthy letter telling him she found the profile "substantially though not precisely correct—its errors are of minor importance." Because Cooper planned to include a variation of the articles in a forthcoming book, Taylor said she felt compelled to correct the errors she had found, including where Jones had been buried. Père Lachaise, she pointed out, didn't open until 1812 (she got the year wrong; it was 1804), well after Jones died in 1792. So Jones could not have been buried there. "He was interred in the old Protestant burial ground, purchased by Lord Viscount Stormont (afterwards Earl of Mansfield) when British Ambassador at the Court of France—it was situated near the Barriere du Combat, and is now, I believe, totally covered with buildings."

Three years after receiving Taylor's letter, Cooper finally published his *Lives of Distinguished American Naval Officers*, which included a chapter on Jones based on the magazine articles. Cooper left out some of Taylor's added details but corrected the burial error from his magazine piece, writing that Jones "was interred in a cemetery that no longer exists, but which then was used, near la Barriere du Combat, for the interment of Protestants. It is probable that no traces of his grave could now be found."[16]

While that 1846 description of Jones's final resting spot seems vague, it was only a half century after Jones's death. To those who knew Paris and Parisian history, there was enough evidence to find the cemetery. Over the centuries, Paris had been encircled by a series of walls, new supplanting old as the city expanded. In 1784, the farmers-general, tax-collecting financiers appointed by Louis XVI, ordered the construction of a fifteen-mile (twenty-four-kilometer) wall around Paris, encompassing some undeveloped areas that had previously been tax-free zones. The wall included sixteen gates aimed at controlling the flow of goods in and out of Paris; they were, in essence, tax collection booths in a customs barrier.[17] The Combat district of Paris was in the northeast and encompassed a low hill called Montfaucon. During the Middle Ages it had been a site of public executions. Bodies would dangle from *le gibet de Montfaucon*—the gallows of Montfaucon—for, in extreme cases, two or three years. Later, the neighborhood earned its

Combat name as the site of animal fights and eventually became a slaughterhouse for horses.[18]

By the late 1700s, the stench of death was gone, but the neighborhood was a crime-ridden slum. When the *barriere* was built through Combat, the ornate gatehouse was erected near present-day Place du Colonel Fabien—just a few hundred yards from l'Hôpital Saint-Louis and its Protestant graveyard, and about two miles northwest of Père Lachaise cemetery. Neither Taylor nor Cooper specified the name of the cemetery nor the street it was on, but a reader with access to old maps and knowledge of some of Paris's history would have found enough clues to locate the cemetery, the only one that had accepted Protestant bodies in that era. But to the uninformed, Cooper's reference just looked like another dead end.

No one, it seems, bothered to look in the obvious place: Paris's l'Hôtel de Ville, or City Hall, where Parisian bureaucrats kept detailed records of burials in city cemeteries. Except one person: Charles Read, the French-born son of Scottish Protestants. In 1849 Read had been appointed assistant director of the department of non-Roman Catholic religions at France's interior ministry, where he helped reorganize the Protestant churches in France, cofounded the Société de l'Histoire du Protestantisme Français, and wrote several books on Protestant history.

Read lost an internal political battle in the interior ministry and was forced to resign his job in 1857, but he didn't give up his work. Over the next few years he continued to write, and as part of his archival research, Read made regular trips to the pre-Commune Hôtel de Ville, where he scoured official records for details on the evolution of Protestant Paris. And he made copies of records pertaining to Protestants—including burial records.[19]

In March 1859 Read published a small item in the French magazine *Correspondance Littéraire* that included the detail that Jones had not been buried in Pére Lachaise as generally believed but was laid to rest in the now-closed Protestant cemetery near l'Hôpital Saint-Louis. It also set the date of Jones's death as July 18, 1792, a fact that had been in dispute among historians. And it reported that he died at home at 42 Rue de Tournon as a "consequence of 'dropsy of the chest' (*hydropisie de poitrine*), in the sentiments of the Protestant religion." The interment came two days later, witnessed by a deputation of members of the National Assembly; Pierre-Francois

Simonneau, the king's representative and a friend of Jones; and several of Jones's American friends, including Blackden.

Translated and truncated versions of Read's article showed up in the American *Atlantic Monthly*, which credited the source but left out the cemetery reference, and in the June 1859 issue of *Russell's Magazine*, which included the cemetery name. The *Russell's* article did not cite its source, but in that era, periodicals often republished material without credit.[20]

Nearly thirty years later, Read revisited the Jones item in an article in the Société de l'Histoire du Protestantisme Français's *Bulletin Historique et Littéraire* that revisited some of the notable death records he had found years earlier in the now-destroyed city archives. Among them was the entry for John Paul Jones.[21] Read's article and notes indicated the original record had come from one of five city registers of burials in a Protestant cemetery near Porte Saint-Martin, which had opened in 1724 after Cornelis Hop, the Dutch ambassador to France, persuaded Louis XV that the city needed a place to inter foreign Protestants who died in France. Catholic doctrine forbade placing non-Catholics in the consecrated ground of parish cemeteries, which forced Protestants to bury their dead on private land, and often in secret. With the opening of the Porte Saint-Martin cemetery, the Protestant dead were accorded some final dignity. That cemetery eventually was closed in 1762 to make way for the extension of Boulevard Saint-Martin. Read, though, discovered that it was soon replaced by another cemetery for foreign Protestants near l'Hôpital Saint-Louis, with the same family of caretakers, the Corroys, in charge. And it was there that Jones was buried.

So the information was readily available—if one knew where to look.

10

---- ☼ ----

A Brush with Fame

ONE PERSON CAME CLOSE to finding John Paul Jones's body: John Henry Sherburne, the politically connected naval bureaucrat who wrote the 1825 book based on a collection of Jones's letters.

Sherburne's interest in the Scottish-born sailor was part of his own family legacy. Sherburne was born in Portsmouth, New Hampshire, in 1794, two years after Jones died. He was the son of a Dartmouth- and Harvard-educated lawyer who left his Portsmouth practice to fight in the Revolutionary War, where he lost a leg during the August 1778 Siege of Newport. While no doubt painful, life-threatening, and a tremendous sacrifice to the cause, the loss of the limb came about in a rather ignominious manner: a British cannonball barreled through Major Sherburne's tent while he was sitting at the breakfast table.

After the war, the elder Sherburne, a quick-tempered and disagreeable man, entered politics, first sitting in the New Hampshire legislature before winning a seat in Congress. He knew Jones from the commodore's days in Portsmouth (they corresponded after the war), and they counted James Madison and Thomas Jefferson among their mutual friends. In 1804, President Jefferson appointed Sherburne to a seat as a federal district judge for New Hampshire. The position came shrouded in controversy. Sherburne had been a key witness in the impeachment of the previous bench-holder, Judge John Pickering, but to avoid cross-examination, he disappeared after giving his testimony. Pickering was duly ousted, and Sherburne then won the appointment to the vacancy he helped create. He remained a federal district court judge until his death in 1830.[1]

The Sherburnes were a family of privilege and thus had connections. Descended from one of the earliest settlers in Portsmouth, the elder Sherburne's sister was married to John Langdon, the shipbuilder with whom Jones had wrangled over the building and outfitting of the *Ranger* and the *America*. Langdon served in the Second Constitutional Congress, was a US senator from 1789 to 1801, passed up Jefferson's overture to appoint him secretary of the navy, and became governor of New Hampshire in 1805. Seven years later, citing his age, Langdon turned down the nomination to stand for election as Madison's vice president in the 1812 election.

The younger Sherburne reaped the benefits of those powerful family connections. He entered Phillips Exeter Academy in 1809 at the age of fifteen, and was married at age eighteen to Mary Ann Hall, a daughter of Elijah Hall, who had served as a naval lieutenant under Jones aboard the *Ranger*. Hall was part of Jones's most daring escapades, including the raid on the Scottish Selkirk estate (in which the lord wasn't home but the family silver was captured). And Jones deputized Hall to sail the captured British warship *Drake* to Brest, France, as a prize. The stories told by his father-in-law, as well as those offered by his father and uncle, intertwined Sherburne's sense of family history with the life of Jones.

Sherburne worked for a time as a correspondent for the *Saturday Courier* newspaper in Philadelphia, traveling extensively up and down the East Coast and into the western territories. In 1825, while his father was still alive and, one suspects, able to pull a string or two, Sherburne was hired as the register for the US Navy, a $1,400-a-year civilian position usually filled as an act of political patronage.

Yet Sherburne styled himself as a writer more than a military man; the same year he took the bureaucratic job, he published his *Life and Character of the Chevalier John Paul Jones*. And he commissioned portraits of himself and his wife by Charles Bird King,[2] an artist noted for his paintings of Native American tribal leaders who passed through Washington, DC. The Sherburnes made a handsome couple. King depicted Mary Ann with a full face, soft hazel eyes, and curled brown hair. In the portrait, Sherburne's eyes are a little darker, as is his hair, which is teased upward above a large forehead and a long, aquiline nose. In a mark of ego, Sherburne had King paint into his portrait a copy of a letter from Jefferson on the table at which he sits, and his book about Jones open in his hand, a nineteenth-century version of an author's publicity photo.[3]

Sherburne returned in late February 1837 to the trove of letters and other documents Jefferson had sent him as he was preparing his book on Jones. This time through, Sherburne discovered something he had overlooked before: a mention of $50,000 that Jones had given to Jefferson, then the minister to France, as a portion of the prize money due his crew members on the *Bonhomme Richard* and the *Alliance*. Digging through Congressional records, Sherburne discovered that the money had never been paid out to the crews or their heirs.

In February 1839, before the wave of books that renewed public interest in Jones, Sherburne went to the District of Columbia's Orphans' Court, an early version of probate court, and sought appointment as the administrator for the Jones estate. As evidence of his legal standing, he provided letters dated 1826 and 1838 from two descendants of Jones's sister, Mary Ann Lowden, who had granted him power of attorney. Both descendants were dead by the time of the court action. Despite writing about the will in his book, Sherburne told the court that Jones had died intestate and that he anticipated there would be no money to claim for Jones's heirs, who had already received some cash from the US government. He did believe there would be a small amount due to Jones's crew. By downplaying the money involved, Sherburne was able to win the court order appointing him administrator by posting a $500 bond instead of a bond equal to the amount of money at stake (as was usual).

Janette Taylor, Jones's niece, got wind of what Sherburne was up to and filed an appeal, arguing that Sherburne had no standing to be administrator because Jones had left a will and his heirs were known. The court let Sherburne keep his authority to administer on behalf of the estate in the United States, but ordered him to post a $30,000 bond. Sherburne missed the deadline, and his rights as an administrator were revoked, a decision that was upheld on appeal on August 22, 1842. The claim itself lingered but was finally paid on July 6, 1848, some fifty-six years after Jones died and on what would have been his 101st birthday.[4]

Sherburne wasn't done with Jones, though. In 1845, he approached navy secretary George Bancroft seeking permission to use a navy ship to bring Jones's body to the United States for a proper burial and memorial. Never mind that he didn't know where the body was. It didn't matter; Bancroft never responded. (Bancroft, in a bit of historical symmetry, also founded the US Naval Academy at Annapolis that same year.)

Sherburne moved on to other projects. When his father died fifteen years earlier, in 1830, Sherburne had inherited the old man's library, which included a copy of *The History of the Administration of John Adams*. A controversial book, it had been published in 1802 and then immediately bought up by some of those scandalized by what the author, John Wood, had written. Aaron Burr, in particular, took umbrage, claiming libel and factual errors, and Wood, in a change of heart, wrote his own publisher repudiating the work, asking that it be scrapped, and offering to pay for the production costs. The printed copies were dumped in a pile and burned, but a few copies escaped the conflagration. One of those copies was in the Sherburne family library; Sherburne claimed (without detailing how he knew) the book had been a gift from Jefferson, a political rival of Adams, to his father.[5]

Sherburne began shopping the book around in 1840 and finally found a taker at Walker and Gillis, publishers in Philadelphia. As the book neared publication, the publisher distributed a pamphlet seeking subscribers, promising that the book would be "printed on fine white paper; new type, bound in cloth of 400 pages and delivered for one dollar." Sherburne sent copies of the prospectus far and wide, including to President James Polk, saying that the former president and son of John Adams, John Quincy Adams, had "personally observed to me at his own mansion that should the work be published, he should publicly notice it in order to correct the early history of the Republic."[6]

The new version, with an introduction by Sherburne detailing the book's history, was published in 1846 as *The Suppressed History of the Administration of John Adams*. Sherburne's additions were a distraction. His writing voice was pompous, spotlighting his family connections and heritage with an overwrought writing style common to the era. Critics found as little to like in it as they had in Sherburne's life of Jones. "Fortunate indeed is it that the endorsement of [Sherburne's] name is not sufficient celebrity to give it currency," the *Southern and Western Literary Messenger and Review* wrote of the book. "A want of method and discrimination is manifest in this volume as well as in the Life of Jones, both exhibiting a dull collection of disjointed documents thrown together without order, taste, or judgment, while to keep up the appearance of legitimate narrative. . . . The conclusions at which Mr. Sherburne arrives in almost every instance, so palpably contradict truth as to excite disgust in every reader conversant with our annals."[7] The review was unfair; the book was written by Wood, not Sherburne, so he wasn't responsible for its disjointed nature. Still, it was hardly the kind of review any writer would want to stomach.

Yet Sherburne kept writing. He had traveled to Europe in the mid-1840s and in 1847 published *The Tourist's Guide, or Pencillings in England and on the Continent with the Expenses, Conveyances, Distances, Sights, Hotels, Etc., and Important Hints to the Tourist* (Philadelphia: G.B. Zeiber and Co.). Later that year he was back in England, part of a tour that would also take him to Ireland and France. He rented a room at 96 Strand, in the heart of the hustle and bustle of London. Part of his trip was to serve as something of a diplomatic courier, "as bearer of dispatches" to, among others, George Bancroft, who had been moved from President Polk's cabinet to the Court of St. James's as the American minister to Great Britain.

Sherburne's mission, though, was primarily personal.[8] He wrote to Richard Rush, a former member of the Monroe and Madison cabinets and the current US minister to France, that he was heading to Paris soon and wanted help finding Jones's body and shipping it to the United States. Rush replied in January 1848 that "I will gladly aid you in any suggestions or steps that may be proper and practical." Rush noted that Sherburne said he planned to have Jones reburied somewhere in Washington, DC, but as in previous endeavors, Sherburne was overstepping his authority. In fact, his approach throughout his adult life seemed to be to act on a whim. In this instance, Sherburne had no claim to the body, no right to have it exhumed, and no authority to determine where it might be reburied on American soil. Rush noted that he himself had little authority to act. "Uninstructed by the Secretary of State on this subject, and uninformed if Congress has passed any resolution in regard to it, I must await your arrival for information on these and other points, preliminary to any steps of mine, official or otherwise, with this government or the public authorities of Paris on the occasion." And he added a telling point: "I have no knowledge of the place of his interment, of which, perhaps, you may know something."[9]

Sherburne took detailed notes of his travels, but they have disappeared, so it's unclear exactly what steps he was taking to try to find Jones's body. British newspapers reported that he delivered a speech in Leicester Town Hall on emigration to America, which sounds like little more than cheerleading as he extolled "the advantages of high wages paid for labour of all kinds, the low price of good land, the cheapness of all kind of provisions, and the numerous chances for an industrious man to improve his social position and elevate himself in the scale of society."[10] It's unclear whether Sherburne even made it across the channel to France. At some point, he returned to the United States, and there is no record of his efforts for three more years, when in 1851 he once again traveled to Europe.

Sherburne arrived in England in early May aboard the *Washington*, an American steam mail ship, this time with a plan. In January, he had written to Daniel Webster, President Millard Fillmore's secretary of state, seeking his help. The letter is a bit disingenuous—Sherburne told Webster that he had received administrative power on behalf of Jones's estate, which was on file in the appeals court in Washington, but he didn't mention that he had subsequently lost that authority for failing to post the required bond. Sherburne invoked his family connections to Jones and reminded Webster that the secretary had known Sherburne's father and uncle. Citing those "friendly feelings," Sherburne asked Webster to write a private letter to the US minister to France, William Cabell Rives, urging him to help Sherburne locate and exhume Jones's body. Sherburne already had raised $500 from American shipping businessmen in Liverpool, so he wasn't seeking money. And, oddly for a man who openly sought publicity, Sherburne asked Webster to keep details of Sherburne's quest from "newspaper writers in Washington who generally write news without a knowledge of what they write and [who have] spies throughout all the Departments, I am informed."[11] Sherburne also sought a second private letter of endorsement for the project, over Webster's signature, which Sherburne could use in Paris, should it be necessary. If Webster ever replied to Sherburne, that letter is lost.

Sherburne also wrote to the secretary of the navy, William A. Graham, soliciting help. Graham in turn wrote to Captain Joshua R. Sands of the frigate *St. Lawrence*, which was slated to sail for England in May carrying some additional US exhibits for the recently opened Great Exhibition in London, the first in what became a long-running series of international world's fairs. Graham instructed Sands to be ready to transport Jones's body, and Sherburne with it, back to the United States.

Once in London, Sherburne sent a note to Sands announcing that he had arrived, and Sands replied on May 6 asking Sherburne when he thought the body might be ready for transport. "The voyage for which the *St. Lawrence* came to this country has been effected," he wrote. With the exhibits unloaded, "there is no further reason for her detention at Southampton." Sands was cooperating, but he also made it clear that he wasn't very happy sitting around waiting.[12]

Sherburne didn't tarry in England. He went on to Paris where he "paid my respects to the American Legation and Consulate, to state the object of my mission to Paris and my anxious desire to proceed at once in order that the frigate *St. Lawrence* should not be detained any longer than necessary." There would be delays anyway. Despite his attempts to move without much media notice, small items appeared in several newspapers about Sherburne's journey and plans. His second edition of *The Life and Letters of John Paul Jones* was due to be published in June (dedicated to Graham, the navy secretary), and one suspects either his publisher in New York or Sherburne himself let the word out, hoping to fan sales. Returning Jones's body to the United States just weeks before the new edition was to hit the streets would have been a significant marketing coup. Perhaps anticipating such timing, the new edition of Sherburne's book included some of the letters Sherburne had received related to his quest.

Once in Paris, Sherburne received a letter from a lawyer identified in the records only as "N. Billings" that stopped him in his tracks. "As your name has been mentioned in the American papers, as superintending the exhumation of the remains of John Paul Jones, it is proper that I should inform you that the legal representative of Jones is Frances E. Lowden [a grandniece], and that, as her attorney I have taken the preliminary steps to prevent any improper interference with the said remains."

Billings and Sherburne met later that day at the US consulate in Paris, and Sherburne managed to talk his way out of the mess. Billings wasn't content with just a conversation, however. He wrote Sherburne the next day asking him to put in writing the gist of their unspecified agreement and Sherburne's intentions. Sherburne complied, though the letter is lost. Billings, his tone now congenial after receiving Sherburne's written assurances, told Sherburne he could meet him at his home in the early morning, or after 4 PM, to discuss plans, and then added an enigmatic postscript: "Please let me know about the spy-glass of Paul Jones."

Sherburne wrote Captain Sands on May 19 about Billings and the delay the lawyer's presence had created. "At so unexpected a proceeding and having no time, or desire to have a controversy on such a subject in a foreign land, [I] have suspended for the present, by advice, further action, trusting that all will yet, on my part, be accomplished." He told Sands to make his own call about whether to wait or sail. Sands replied that he too had received a note from Billings, which he had ignored. With his ship and crew idle and business to attend to, Sands couldn't accommodate an indefinite delay. With regrets, the captain sailed.

Billings and Sherburne eventually agreed to work together to search for Jones's burial place, though it's unclear if they had reached agreement on whether to move the remains to the United States. Sherburne and Billings poked into Parisian archives, and while nothing indicates which records they consulted, they apparently missed the city hall records detailing Jones's burial site near l'Hôpital Saint-Louis that Charles Read would soon find. Sherburne and Billings concluded instead that Jones had been buried in an area set aside for Protestants behind the Hôtel-Dieu hospital on Île de la

Cité, the island in the Seine that also holds Notre Dame Cathedral. That cemetery, though, was long gone. "The land devoted to such purpose was subsequently sold, and all the bones collected and placed in a pit, or carried to the Catacombs," Sherburne reported to Graham, the navy secretary, in a letter dated July 14, 1851.

The mission was a bust, Sherburne concluded. The bones were gone. Or at least irretrievable. So Sherburne set sail for home. A year later he was dead, unaware of the error that had kept him from finding Jones's body.

11

The Search Begins

IN THE YEARS AFTER losing the White House to Grover Cleveland in the 1892 election, Benjamin Harrison returned to civilian life and a lucrative legal practice in Indianapolis. As a former president, he was in demand as much for his legacy and connections as for his legal acumen, and he took great advantage of it. Among his new clients was the country of Venezuela, which hired him in January 1898 to handle negotiations in a dispute with Great Britain over its border with British Guinea. Harrison's fee: $100,000, or about $2.4 million in current dollars.[1]

Great Britain was in a tight spot. The United States, invoking the Monroe Doctrine, cast a wary eye over the border dispute, ready to push back against any attempts by England—or any other European power—to expand its presence in the Western Hemisphere. President Cleveland upped the pressure on Great Britain by asking Congress to create a boundary commission to unilaterally impose a solution and then be ready to enforce it with military action, if necessary. Great Britain was already wrangling with European rivals over colonies in Africa and trade with China, as well as fighting off a rebellion by the Boers in South Africa. Not wanting another international flash point, the British agreed to arbitration, and three months later the Venezuelans agreed also. It took months to hammer out the details, but the groundwork was set, and the agreement was made to hold the arbitration hearing in Paris in the summer of 1899.[2]

So it was that ex-president Harrison found himself and his wife boarding the Europe-bound *St. Paul*—the same passenger ship that ferried the Porters in 1897—for Paris. The Harrisons arrived in late May, and as a former head of state, Harrison wasn't just any lawyer showing up for a hearing. Porter prepared the embassy staff for Harrison's arrival, and throughout his summer-long visit, Harrison was the guest of honor at formal dinners hosted by Porter, French president Loubet, and others. With such an eminent American in Paris, the organizers of the annual Decoration Day celebration at the Marquis de Lafayette's tomb in Paris's Picpus Cemetery decided to ask him to give the main speech. Harrison obliged, and on the cool and sunny morning of May 30, Harrison delivered a simple message of peace and friendship between the United States and France, framed around Lafayette's role as a military leader in the American Revolution.

"The nation that cherishes the graves of its soldiers and assembles to honor them is the nation that preserves and enlarges national life," Harrison said. Monuments in the United States, he added, celebrated emancipation. That quest for freedom united the Americans and the French, a relationship personified by Lafayette, "the crusader of liberty, who came to our aid in a time of stress, whose name is perhaps more closely than any other connected with the name of [George] Washington. Let the president of France and all Frenchmen be assured of the sentiment of amity and gratitude felt by all Americans."[3]

As speeches go, it was pretty pedestrian, but it served its purpose and was duly reported in the American newspapers back home. James G. Johnson, a lawyer and local Republican Party figure in rural Randolph, New York, some sixty miles south of Buffalo, read an item about the speech in his local paper. It stirred Johnson, a Union Army veteran, to pick up his pen and write to McKinley at the White House.

"Ex-President Harrison seemed to indicate that the Marquis was the only American officer of prominence during the revolution, buried in France," Johnson wrote. But that wasn't the case. John Paul Jones had also died "in Paris and was buried with highest honors by the French government—perhaps in the same cemetery that contains the remains of Lafayette." Johnson speculated that Jones may have been interred in a grave that had been rented for a number of years, a custom in France at the time, then tossed

> . . . into a potters field, there to mingle with those of uncounted dead of the French Revolution. Yet, there may be a possibility that owing to Paul Jones having received a national burial, this is otherwise. Cannot you, dear Mr. President, as the head of our great nation, cause search to be made so that these remains, if identified, may be brought home for burial; or if not, that the spot where he was laid to rest may be so designated so that on next Memorial Day loving hands can cover it with flowers in memory of a simple republican hero whose wise states-manship, cunning seamanship and desperate valor so largely aided in our national deliverance?[4]

McKinley's office sent the letter to Hay at the Department of State, who forwarded it to Henry Vignaud, the first secretary in the Paris embassy. Hay asked Vignaud to look into the matter, apparently either unaware of Gowdy's efforts six months earlier in response to Congressman Landis's letter, or dissatisfied with the results.

Vignaud, too, had been making some inquiries of his own. In Febru-ary 1899, the Parisian papers were full of articles about the successful effort by Alfred de Ricaudy, editor of the conservative weekly *L'Echo du Public*, to find the grave of eighteenth-century French laissez-faire economist Anne-Robert-Jacques Turgot. The economist died in 1781, and, like Jones, over the ensuing decades his burial spot was forgotten. Ricaudy decided to see what he could find by diving deeply into Parisian and French records. He discov-ered that Turgot had been buried in a lead coffin at the Hôpital Laennec in Paris, and not in Bons, Normandy, as legend had it. With Turbot's descen-dants standing around, the crypt was opened, and the mystery solved.

Vignaud wrote to Ricaudy congratulating him on the discovery, and as a long shot asked the French editor whether he had seen during his research any hints of where Jones's grave might be.[5] The embassy records don't include a response from Ricaudy, but if he had written back to Vignaud, the answer apparently was no, he didn't know where Jones's body was buried. In late June, Vignaud wrote back to Secretary Hay that "I have had more than one occasion to look into this matter and all inquiries made of the city authorities or persons to be informed failed. One thing however is certain. Paul Jones was not buried in the cemetery where the remains of Lafayette lie. At the instance of a gentleman from Boston, who wrote me on the subject, I am making another effort in that direction and if successful I will inform you at once."[6]

The "gentleman from Boston" was most likely a woman by the name of Marion H. Brazier, an activist in the Daughters of the American Revolution. Vignaud had mischaracterized Brazier as a man "who takes particular interest in all matters pertaining to Paul Jones" in an earlier letter—dated November 15, 1898—to a woman in France who was also seeking information on Jones.[7] And the other effort Vignaud mentioned was a bit of a whim. The same day he responded to Secretary Hay, Vignaud wrote to the prefect of the Seine and president of the Commission of Old Paris. When Jones was buried, the funeral cortege had wound through the old Parisian streets. Might the prefect have some records of that long-ago event that would suggest where the funeral procession had ended? It was a good instinct, but apparently fruitless.[8]

The range of inquiries into Jones's fate from fellow American citizens, not to mention the secretary of state, struck Ambassador Porter as deserving more than a simple rehash of what had become the adopted US position in the matter: that Jones's bones were beyond retrieval. Porter would write later that he was moved not only by a sense of patriotism but also by empathy for the war hero. As the force behind construction of Grant's Tomb, Porter knew the power a public monument had in preserving public memory. "I felt a deep sense of humiliation as an American citizen in realizing that our first and most fascinating naval hero had been lying for more than a century in an unknown and forgotten grave and that no successful attempt had ever been made to recover his remains and give them appropriate sepulture in the land upon whose history he had shed so much luster," Porter wrote. "Knowing that he had been buried in Paris,

I resolved to undertake personally a systematic and exhaustive search for the body."

Porter was uncertain about the extent of the earlier searches, and by nature a methodical man, he thought that a more diligent effort would either turn up the body or confirm that it was, indeed, beyond finding. At the very least, a spot might be found in Paris to erect a memorial to the dead war hero.

The timing was ripe. Public interest in Jones was growing back home, fanned by the publication of a historical novel about a young American during the pre-Revolution years that featured several chapters on the naval hero. The novel, by Winston Churchill—not to be confused with the future British prime minister—was called *Richard Carvel*, and after its publication in June 1899, it went on to become the bestselling book in American history to that point, cementing Churchill as one of the top American writers of the day. Churchill's portrayal of Jones "presenting him for the first time as an actual man" infused public interest in Porter's quest, once details of the search began surfacing.[9]

Porter turned the search over to the embassy's second secretary, Arthur Bailly-Blanchard, who, like Vignaud, was a native of New Orleans and spoke fluent French. Bailly-Blanchard effectively started from scratch, seeking new sources of information even as the embassy was reporting back to Washington that the body likely was irretrievable. There were leads to follow. The Taylor edition of Jones's letters contained an August 9, 1792, letter from Samuel Blackden, the Revolutionary War veteran and friend of Jones, to Jones's sister, detailing the commodore's last days. Blackden, who had been in London at the time, began his letter with a reference to the query from Taylor dated August 3, in which she apparently had asked Blackden if he knew details of what had happened to her brother. Jones, Blackden replied, had been ill for about a year, "but had not been so unwell" that he couldn't maintain his apartment. Two months before his death, Jones's color began to yellow and he lost his appetite; he began taking unspecified medicines that seemed to help. "But about ten days before his death his legs began to swell, which increased upwards, so that two days before his exit he could not button his waistcoat, and had great difficulty breathing." He died on July 18 and was buried two days later in "a leaden coffin . . . in case the United States, whom he had so essentially served, and with so much honor to himself, should claim his remains, they would be more easily removed." That was all, he wrote, "that I can say concerning his illness and death"[10]

The lead coffin would prove to be the most significant detail for Porter in his search. How deeply involved Porter became in the physical work of reviewing records and chasing down slivers of information remains a question, given that he directed Bailly-Blanchard to steer the investigation. But his commitment was inarguable. He paid for the search on his own and conducted it quietly, trying to keep it out of the newspapers (he was unsuccessful on that front) and initially without informing his superiors in Washington what he was up to.

It quickly became clear the Americans would need some French help. Bailly-Blanchard might have been fluent in French, but he was not intimately familiar with the workings of Parisian municipal bureaucracy and various public and private archives. What they needed was a French historical detective. With Paris history buffs still buzzing over the discovery of Turgot's grave, Sims, the naval attaché, suggested that Ricaudy was the obvious man for the job of finding John Paul Jones's body.[11] Vignaud approached the editor, who agreed to help undertake a painstaking review of records in hopes of picking up the threads of history and unwinding fact from legend. It took several months, but they pieced the story together.

---------- ✿ ----------

The search began in earnest in late June 1899, with a series of letters and inquiries to various French political figures and bureaucrats. Vignaud, a voracious reader of the Parisian press, had seen an article in the *Bulletin Municipal* by municipal councilor Alfred Leroux that mentioned Paul Jones and an old cemetery for foreign Protestants on Rue de l'Hôpital Saint-Louis. Vignaud wrote to Leroux asking for more information about that cemetery, including whether it still existed, but there is no mention of a response.[12]

By the end of the summer, Ricaudy had been enlisted, and his first step was to verify exactly when Jones had died, a date that was still in dispute among historians.[13] The logical place to find that detail was in the Hôtel de

Ville, but once again, Paris's revolutionary history got in the way. Those records had been destroyed during the Paris Commune.

Charles Read, the Protestant researcher and historian who had copied Jones's death information from the city records, died in 1898, the year before Porter began his search. Read's personal and research papers were donated to the Bibliothèque de Rue des Saints-Pères, a library. Both Bailly-Blanchard and Ricaudy soon found Read's 1887 article on the history of Protestant cemeteries and Jones's likely burial spot. Ricaudy took the additional step of consulting Read's personal archive at the library.

In his early reports to Porter, Ricaudy held back one key detail from the ambassador: that Jones had been buried "in a cemetery for foreign Protestants." The significance of that withheld fact didn't become clear until later, even though it wasn't withheld for very long.[14] Bailly-Blanchard had the same material from Read's article, and he and Porter were becoming convinced they were on the right trail. Porter, whose skepticism of Ricaudy was growing, directed Bailly-Blanchard to undertake a process of elimination of other potential burial sites.

Over the next few weeks, Bailly-Blanchard reviewed more than one hundred publications for hints that their assumption—that Paris was home to only one Protestant cemetery at the time—was correct, and for other clues. They found records that identified Simonneau as the man who had paid for the burial, an act of charity that galled Porter. "This brought to light for the first time the mortifying fact that the hero who had once been the idol of the American people had been buried by charity, and that the payment of his funeral expenses was the timely and generous act of a foreign admirer." Simonneau was also the king's commissar overseeing the burial of Protestants, which further cemented Porter's belief that he was on the right track. And they found that Marron, the minister who had overseen the graveside service, had at that time buried all the dead from his church in Saint Louis cemetery. "I found the book containing the minutes of the meetings of the consistory of M. Marron's church, but just at the date of Paul Jones's death, four pages had been torn out," Porter wrote. He sent Bailly-Blanchard to try to find them, tracking down the heirs of one M. Coquerel, a former pastor of the church, who "was mentioned in a publication as an enthusiastic collector of papers relating to Protestantism in Paris." Bailly-Blanchard also dropped in at junk and antiquarian shops whose owners "revealed the fact that M. Coquerel's heirs had sold some old papers which had afterward been purchased by the Society of the History of Protestantism, and in its library were finally found the four lost pages. I now ascertained positively that M. Marron buried his parishioners in the Saint Louis cemetery, and the fact that he had delivered the funeral oration of Paul Jones would be some indication that he had also buried him there."

Other details seemed to cement the conclusion that they had found the right cemetery. One old map showed that a now-missing street that ended at the cemetery gate was called Rue des Mortes—Street of the Dead— which Porter took as confirmation. Another still existing street that entered the intersection from the other corner was called Rue Vicq d'Azir, named after the doctor who had attended Marie Antoinette and who had been summoned to Jones's apartment the night of his death. "When a person's name is given to a street in Paris, it is generally in a quarter connected with events in his career," Porter wrote later. "It is possible that the distinguished physician's name was given to the street because of its leading to the place which held the remains of his illustrious friend and patient."

The cemetery site ascertained, Porter faced a second, even more vexing question: was the body still there? Over the decades, as Paris grew outward, older cemeteries were routinely closed down, the bodies exhumed and moved, most often to the Catacombs in the vast network of the city's subterranean passageways, mines, and quarries. The process began in the 1780s with the closure of the centuries-old Cemetery of the Innocents near the heart of Paris, a burial ground so overcrowded that the dead were heaved into mass graves kept open for six months so they could be more easily filled. The stench—as it mixed with human excrement, kitchen offal, and other household wastes tossed to the streets from homes—was legendary. It reached the crisis point in late 1779 when people entering their basements in nearby neighborhoods were overcome by fumes; candles and lanterns would go out in the fetid air; wine stored against walls closest to the cemetery turned bad in their vessels. The final straw came on May 30, 1780, when a house's foundation wall collapsed inward and stacks of moldering corpses tumbled into the basement. City health officials were called in and tried venting and other potential solutions but ultimately admitted failure.

The Cemetery of the Innocents was closed, and five years later night shifts of workers began exhuming the grave pits and moving the bodies to the Catacombs. Bodies from other cemeteries followed over the years in a morbid forced exodus of the dead.[15]

Porter had the Catacombs records searched for clues that bodies from the Saint Louis cemetery might have been part of the relocation drive. Unspecified city files (perhaps Read's copies) included a reference to the exhumation of a woman identified as Lady Alexander Grant and the return of her remains to London in 1803, as well as receipts at the Catacombs for the bones of dead paupers who had been exhumed from graves outside the cemetery walls. There were no records of transfers from the cemetery itself. He took omission as proof.

Porter still feared misdirection. He had Ricaudy and Bailly-Blanchard run down and dispel other stories of Jones's whereabouts. Dumas's novel said that Jones had been buried in Père Lachaise. Even though that cemetery opened more than a decade after Jones's death, Porter had the records searched anyway "to be sure that his body had not been transferred there in later years." They found five listings for people named Jones, but none were John Paul, and none of the burial dates matched that of the commodore. "There was another fanciful story that he had been interred in Picpus cemetery, where Lafayette was buried," something Porter discounted since Protestants would not have been allowed in that consecrated Catholic ground. "Still a search was made, and it disproved the rumor."

Porter checked with the minister of the Jones's family church in Dumfries, Scotland, to ensure the seaman wasn't buried there, as one rumor had it. The minister, D. W. McKenzie, reported back that his graveyard held but one John Paul, "the tomb of the father," with the headstone inscription IN MEMORY OF JOHN PAUL SENIOR, WHO DIED AT ABIGLAND THE 24TH OF OCTOBER 1767 UNIVERSALLY ESTEEMED. Beneath it was inscribed, ERECTED BY JOHN PAUL, JUNIOR. So the commodore's name—but not his body—was in the cemetery.

Another story to debunk arose from the French Revolution itself. Lead bullets were in short supply, and legend had it that the cemeteries were scavenged for lead coffins, which were then melted down for bullets, the bodies tossed back into the ground to rot. Porter pursued the legend through old records and "talks with the 'oldest inhabitants,' to whom traditions of a former age are handed down." He concluded that the French cultural reverence for the dead and "the sacredness of places of burial" made it unlikely they would, even in the midst of revolution, dig up old coffins for their metal. This was an especially sensible line of reasoning since easier targets such as statues and "extensive lead piping to carry the water from the Seine to Versailles" had survived the revolution. So it seemed unlikely the graves would have been disturbed. "Moreover, the metal contained in the few leaden coffins to be found at that date in a Paris cemetery would not have paid the digging or furnished bullets for a single battalion."

Ultimately Porter concluded that "local traditions or printed documents suggest nothing at variance with the accepted opinion that he died in Paris and was buried in the Protestant cemetery there." Consulting old maps and Read's work, Porter, Bailly-Blanchard, and the others pieced together more details about the burial ground and its history. "The surface of the garden was about eight feet lower than that of the courtyard, the descent to which was made by a flight of steps. Thirty years later the grade of the street had been changed and the garden had been leveled up even with the courtyard, and the fact seemed to have been lost sight of that there had ever been a cemetery beneath. . . . The whole property was surrounded by a wall between six and nine feet high. There was a house in the courtyard and a shed, but no buildings in the garden."

Ricaudy visited the site and found nothing like the low garden with fruit trees described in the early records. The cemetery had closed some six months after Jones's death and just weeks after the bodies of some of the six hundred Swiss Guards killed defending Louis XVI had been unceremoniously dumped in a mass grave. After the cemetery was officially closed, the caretakers continued to accept the occasional body until the government sold the land in 1796 to a developer named Phalipaux.

In addition to raising the ground level eight feet to near street level by moving in loads of earth and fill, occupants had erected cheap buildings around a courtyard and garden. The property changed hands over the decades, and the land was used as a dumping ground for night soil— a charming euphemism for human waste collected from homes by special cartmen—for rendering the carcasses of dead animals, and as a laundry, among other things. The filth and runoff of all those uses percolated down to mix with countless decaying bodies, nearly all of which had been buried in degradable wooden coffins or simply rolled in sheets and dropped in graves.

Shortly before Ricaudy visited the site, the owner of the laundry that occupied part of the space had dug down more than eight feet "to increase the depth of the pit where his boiler was placed." He struck a layer of corpse loam, "a viscous black substance containing fragments of human bones." Other ditches and holes over the years had uncovered shinbones and shoulder blades. A man seeking to bury his dead dog unearthed two skulls.

Porter was taken aback by what he saw as the desecration of the dead— particularly of Jones. "One could not help feeling pained beyond expression and overcome by a sense of profound mortification," Porter wrote later. "Here was presented the spectacle of a hero whose fame once covered two continents and whose name is still an inspiration to a world-famed navy, lying for more than a century in a forgotten grave like an obscure outcast, relegated to oblivion in a squalid quarter of a distant foreign city, buried in ground once consecrated, but since desecrated."[16]

In an interesting and hard-to-assess side note, Johnson, the lawyer from rural western New York, cropped up again in August with another letter to McKinley. The embassy in Paris had responded to Johnson's first letter, informing him that while it seemed likely Jones's body was in the Catacombs or otherwise beyond retrieval, they could say with certainty that he was not buried in the same cemetery as Lafayette. In early August, Johnson replied that if the embassy didn't know where to find the body, his research might provide some insight. He sent along details from Read's article. The records don't indicate where Johnson had encountered the article, but it's clear that the information was neither obscure nor limited to Parisian Protestants and historians.[17]

---❖---

Ricaudy sent his report to Porter on October 29, 1899, the day after he printed a short article about his findings in his own newspaper, *L'Echo du Public*. He concluded that Jones's remains could not be anywhere but beneath the buildings and courtyard off Rue de la Grange-aux-Belles, a property of some thirty thousand square feet. The land was owned by one Mme Crignier, a widow, but it held five buildings under the control of tenants with long-term leases. A man named Bassigny operated a two-story granary with a large paved courtyard partially ringed by storage sheds. The laundry next door was built without a foundation but had a cement floor with drains that led to the street. Along with a three-story hotel sat yet another single-story building "of cheap construction . . . and in dilapidated condition."

Since Jones had died six months before the cemetery was closed, Ricaudy speculated that he would have been buried near the main entry off Rue de la Grange-aux-Belles, the last part of the property to be used for graves. Whether Jones's body could be found beneath the buildings was the big question. Ricaudy advised Porter that if Jones had been buried in a wooden coffin, the remains would likely be unrecognizable. A leaden coffin would improve the chances. "In any event, even if his bones cannot be identified it is nevertheless absolutely certain that he is there, and that the acquisition of the site could be made under advantageous circumstances," Ricaudy wrote, suggesting the Americans buy the land and turn it into a park with a memorial to Jones "without prejudice to any excavations that might be hereafter deemed advisable."

Porter sent Ricaudy's report, attached to his own, to Secretary Hay in Washington, referring to the June reply by Vignaud that Jones's body was most likely beyond recovery. "I am now in a position to inform you that the place where he was buried has been found and that I have also procured a copy of the burial" record, Porter wrote. He credited Ricaudy for the research and added that Ricaudy "believes that he could locate within eight or ten yards the spot where the body was interred." Porter also oddly passed along Ricaudy's suggestion that a committee be formed to raise the funds for the project, an idea Porter didn't support. And Porter also seemed to miss the point that Jones had been buried in a lead coffin, telling Hay that it "was in all probability [made] of wood, and unless there was a metal plate bearing the name of the deceased, or a sword or some article, not perishable, it might be difficult to identify whatever may be left of the body." Porter then tossed the decision on how to proceed to Hay, saying he would "cheerfully cooperate in any action having to do with the removal to the United States of the body of Paul Jones."[18]

By the time Hay received Porter's letter, newspapers in France, England, and the United States had reported that the former war hero's remains were within potential reach. In Paris, proposals were made to persuade the French government to turn the spot into a park in time for the Exposition the next year, which would offer another draw for American tourists. Others urged the site be excavated, despite the buildings, so Jones's body could be found and transferred to the United States. *New York Tribune* correspondent Charles Inman Barnard had followed the search—he wrote later that he joined Ricaudy in his visit to Père Lachaise and on other research jaunts—and his reports were the most detailed in the American papers.[19] They fanned significant public interest in recovering the body if possible. Members of the US Congress introduced a joint resolution to pay the costs of digging up Jones and reburying him in Arlington National Cemetery, one of several locales that began lobbying for the privilege of hosting Jones's permanent grave. (The measure died after being referred to the House Committee on Naval Affairs.)

Porter was among those who thought Jones's body should be exhumed and moved to the United States. Though he had hoped to work outside of the public spotlight, it was too late for that as photographers took pictures of the site and news columns were filled with speculation about what would happen. Porter decided to approach Mme Crignier, who owned the property, and the tenants to see if they were interested in selling or would at least let the Americans buy access to the site to try to unearth Jones's coffin. He soon discovered, though, that there was a very good reason why Ricaudy knew the terms for purchase could be "advantageous." During his visits to the site, Ricaudy had secured options on the land himself.

Porter found himself negotiating with the man he had hired to find the burial spot.[20] The talks went nowhere. Porter was angry and wounded by the duplicity but, ever the diplomat, blamed public exposure of the project "through the indiscretion of persons who had been consulted on the subject. Self-constituted agents immediately began to busy themselves with circulating fantastic stories regarding the fabulous prices that were to be paid for the property, the whole of which it was said was going to be bought by a rich government." He didn't identify Ricaudy publicly as the person behind the "indiscretion" in his reports on the search. He was more direct a few years later in a private letter when Ricaudy was pressing a claim against the US government over payments for his research work. In a letter to Bailly-Blanchard written after Porter had retired from his post, the ambassador wrote that Ricaudy had delivered a "garbled" account of the burial and initially omitted the key detail about Jones having been buried in the Protestant cemetery. "He got this from Charles Read's assertion, no doubt, and we knew of this ourselves—you, I think, ascertained that fact before Ricaudy's report." Porter said Vignaud had told Ricaudy at the time that he would be paid nothing for his work because of his duplicity, and Porter now urged Bailly-Blanchard to ensure Ricaudy received no money other than possible expenses.[21]

But in November 1899, with the body within potential reach after more than a century, Porter decided that "there was but one course to pursue, however reluctantly, which was to drop the matter entirely for a couple of years, in order to let the excitement subside. . . . This was altogether the most discouraging episode in the history of the undertaking." Once again, though, Porter dissembled. The public excitement had little to do with his decision to postpone the project. Ricaudy's options on the property were for two years. Jones's body wasn't going anywhere. And neither was Porter.

The ambassador—and the recovery—could wait.

12

---- ☀ ----

Dreyfus, the Exposition, and Other Distractions

THE EXCITEMENT OVER THE discovery of Jones's likely burial ground faded as it became clear that the body would not be dug up. Media accounts blamed uncertainty for the decision; the cemetery might have been tracked down, but the expense of trying to find one body in that buried haystack was formidable, and the odds of success long. Eventually, public discussion about buying the site and turning it into a public square faded away too.

Porter was happy to let the talk die down. Smothering his disappointment and his anger at Ricaudy, Porter focused on other parts of his job, including preparations for the Exposition Universelle opening in April 1900, diplomacy tied to the disintegrating situation in China that gave rise to the Boxer Rebellion, and the looming reelection campaign of his friend and patron, President McKinley.

There had been some political changes for Porter to wrestle with as well, beginning with the death of his friend Félix Faure, the French president. The former leather merchant who had risen to the presidency of the Third Republic was notorious for his appetite for food and women. In late 1898, the married Faure had begun an affair with Marguerite Steinheil, the wife of artist Adolphe Steinheil, who had painted a portrait of Faure. The president and his mistress met regularly in a secluded room at the Palais de l'Élysée, sessions that Steinheil wrote in her autobiography were private meetings in which she worked with the president on his memoirs. Steinheil didn't admit to the sexual affair but painted a picture of such secrecy—she'd enter the palace by a little-used side door under prearrangement—that it's hard to believe there was nothing more than memoir-writing at hand, especially since she had no notable literary expertise. On the afternoon of February 16, 1899, Faure called Steinheil and asked her to meet him at the palace that evening. They retired to the private room, and, a short time later, one of Faure's aides heard Steinheil calling for help. When the aide entered the room, Steinheil was rearranging her clothing, and Faure was dead on a couch; he had suffered a fatal stroke mid-act.[1]

Faure was succeeded by Émile Loubet, whom British journalist Walter F. Lonergan summed up as "a dumpy little man . . . known as a plain, practical politician, nowise brilliant, but a ready speaker, versed in the law, experienced also in other ways, and there are no scandals about him."[2] There was speculation that one of the contributing factors to Faure's fatal stroke was the relentless stress from the Dreyfus affair, which Loubet had inherited along with the job. At first, it was unclear where Loubet stood. Some believed he was sure of Dreyfus's guilt and would take as hard a line as Faure had. Anti-Dreyfusards sensed a softening and feared he would side with Zola and the left intelligentsia against the military. So Loubet was a target for all. As his carriage took him from Versailles to the Palais de l'Élysée, onlookers tossed eggs. When the gathering for Faure's funeral broke up after the burial at Père Lachaise cemetery, Faure's longtime friend and former aide Paul Dèroulede sought to instigate a coup. It was poorly planned and quickly collapsed when the military officials he was counting on returned to their barracks instead of storming the Palais de l'Élysée. Dèroulede was eventually exiled.

So Loubet was facing his own circle of stresses, which increased less than four months after he took office, when the appeals court threw out Dreyfus's conviction and ordered a new trial, convulsing France with a fresh round of protests. At the Auteuil horse race track a few days after the decision, a fight broke out between Dreyfus's supporters and those who believed him guilty; Loubet was present, and one of the anti-Dreyfusards struck him over the head with a cane.

Within a few weeks Dreyfus was returned to France from Devil's Island. Malaria and malnutrition had taken their toll during his five years of mostly solitary confinement in the tropical island prison. Dreyfus's face bore a permanent flush, and his gums were swollen, red, and painful. Wiry to begin with, his muscles had wasted away to the bones and sinew. His thinning hair, though he was only thirty-nine, had gone white. Living in near total silence had robbed his voice of its resonance; he spoke in soft rasps and hisses. The career military man was a physical wreck.[3]

The new trial took place in Rennes in August 1899, as Porter was directing the search for Jones's burial spot in Paris. Despite evidence of forgeries, another verdict of guilty was inevitable given the military's closed ranks and fear of exposed wrongdoing. Loubet, citing Dreyfus's medical condition, granted a pardon, which Dreyfus accepted with the proviso that he could continue to try to prove his innocence. Dreyfus was finally exonerated in 1906, though the affair would percolate through French society for years to come.

Where the Dreyfus affair laid low France's international reputation, the Exposition Universelle of 1900 was the nation's chance at redemption. It was the fifth world's fair to be hosted by France; the first had taken place in 1855, just four years after the first international expo was held in London's Hyde Park. The most recent French expo had come in 1889, marking the centennial of the French revolution. That gathering introduced the world to Gustave Eiffel's magnificent tower near the Seine, but overall the *exposition* was more French than *universelle* and thus a bust. The problem was the concept. Celebrating the overthrow of Louis XVI and the monarchy might have appealed to the French, but other royalty-led nations—from Russia to Arab sheikdoms—saw little reason to celebrate the kind of transition they didn't particularly embrace.

Ostensibly the expositions brought together in one setting the best the industrial world had to offer. In reality, they were massive marketing programs that heralded the rise of modern consumer society. The previous exposition, hosted by Brussels in 1897, was a lackluster affair focusing on automobiles; it drew 7.8 million visitors. The one before that was the 1893 "White City" of the World's Columbian Exposition in south Chicago, a massive event that drew more than twenty-five million visitors and introduced the world to the Ferris wheel, displayed the versatility of electrical power, exhibited a series of gas-powered carriages, and involved the first use of spray paint in construction of the massive fair site. It was an international success for American consumer products, and Porter was anxious to ensure that American businesses were front and center at the upcoming Paris exposition. He feared, though, that the war with Spain might have dampened European enthusiasm for American products and dissuaded American businessmen from making the trip to display their goods. "I trust our people will not prevent our merchants and manufacturers and farmers from being represented at the Exposition of 1900," he wrote to William R. Day, then secretary of state. Attending and exhibiting a wide array of American products would be "in their own interest, for I am convinced that the effects of an important exhibit here will increase very largely the American export trade to all Europe, for all Europe will attend and have an opportunity to see and admire our superior production."[4]

The previous French expositions had, for the most part, been privately financed by business groups seeking markets for their products. The Exposition Universelle 1900 would be different. Expositions were usually announced a year or two before they were to be held, but this time the French government invited foreign nations to take part eight years ahead of time, partly to trump plans by the Germans to hold a similar gathering. And it would be a government-run affair, an effort to reclaim some lost luster. France, while still one of the world's leading nations, had seen both its power and its cultural standing erode over the previous few decades. In the mid-1800s, France had been the richest nation in the world; by the end of the century, it had fallen behind the United States and other industrial powers. Its colonial reach was not on par with some of its European rivals, such as Great Britain, and it had suffered embarrassing military defeats at the hands of the Prussians. With the Dreyfus affair tearing at the country's domestic fabric, a national malaise had settled in. It was hoped that the Exposition Universelle—bigger and bolder than the previous gatherings—would revive France's fortunes and spirits, and usher in the new century with Paris at its symbolic center.

Stripped of the revolutionary subtext and with industrial powers seeking ways out of a persistent economic depression, the Exposition Universelle received early exhibit commitments from more than forty nations. The grounds would cover both sides of the Seine, stretching northwest and southeast from the Eiffel Tower, then northeastward along the river. As the opening neared, French officials announced that they expected sixty million visitors, more than twice the number drawn to Chicago in 1893 and an eightfold increase over Paris's last expo in 1889.[5]

The exposition almost didn't get off the ground. Parisian officials intended to use the event to introduce the first stretch of its planned Metropolitan subway system, a project that was fraught with problems. Rather than tunneling below ground, engineers designed a project that involved digging wide, deep ditches, laying the track bed then building the tube to encase it, and filling in the remaining ditch. The first stretch of line was to travel beneath Rue de Rivoli on the Right Bank, linking an auxiliary exposition display area near Porte de Vincennes with the main exposition grounds. Construction problems, including collapsing walls along the ditch, added delays. "The whole *Rue de Rivoli*, from the *Concorde* to the *Rue Castiglione*, caved in in different places," Elsie Porter noted in her diary. "At the *Etoile* I walked out one fine morning to find a huge hole in front of a private house—all caved in, taking a tree and men along between the *Champs Elysèe* and *Avenue de Friedland*. Everything was barred off and full of dust and dirt."

Organizers, who had set April 14 as the day for the opening ceremonies, saw no reason to change the date, even though the fairgrounds were still a work in progress when it arrived. Landscaping was hurriedly emplaced for the opening, but most of the buildings were far from finished. The Art Palace, one of the centerpieces, had yet to get a roof, and only half of its grand staircase was in place. The Pont Alexandre III bridge linking the Grand Palais on the Right Bank with the manufacturing pavilion on the Left Bank—a bridge already four years in the making—was barely done in time. That didn't much matter, since neither of the exhibition spaces was ready either. The whole affair was a jumble of chaos, and it would be late May before the exhibits were ready, though the Americans were ahead of most of the other exhibitors. Even though there would be little to see—leading to wide frustration—some fifty thousand people had arrived in Paris from around the country and the world to celebrate the opening at the dawn of the new century.[6]

One of the few large spaces ready for use was the massive Salle de Fêtes at the southern end of the Champs de Mars, surrounded by halls that would exhibit advances in mining, metals, transportation, and other industries, including the brilliantly lit hall devoted to innovations in electricity. The Salle de Fêtes was a circular room within a square building, topped by a glass dome and with a sweeping staircase at one side. Organizers invited fourteen thousand people to the opening ceremonies, and Paris, for the most part, was closed as if on holiday. President Loubet, to mark the occasion, pardoned scores of military men in jail on minor offenses, and ordered an extra ration of wine for the nation's troops. But his main role that day was to deliver the opening speech.

The president left the Palais de l'Élysée by carriage and was carried to the Salle de Fêtes through thronged streets framed by bunting-clad buildings, as though leading a short parade. It was a cold and windy but clear-skied spring day, and traffic on nearby streets was snarled for hours, exacerbated by a maze of carriages abandoned by those rushing to get to the ceremonies on foot lest they miss them. Loubet's path was clear, though, and he entered the Salle de Fêtes with a grand fanfare. A volley of artillery was fired outside the hall as large, red velvet–covered doors swung open. Loubet, dressed in a dark suit with the wide red sash of the Legion of Honor, strode in as the Republican Guard band struck up "La Marseillaise."

Ambassador Porter, his wife, and his daughter were among the sea of diplomats, exposition officials, and *grandes dames et messieurs* of Parisian society that flowed across the open floor and out into the open air of the Champs de Mars, with the Eiffel Tower beyond. While most of the Europeans were in conservative business suits and evening gowns, the wardrobes of the world added splashes of color, from green-and-red Hungarians to white-clad Arab sheiks to red-cloaked Cossacks and Chinese representatives in fine silk. The speeches were mercifully short; Loubet spoke of Europe and his hopes that the international cooperation that had made the exposition possible augured a lengthy peace in a region that had seen so much war. "I am convinced that, thanks to the persevering affirmation of certain gener-ous thoughts with which the expiring century has resounded, the twentieth century will witness a little more fraternity and less misery of all kinds, and that ere long, perhaps, we shall have accomplished an important step in the slow evolution of the work towards happiness and of man toward humanity," Loubet told the crowd, which erupted in a prolonged outburst of cheers.[7]

It was the only high point in an otherwise inauspicious start. People who had traveled to Paris expecting an extravaganza were bitterly disappointed. "Imagine if you will an exhibition which exhibits absolutely nothing, an exposition which exposes naught but the incompetency of its management," the *Los Angeles Times*'s George Grantham Bain reported. "Conceive a lot of buildings magnificently planned and in part finely executed, solemnly, and formally opened to the public, which enters them to the number of 180,000 in one day, to find only scaffolding, rubbish, plaster, dirt, dust, and half-finished showcases." And it was not a cheap place to be. "The French people have reduced the business of squeezing the last penny from a plea-sure seeker to a science."[8]

The Exposition Universelle eventually hit full stride and became a massive affair. It was so large, in fact, that few realized that Paris was simul-taneously hosting the second modern Olympic Games, most of which were conducted in front of empty stands. The Exposition ultimately drew some 30,000 exhibitors from France, followed by 6,600 from the United States, 2,500 from Belgium, 2,000 each from Germany and Italy, and another 1,500 from Russia. That the United States, though separated from the expo by an ocean, sent the second-highest number of exhibitors indicated how much significance American industrialists and businessmen put on the event, much to Porter's satisfaction. While there would be food and music and exotica, the Exposition Universelle was, at heart, an international trade show, and the Americans were there to try to crack open European markets. The US Congress had budgeted nearly $1.4 million to help under-write the nation's exhibits. The feckless Ferdinand W. Peck of Chicago, son of a wealthy real estate developer and a philanthropist in his own right, was named head of the American delegation, largely based on his role as a vice president and fundraiser of the Chicago World's Fair. His hubris and lack of tact (he was a no-show when Loubet, the French president, made a scheduled tour of the American pavilion) became a source of continual embarrassment to Porter and other Paris-based Americans.

The American footprint spread across the exposition grounds. A build-ing to house the forest-products exhibition was created in Chicago and shipped in pieces for final construction. Individual exhibits, including one to display different methods of cooking corn, were designed and created and shipped over to take their places in the various halls. The main US pavilion, a domed octagon on the riverfront, dismissed by one critic as look-ing like "a bleached interpretation of a Roman pantheon," went up on the Left Bank just west of the Invalides bridge, between pavilions for the declin-ing empires of Austria and Turkey. The American pavilion was set up as something like a hospitality suite for businessmen, with stenographers on standby and supplies of typewriters, American newspapers (the *New York Times* published a special Paris edition for the duration of the exposition), and daily stock updates. At night, the space was given over to lavish recep-tions and parties, all designed to facilitate business deals.

In an era of jingoism, there was nationalist pride to display as well. Over the previous decades, fine arts had played increasingly important roles in the world's fairs, with medals and other honors making or breaking artistic careers. In an effort to push American artists, the American jury selecting the US entries was based in New York City instead of Paris (which had selected mostly Paris-based American artists for the 1889 exposition). This time the cream of domestic artists—many of whom had studied in Paris at some point—were selected to exhibit, including James Whistler, Winslow Homer, and John Sargent.

Ambassador Porter was the face of America in Paris, and the embassy played host to a revolving door of American dignitaries and business leaders, many of whom knew Porter from his role at Pullman, his work within the Republican Party, and his years moving among New York City's moneyed circles. Some demands were a bit odd: one woman asked embassy officials to store her sealskin coat, and another asked for space for her trunks. The embassy also served as the safety net for unfortunate tourists who ran out of money, were robbed, or faced other crises while in the country. "Shortage of money was, of course, a very common reason to appeal to the Ambassador," Elsie Porter wrote in her biography of her father. "Some of these unfortunates confessed to a night on Montmartre and in consequence the disappearance of all their worldly goods." Others were simple scam artists, including non-Americans who showed up with "the stars and stripes in their buttonholes and who spoke broken English." Some were young Americans who had budgeted too little or spent all their cash to get to Paris, planning to find temporary jobs to finance their stays and eventual trips home—jobs that didn't materialize.[9]

Elsie, for one, was unimpressed with the exposition. "My impression is that, for the people who had never travelled, or for engineers and manufacturers, the Exposition filled its special function. For a person who had travelled and seen all the exhibits in their own country and surroundings and who was not interested in manufacture or engineering or boats, it was not a very interesting show. The buildings on the whole were in wretched taste and many of the exhibits very cheap. Everything was over-crowded and rather poorly done." She was particularly displeased with the "disgrace" of the American pavilion, which she said paled in comparison with "the beautiful English Tudor house and the Belgian Gothic building, a copy of the *Hotel de Ville* at Antwerp. . . . But ours—oh dear, how it made my blood boil. The inside was a large rotunda with galleries all around and draped in American flags. On the ground floor was a Post Office, at the back was a large sitting room with some plain oak furniture."

The dedication of the US pavilion was put off until early May, when the building was ready. Peck and other leaders of the American delegation decided to invite the entire diplomatic corps—and, it seems, anyone else who was interested—to the ceremony. It was so crowded that many key guests, including speakers such as Porter, couldn't get to the main door, which remained closed and locked as the throng grew. Porter extricated himself from the mess out front and went around to the rear where a guard, not recognizing the ambassador, refused to let him in. Another official already inside spotted Porter arguing with the guard and intervened. The plan had been for the speakers to be in place before the doors opened, and there was a lengthy delay before everyone was ready. "The doors were opened and every straggling American climbed in," Elsie wrote. "They got all around us, so that I was nearly stifled. They stood on seats and chairs, so that there was no chance of getting out, and it was a very warm day. The only refreshing thing was Sousa's band."

John Philip Sousa, in fact, was one of the highlights of the exposition. His band performed at a wide range of pavilions and evening concerts, filling the expo grounds with his driving marches. American artists also grabbed attention, with awards going to works by Whistler, Homer, Sargent, and others. In some ways, the Exposition Universelle marked a transition in the art world. Among the attendees was nineteen-year-old Pablo Picasso, who finagled a press pass through the Spanish journal *Catalunya Artística* and arrived in Paris in late October, just before it closed, to write about the extravaganza (though he apparently never published any articles).

A Parisian crowd overwhelms the American pavilion at the Exposition Universelle 1900.
Courtesy of the Library of Congress, Horace Porter Collection, Manuscript Division

He also had his first painting to be exhibited outside Spain hanging in the Spanish section of the Grand Palais exhibit, a piece called *Last Moments* that was singled out by reviewer Charles Ponsonailhe as representative of the new wave of painters coming out of Barcelona.[10]

Overall the Exposition Universelle was light on innovations; there was no new Eiffel Tower or Ferris wheel. It was the first world's fair in which automobiles were featured prominently, on the eve of their transformation of the world. An elevated, wooden, three-speed moving walkway carried attendees around the interior edge of the Left Bank exhibition areas. The entire grounds were illuminated by electric lights, also a first. (Chicago had been only partially lit.) So the displays were mostly innovations on pre-existing ideas, a focus on doing what was already known faster, larger, and better. American industrial and commercial products fared well. Of nearly 2,000 medals awarded to American products and exhibitors, 220 were grand prizes in their categories, 486 were gold, 583 were silver, and 422 were bronze. Each award carried with it marketing potential and bragging rights; some Campbell's soup varieties still bear a copy of the medal its three-year-old product won that year.[11]

In the end, the Exposition Universelle didn't live up to French expectations. Some fifty million people attended, setting a record that still stands, but this was a full ten million people fewer than anticipated and budgeted for. Private businesses and vendors lost money, particularly restaurants that had paid high fees and endured high overhead costs in their temporary locations. They badgered the French government for rebates based on the unmet attendance promises, and eventually received partial settlements. For months after the fair closed, the shells of abandoned or bankrupt exhibits dotted the grounds; these were slowly eviscerated by scavengers before finally being razed. Still, the Exposition Universelle did what the organizers had hoped: it buffed up the French image internationally, spurred the economy in the short term, and was viewed as a success, even if it didn't meet expectations.

Porter, though, must have been happy to see the last of the Americans leave.

In the fall of 1898, Garret Hobart, a friend of Porter's and a well-known and well-liked New Jersey politician, began having trouble catching his breath. Then he developed a steady and tight pain across his chest. He talked with his doctors, who diagnosed myocarditis—an infection and inflammation of the heart tissue. While the exact treatments the doctors prescribed are unknown, they apparently had some effect, and Hobart began feeling better. But only for a time. He was, in fact, gravely ill, and despite several rallies, his condition deteriorated over the ensuing months, exacerbated by a bout of influenza that winter, work stress in the spring, and an ill-advised strenuous travel schedule in the summer of 1899.

By fall, a year after he first began feeling poorly, Hobart was effectively confined to his house and bed in Paterson, New Jersey. He had a large public following, and periodic updates about his health showed up in the nation's press. The articles offered few details, but Hobart's wife noticed that every time he read about his own illness he seemed to get worse. So she limited public updates to trends—that he'd had a good night or a bad night, he was feeling strong, or was resting quietly. But Hobart was, without a doubt and despite the best hopes of his family and friends, dying.

And that posed a problem, for Hobart was also the vice president of the United States. And his boss, President McKinley, was expected to run for reelection in the fall of 1900. Discussions began about what the Republicans should do. At first, it was quiet talk framed in general terms of having a backup plan in case Hobart's health precluded him from running again.

In late October, the vice president's health failed rapidly, and he nearly died on Halloween night. The next day his family announced that while he was not resigning, Hobart had, in effect, retired from duty and would not return to Washington. Three weeks later, Hobart, surrounded by his family, died. "The saddest news I have received since I left home was the announcement of this death," Porter wrote in a private letter to Secretary of State Hay. "Hobart and I for many years were personal, club, and political friends, and the news came to me with a touch of sadness that was akin to the sorrow of a personal bereavement."[12]

By the time Hobart died, the jockeying to succeed him was already in full fury. To balance out the national ticket and mollify powerful political bosses, the expectation was that whoever replaced Hobart would be a New

Yorker and would have the support of McKinley's political enemy, Thomas Platt, the New York political boss.

Ambassador Porter's name came up in several places as a potential candidate. And his candidacy made sense. As a New Yorker, he would bring balance to the ticket. He had a decorated military record in the Civil War and was a living connection to President Grant, still a revered figure despite his scandal-scarred years in the White House. A tactful and polished orator, Porter also had significant connections with New York's financial powers, which he had tapped with such efficiency for McKinley's first presidential campaign. And he had developed a good reputation for his diplomatic work in France.

But Porter was not a Platt man. And, even more significantly, Porter wasn't interested, which he told any reporter who raised the question. While such denials are often more show than substance, it seems likely Porter was sincere. If the political battles that would have come with a cabinet position had dissuaded him from going to Washington in McKinley's first term, it seems unlikely that the stresses and pressures of a national campaign would have appealed to him the second time around.

Regardless, an offer never came. McKinley contemplated a few other men, such as war secretary Elihu Root and treasury secretary Cornelius Bliss, both friends of Porter, but McKinley either changed his mind or was turned down. (Bliss backed out after failing to get support from Platt, now a senator from New York.) After months of dithering, and fearing he'd be tarnished by an intramural Republican squabble if he made a selection, McKinley ultimately left the call to the attendees of the 1900 Republican National Convention in Philadelphia. And the rank-and-file of the party already had their man: Theodore Roosevelt, who had won a two-year term as New York's governor in November 1898, just weeks after returning to civilian life from the war in Cuba.

Born on the cusp of the Civil War, in October 1858, Roosevelt was not even forty-two years old, but he was one of the best-known political figures in the country and something of a leader in a generational shift in politics. McKinley and most of his contemporaries—including Porter—had fought in the Civil War. Roosevelt was at the vanguard of the generation that came after, men for whom the Civil War was at most a childhood memory. An author and historian of some note, he had entered politics as a New York State assemblyman in 1881, quickly earning a reputation as a reformer and an enemy of Tammany Hall and other political machines, including that of fellow Republican Platt. Roosevelt quit politics for a while after he was on the losing side of a floor fight during the 1884 Republican convention that made former Maine senator James G. Blaine the party's presidential candidate. (Blaine lost the November election to Democrat Grover Cleveland.) Roosevelt fled to the Dakota Badlands to be a rancher for a couple of years before returning to the East. He lost a bid for mayor of New York City but was later appointed police commissioner and began cementing his reputation as a reformer by ferreting out corruption, adding to the bad blood with Platt and his cronies. Roosevelt was assistant secretary of the navy under McKinley, a job he quit to go to war in Cuba. Back in New York, he won the governor's office and by the summer of 1900 was a respected author, celebrated war hero, and political reformer, which made him something of a populist political celebrity and a natural addition to the list of potential McKinley running mates.[13]

Yet McKinley—and Mark Hanna, McKinley's political guru—didn't like Roosevelt, either personally or politically. McKinley was at heart a conservative man; by contrast, Roosevelt was propelled by an overpowering personality. And at first, Roosevelt didn't want the post. He had his eyes set on the White House in 1904 and feared that serving as McKinley's understudy would put him out of the public eye and force him to defer to McKinley's policies rather than stake out his own public positions. Roosevelt figured he would have a better chance in 1904 if he stayed in Albany as governor, giving him a high-profile platform from which he could reach a national audience. But Platt's friends, who feared Roosevelt's reform agenda, wanted the former Rough Rider out of Albany. Thus, so did Platt. "I want to get rid of the bastard," Platt confided to a political friend. "I don't want him raising hell in my state any longer. I want to bury him." Ultimately, Roosevelt came around to the idea of the vice presidency and allowed himself to be drafted on the floor of the convention.[14]

The 1900 election was essentially a repeat of the 1896 showdown. The Democrats again nominated Bryan, and McKinley again did very little campaigning, letting Roosevelt be his stump surrogate. Bryan's oratorical skills were by then old news. Roosevelt, on the other hand, was a fresh voice and a natural barnstormer. Often accompanied by former members of the Rough Riders—as if voters needed a reminder—Roosevelt gave some six hundred speeches while traveling some twenty thousand miles, mostly by train, and spoke before an estimated three million people. Come Election Day, McKinley and Roosevelt received 52 percent of the popular vote to 46 percent for Bryan and running mate Adlai Stevenson; McKinley won reelection with a nearly two-to-one margin in electoral votes, but Roosevelt was the talk of the nation.[15]

Given the distance and his role as ambassador, Porter stayed out of the race, though he was champing at the bit in Paris amid the hustle and bustle of the exposition. "One of the greatest disappointments that I ever experienced was not being able to leave my post here at such an important period and go home to take part in the electoral campaign, the first one in which I have not participated in thirty years," he wrote to McKinley in a private post-election letter. "I felt like a hound struggling in the leash, and the homesickness from which we all suffer over here was largely increased every time I read of the activity that was taking place at 'the front.'"[16]

What Porter didn't mention was that McKinley's reelection meant he would stay on in Paris for a few more years. That would give him more time to try to recover the body of John Paul Jones.

13

An Assassination

A FTER THE SUCCESS OF the Spanish-American War and his resounding reelection to the White House, McKinley was ready to take a victory lap around the nation.[1] He planned to travel by train for six weeks with an entourage of cabinet members, through the South, up the West Coast, and then back along the northern tier of the country to Buffalo for a speech at the Pan-American Exposition of 1901, the successor to the Parisian Exposition Universelle 1900.

The trip began on April 29, and McKinley was greeted as a national hero at every stop, with brass bands, cheering crowds, and local politicians and businesspeople anxious to shake his hand, sing his praises, and get their names mentioned next to the president's in their local newspapers. First Lady Ida McKinley, always frail, developed a painful and swollen finger from an infection as the tour hit the desert Southwest. When they reached Los Angeles, her doctor decided to lance the infection, which was attached to a bone. After the procedure, the tour continued on to San Francisco, but

Ida's health worsened. Instead of helping cure the infection, the lancing procedure had spread it through her blood stream, and she fell gravely ill. The tour was delayed as Ida's fever spiked and wouldn't relent; fears rose that she might die. She fought through it, however, and began to recover. The McKinleys headed east after deciding to cut the trip short and hole up for a three-month summer's rest at their home in Canton, Ohio. McKinley postponed the speech at the Pan-American Exposition in Buffalo until the first week of September.

McKinley had an odd personality for a political figure. Inherently a quiet man, he had learned over the years to keep his own counsel and could often be hard to read. In a crowd, he came across as cold and distant; but on a personal level, McKinley was warm and curious. He delighted in meeting and talking with people, often trying to draw from them perspectives on national issues. Even after winning elections to the US Congress, the governor's mansion in Columbus, Ohio, and now, his second term as president of the United States, McKinley still enjoyed—and insisted on—meeting with the public. It was a regular point of contention with his closest advisors and his security detail as McKinley balanced out a sense of invulnerability and of drama. He couldn't conceive of why anyone would wish him violence, despite his role leading the United States to war against Spain, the brutal US suppression of the Philippine insurrection, the always simmering anarchists, and the reality that a single person with a broken mind could trump the best efforts of bodyguards. Yet McKinley also had a sense of fatalism. He once told a friend that "if it were not for Ida, I would prefer to go as Lincoln went."[2] And so McKinley insisted that time be set aside during his trip to Buffalo for an open reception in which he could meet as many people as could shuffle through a receiving line.

The summer in Canton was intentionally uneventful, and Ida slowly regained her health. The couple hosted some gatherings, and McKinley kept fairly regular office hours, meeting with a steady stream of official visitors while monitoring events in Washington by wire and press reports. He chatted with old friends and neighbors and oversaw renovations to the house and grounds. But mostly he and Ida relaxed and recharged, and toward the end of August they began preparing for the trip to Buffalo and then back to Washington.

It was a relatively short ride on the presidential train from Canton to Buffalo, some two hundred miles to the northeast. The McKinleys made the trip on September 4, the day before the president's speech. Throngs of people waited at stations and crossings in Ohio, northeast Pennsylvania, and western New York to wave at the president, strike up bands, and, in one ill-advised instance, fire off a salute of cannons, which shattered windows in one of the train cars and rattled Ida's already taut nerves.

The presidential train arrived at the Exposition terminal at about 6:20 PM. A horde of people greeted the president and his entourage, jostling and pressing forward in such a rush that a protective detachment of police had to push the crowd back. One man in particular was trying to push forward against the surge, trying so hard in fact, that he raised suspicions in one of the officers. But the moment passed in a mass of confusion and cheering and shouts. The man faded into the crowd, his face remembered but his mission unexplored. History might have progressed differently if the officer whose curiosity was raised had managed to reach the man, Leon Czolgosz, a mentally disturbed anarchist from Detroit with a gun in his pocket and a plan to murder the president.

The next day, some fifty thousand people packed the exposition grounds to hear McKinley's speech, delivered from an elevated stage. The president talked about peace and prosperity, and about the themes of such expositions—trade and technology—and their role in a shrinking world. "Modern inventions have brought into close relation widely separated peoples and made them better acquainted," McKinley said, right hand in his pants pocket, the left holding his speech as he projected his unamplified voice out over the crowd.

> Geographic and political divisions will continue to exist, but distances have been effaced. Swift ships and fast trains are becoming cosmopolitan. They invade fields which a few years ago were impenetrable. The world's products are exchanged as never before and with increasing transportation facilities come increasing knowledge and larger trade. . . . We travel greater distances in a shorter space of time and with more ease than was ever dreamed of by the Fathers. Isolation is no longer possible or desirable. The same important news is read, though in different languages, the same day in all Christendom. The

telegraph keeps us advised of what is occurring everywhere, and the press foreshadows, with more or less accuracy, the plans and purposes of the nations.

McKinley saw the merger of the inventor and the investor as the driving force behind the advances, a marriage of purpose that propelled nations. "So accustomed are we to safe and easy communication with distant lands that its temporary interruption, even in ordinary times, results in loss and inconvenience," McKinley said. "God and man have linked the nations together. No nation can any longer be indifferent to any other. And as we are brought more and more in touch with each other, the less occasion is there for misunderstandings, and the stronger the disposition, when we have differences, to adjust them in the court of arbitration, which is the noblest forum for the settlement of international disputes."

With the aim of further shrinking the world and increasing trade, McKinley repeated his earlier support for building a canal across the Central American isthmus to "unite the two oceans and give a straight line of water communication with the western coasts of Central and South America and Mexico. . . . Let us ever remember that our interest is in concord, not conflict; and that our real eminence rests in the victories of peace, not those of war."

As McKinley spoke of peace, Czolgosz, near the front of the crowd, weighed his options for violence. He was too far away for a definitive killing shot, and as he thought about how to get closer, or whether he should take the chance from where he stood, McKinley abruptly finished the speech, waved to the cheering horde, and disappeared into a crowd of bodyguards and dignitaries for a short tour of the exposition grounds, followed by lunch and that evening a fireworks display. Czolgosz again melted away into the crowd.

The next day, McKinley took an unannounced dawn walk, and then he and Ida boarded a train for a morning trip to Niagara Falls. Czolgosz read about the president's plans and boarded a separate train to the tourist attraction. Discovering he would not be able to get anywhere near the president as he toured the falls, Czolgosz returned to Buffalo and made his way to the exposition grounds, where McKinley was scheduled to hold his public reception at the Temple of Music display. This would be Czolgosz's last, best chance. And he made the most of it.

By the time McKinley's carriage arrived a few minutes before four o'clock, there was already a long line of well-wishers waiting to shake the president's hand. Czolgosz was near the head of the line. He kept his right hand in his jacket pocket, where he clutched a small handgun wrapped inside a white handkerchief. The man in front of Czolgosz, a small and intense-looking Italian, drew the attention of the security force, especially when he grasped the president's hand and wouldn't let go. Apparently, the man was no anarchist; he was simply enthusiastic about meeting the president.

McKinley finally freed his hand and turned to the next person in line, Czolgosz. The president smiled as he extended his hand; Czolgosz pulled his right hand from his pocket, lunged toward the president and fired two shots into McKinley's abdomen before the next man in line punched him in the neck and grabbed for the gun as others piled on. McKinley, bleeding badly from his chest, told his protectors to not hurt Czolgosz, probably saving the gunman's life. He then told George Cortelyou, his secretary, "My wife. Be careful, Cortelyou, how you tell her." McKinley was then whisked away to the house at which he had been staying during the visit, where doctors struggled to save his life.

The technological advances McKinley had so thoroughly endorsed the previous day spread word of the shooting around the world. It's unclear from whom Porter, in Paris, first heard of the assassination attempt, but it most likely came from news reports and then by telegram from Hay in Washington. It was a particularly painful moment for Hay, who was still trying to regain his emotional equilibrium from his own tragedy that June, when his twenty-four-year-old son, Del Hay, died after falling thirty feet from a window in New Haven, Connecticut. The younger Hay, a popular figure in the close personal circles of the McKinley White House, had been about to join the president's staff as a secretary. "Every word of praise and affection which we hear of our dead boy but gives a keener edge to our grief," Hay wrote to a friend in the days after his son's death. "I must face the facts. My boy is gone, and the whole face of the world is changed in a moment. . . . Have you heard how it happened? The night was frightfully hot and close. He sat on the windowsill to get cool before turning in, and fell asleep."[3]

As word of the assassination attempt ricocheted through the Paris diplomatic corps and top levels of the French government, people anxious for news descended on the embassy, the consulate, and Porter's home. Porter and Consul General Gowdy, who both counted McKinley as a personal friend, were stunned, as well as frustrated by the slow release of news from Buffalo and Washington. Porter's wife, Sophie, was staying at the Townsend Hotel Kulm in Saint Moritz, and Porter fired off short telegrams to her as he received updates. "First ball not dangerous. Second passed through stomach thought not to have touched intestines. Severe but not necessarily fatal. President conscious and tranquil. Porter."[4] Crowds also gathered outside the Parisian news offices, gambling that the first and best details would come over their wires.

For the French, the shooting of the American president was eerily reminiscent of the murder of French president Carnot seven years earlier, when Italian anarchist Caserio had leaped onto the presidential carriage as it left a speech in Lyons and plunged a knife deep into the president's stomach, lacerating his liver. Carnot had died a few hours later. Caserio, in what had become the mark of the anarchist assassins, was cavalier about the killing. At his subsequent trial, the prosecutor told the court that Caserio wanted to kill the pope and the king of Italy. Caserio laughed and said he wouldn't have killed them at the same time because the two men never traveled together.[5]

Carnot's murder was part of a spree of killings and attacks through the 1880s and '90s during which Parisian high society lived in fear of annihilation. Scores of people were killed or maimed by terror bombs tossed into cafes, police stations, and salons, or detonated on the street, each a blow by anarchists against the state. Rarely were the motives personal, outside of vengeance attacks committed after convicted anarchist murderers were guillotined. Rather, the attacks were blows against the capitalist system, and they shook France—and the rest of Europe—to the core. By the turn of the century, the world had hoped that the spasm had passed. But in Buffalo, an anarchist had struck again. And the leaders of Europe ratcheted up their own security, not knowing who might be next.

McKinley, though critically wounded, seemed to be on the mend. Surgeons removed one of Czolgosz's two bullets, but, unable to find the other, speculated that it had lodged relatively harmlessly in the president's back muscles. Still, the nation and the world tracked McKinley's condition through terse regular reports, including the indelicate detail that McKinley had developed a fever of 102 degrees measured with a rectal thermometer. The doctors exuded caution, saying that there was still a high risk of complications from the wounds but that they felt he would recover.

The worst fears of worried friends and supporters began dissipating as McKinley slowly seemed to overcome the wounds. Six days after the shooting, White House officials started thinking about how to move the healing president back to Washington; McKinley—still sequestered by his doctors—began complaining of boredom. The next day, McKinley had recovered sufficiently to eat, a step that was greeted as a harbinger of a full recovery. So when he fell ill later that night and quickly spiraled downward, it came as a shock, as did his death on the morning of September 14. An autopsy found that McKinley's internal tissues along the paths of the bullets had turned gangrenous; he had been doomed from the moment the bullets had torn into him.

In Paris, Porter was having health problems of his own. The details are murky—it was described delicately in the press as "a local problem" that required painful but not dangerous surgery. Porter had become distraught at word of McKinley's relapse, and when the news flashed around the world that McKinley had died, Porter's doctor kept it from him for several hours to let him rest. As a parade of officials and other dignitaries—including French president Loubet—began arriving at the ambassador's residence, he had to be told.

Porter, along with Gowdy, was devastated. Gowdy had already cabled the rest of the American consulates in France of the death and then shuttered the Paris consulate while issuing a statement to the press: "President McKinley was my true friend. Words cannot express my sorrow at his untimely death. He honored the manhood of the country by his nearly faultless life. His official record is stainless, and the marked integrity and honor of President McKinley will, I believe, equal that of Lincoln in the world's appreciation. His administration stands out as our first introduction to the world as a force to be considered for all future."

Hay, still reeling from his son's death, was staggered. Yet he found time to respond to personal telegrams of sympathy, including one from "Lady Jeune," the British journalist and socialite Susan Mary Elizabeth Stewart-Mackenzie. Hay wrote within hours of McKinley's death, "a day when my personal grief is overwhelmed in a public sorrow," that McKinley had been fond of his own late son and was ready to take him under his wing when the young man died. "The president was one of the sweetest and gentlest natures I have ever known among public men. I can hear his voice and see his face as he said all the kind and consoling things a good heart could suggest. And now he too is gone and left the world far poorer by his absence. I wonder how much grief we can endure. It seems to me that I am full to the brim."

Then, in a note of poignancy, Hay, the one-time secretary to Lincoln and a close friend of James Garfield, traced the threads of public tragedy through his own life. "What a strange and tragic fate it has been of mine to stand by the bier of three of my dearest friends, Lincoln, Garfield, and McKinley, three of the gentlest of men, all risen to the head of state, and all done to death by assassins." Despite his close association with McKinley, Hay would skip the wake in Buffalo. Under the Presidential Succession Act of 1886, with the death of the president, the vice president assumed the presidency; if the vice president died, the job would go to the secretary of state—Hay. Vice president Roosevelt was on his way to Buffalo, where he would take the oath of office, and "as I am the next heir to the Presidency, he did not want too many eggs in the same Pullman car."[6]

Porter didn't have as close a relationship to McKinley as did Hay, but his grief was profound nonetheless. And he was, as it turned out, alone in Paris. His daughter Elsie was in the middle of an extended trip to New York City; Sophie was still in Saint Moritz. Even Porter's friend General Winslow was out of town, vacationing in Italy. The ambassador sent them all the same terse telegram: "President died two fifteen this morning." Then Porter made himself the face of official mourning in Paris, helping arrange a series of public memorials as an international act of catharsis, and hosted at least one wake at his residence.

He also kept his focus on his job. On September 24, Porter wrote to the new occupant of the White House. After congratulating Roosevelt on his ascension, Porter added what can only be read as a note of fealty. "You know that no one has watched your onward career for more than fifteen years with greater pride and satisfaction than I, and I want to say to you now, man-fashion, what I am sure you already feel, that any energies which I possess will be devoted at all times loyally and faithfully to your support."

If Porter was trying to ensure Roosevelt didn't ask for his resignation—a possibility with a change in administration—he need not have feared. Roosevelt viewed his immediate role as extending the goals and policies of the McKinley administration, and he didn't plan significant personnel changes (though he quickly began putting his own stamp on public issues). So Porter stayed on in Paris, overcoming his shock and grief and recovering his own health—until death struck again, this time within his own family.

As the McKinleys were taking their train tour of the United States, Porter's wife, Sophie, was once again away from Paris. The months of receptions and crowds and entertaining she had endured during the Exposition Universelle 1900 had left her exhausted, and she failed to regain her health during the winter. With her chronic heart issues, she tired easily and seemed vulnerable to whatever cold or flu happened to make the rounds of Paris. Still, as the ambassador's wife, she insisted on maintaining as much of a social schedule as she could, with Elsie filling in at her father's elbow as needed. But the encounters drained her. The Porters also traveled often through Europe—they attended the wedding of Queen Wilhelmina of the Netherlands in March 1901—and spent many evenings at dinners and receptions. Porter, for his part, was solicitous of his wife's frailties and spent a significant amount of money for treatments, weeks of recuperative seclusion, and other potential cures.

Porter's papers suggest the lengths they pursued in hopes of improving Sophie's health. In September 1901, the day before McKinley died, Porter paid 960 francs—about $185 US, equal to about $5,000 today—for "medical attendance" by Dr. Otto Veraguth, a Swiss neurologist, whose expertise was in electrophysiology and whose research explored links between external stimuli and increased electrical activity in the human body. That fed into the Porters' apparent belief that rest and quiet would be best for Sophie's health and her weak heart.

Much of Sophie's care was overseen by Dr. Theophile Mende, a Zurich physician who subscribed to homeopathic remedies, including extended rest to let the body's natural healing processes work. Sophie made repeated weeks-long trips to Switzerland. Away from the stress of Paris and the embassy, and in the fresh mountain air, her health usually bounced back. "His rational treatment, the quiet living, the walks in the Dolder woods [outside Zurich] always greatly helped her," Elsie wrote. "But a few months of Paris life seemed to undo any benefit she had derived from her stay."[7]

In the summer of 1901, Sophie spent several weeks in Mende's care before returning to Paris and then joined her husband and Elsie on an extended tour that included Berlin and Saint Petersburg. It was a steady stream of exhausting balls and receptions to hobnob with the diplomatic corps and the political powers of different nations and empires.

Back in Paris, Sophie fell ill again during the winter of 1902, and by spring she was headed back to Zurich, accompanied by Elsie and some visitors from America: her son Clarence, his wife, and the ambassador's sister, Elizabeth Wheeler. The company seemed to help, and a restored Sophie returned to Paris by mid-May and was on hand to join her husband in hosting a dinner party for "Mrs. Astor," as she was known in public and in the press—Caroline Astor, the wife of William Backhouse Astor Jr. and grande dame of Manhattan society, who spent part of her summers in her Champs-Élysées apartment.[8]

Shortly thereafter, Porter made his first return to the United States since assuming his ambassadorial duties five years earlier. Traveling alone, he arrived in New York on May 17, 1902, aboard the *St. Louis* steamship and spent nearly three months with family and old friends, mostly in New York City, where Porter's peers in the Union Club and other exclusive social groups feted him at a series of dinners. (Mark Twain spoke at one of them.) Porter also joined President Roosevelt for a luncheon aboard a French battleship moored near Annapolis. He took part in the dedication of a statue in Lafayette Square across Pennsylvania Avenue from the White House to

memorialize Comte de Rochambeau, the head of the French Expedition-
ary Forces that had fought with the colonial army during the American
Revolutionary War.

On a side trip, Porter guided the French delegation on a tour of Grant's
Tomb in Manhattan. And Porter joined Roosevelt, secretary of war Root,
and other top officials in a program at West Point celebrating the military academy's centennial, where Porter—among West Point's oldest high-
profile graduates—was one of the main speakers. Most of the trip was personal, though, and social. When in New York, Porter stayed with his son
and daughter-in-law, but he also traveled to Newport, Rhode Island, to
attend a Vanderbilt wedding and vacationed for several days in Bar Harbor, Maine, at the start of the "summer season." It was a warm and welcoming return to the home soil.[9]

While Porter was in Washington, Root took him aside and asked the
ambassador to prepare a brief statement about his long-ago actions during the Civil War battle of Chickamauga, with an eye toward nominating
him for the Congressional Medal of Honor. A significant and rare honor
now, in that era the Medal of Honor was bestowed for the slimmest acts of
valor. For years, military men could nominate themselves, and while still an
honor, the awarded medals didn't necessarily recognize bravery under fire.
One entire Civil War regiment received awards for simply doing its duty in
Washington. And there had been a rush of applications in the 1890s, more
than eight hundred requests, for Civil War–related acts that had taken place
a generation earlier. Porter was duly awarded his—the final decision was
Root's, so there was never any doubt—as part of a group of more than a
dozen granted at the same time. In 1917, fearing a dilution of the medal's
significance, the military would purge more than nine hundred names from
the list of honorees after a blind review of the soldiers' actions. Porter would
keep his medal, though—his efforts at Chickamauga were harrowing and
decisive—and it remained a point of pride for the duration of his life.[10]

Porter returned to Paris in late July on the French liner *La Savoie*,
accompanied by Root and his wife, who were off for a European vacation. Porter spent a few days in Paris then traveled to Germany with the
exhausted and ailing Sophie, who then headed for Switzerland while the
ambassador returned to the embassy.

By late August, the family was reunited in Zurich, where Porter had booked rooms at the three-year-old Dolder hotel and spa, an ornate complex on a hill overlooking the city. The grounds included tennis courts and other areas for outdoor exercise adjacent to hiking trails through the Dolder woods. Elsie particularly enjoyed the setting and the attentions of a young tennis player she met, Edwin Mende, the son of her mother's doctor. He began stopping by the family's suite and persuaded Elsie to join him on day trips around the region. "I found myself not wanting to go back to Paris, with all its rush and turmoil and all the endless society functions," Elsie wrote later in her diary. "I was quite contented to wander through the green fields and autumn-tinted woods with the boy for the rest of my life." She did return to Paris without him, but the couple would marry three years later.

The winter of 1902–03 was particularly bad for illness in Paris and across Europe. Porter fell ill, as did most of the embassy staff, all knocked off their feet by a virulent strain of the flu. And it was a deadly bug. Gowdy's vice consul, Edward P. McLean, died on January 6 of pneumonia, which began with the flu. A month later, John H. Carroll, the US consul in Cádiz, Spain, died of congestion of the lungs also brought on by the flu. Sophie escaped it, but as the illnesses spread, she again fled Paris for Switzerland and the ministrations of Dr. Mende. The flu was persistent, as well. In March, Porter mentioned in a letter to the new American ambassador to Germany, Charlemagne Tower Jr., that he had been bedridden with the grippe for a week and nine other embassy staffers were ill. It took Porter a month to recover, forcing him to cancel a planned trip to Greece.[11]

Sophie's visit to Switzerland, usually a palliative to her weak health, didn't help much that winter and spring. She arrived in Switzerland feeling tired and drained, and left the same way. She boarded a train for Paris at the start of April in order to be back at the embassy in time for the spring entertainment season, but en route she was overcome by a sudden and severe flu. She went to bed once she arrived at the residence, and for the next few days, Porter barely left her side as a pall of anxiety descended on the embassy. By April 6, Sophie was looking and sounding better and regaining strength; she seemed to have weathered the worst of it. Porter had abandoned his customary daily walks during Sophie's illness, but around four o'clock that afternoon he decided to step out for air and exercise. He slipped into his coat while still in Sophie's room, bade her good-bye, and headed downstairs for the door; before he could reach it, the housekeeper called out to him, and he went racing back to his wife, who was suddenly having trouble breathing. Her lungs were filling with liquid; the doctor's treatments made little difference. Her decline was rapid. Within an hour, Sophie, Horace Porter's wife of forty years, was dead.[12]

Her death devastated Porter. He dictated terse telegrams to relatives in the United States. "Sophie died five this afternoon congestion of lungs," Porter wired her brother, John McHarg, in Stamford, Connecticut, who was overseeing Porter's financial affairs while he was in France. He asked McHarg to inform Sophie's other brother and his own sister with a direct "Advise John and Lizzie," then signed the message simply "Porter."[13] And he sent a personal wire to his boss Secretary Hay: "It is my sad duty to inform you that Mrs. Porter died at five this afternoon of congestion of the lungs."[14]

Porter spent that night sitting in a chair in his wife's death chamber, crying into his hands as he awaited the arrival of Elsie, who cut short a trip to Germany to return to Paris. He couldn't bring himself to make the funeral arrangements and left it to Vignaud, the embassy secretary. He sat stoically through the memorial service at the American Church in Paris, then took a few weeks off to try to regain his footing. His son, Clarence, and daughter-in-law arrived from New York, and with Elsie they took Porter to Venice, one of his favorite spots. The ambassador couldn't shake his grief, and as they left the Piazza for the last time before returning to Paris, Porter spoke in maudlin terms. "I am saying good bye to all this beauty," the daughter recorded her father saying. "I shall never see it again." He was, Elsie suddenly realized, sixty-six years old.

Back in Paris, Clarence Porter took charge of his mother's body, and without fanfare her remains were taken by train to the coast then ferried to Southampton, where the coffin was loaded onto the steamship *New York* and returned to New York. On June 15, she was buried next to the graves of her two sons in the West Long Branch Cemetery in Long Branch, New Jersey, the coastal village where the Porters had for years maintained a summer residence.

Sophie's death took the joy from Porter's life, and his grief turned to depression. He lost interest in the job of ambassador and began talking about resigning and returning to the United States. "More than ever he longed for America," the daughter wrote. Ultimately he didn't resign—Elsie wrote that Roosevelt talked him into staying through the end of the president's term, though there are no records to support that. Porter lost his heart for much of the socializing that came with the ambassadorship. The rented mansion itself depressed him. He ordered the reception rooms closed up, and in June he and Elsie left the city for two weeks in Dinard, a favorite getaway spot on the north Brittany coast. Even that couldn't dispel the gloom. Porter "had lost his old buoyancy of spirit, and this time forever." He rarely tended to business at all that summer but finally resumed a full schedule of work in late September. Even then, he was something of a recluse, no longer hosting dinners and turning down nearly all social invitations, even those from old friends.[15]

In early October 1903, Porter received a letter from Roosevelt, circumventing Secretary Hay, the usual intermediary for communications from the White House (though Roosevelt wasn't particularly wedded to such protocols). It could be that Roosevelt, aware of Porter's floundering emotions, sought to lift the ambassador's spirits by giving him something other than the mundane duties of the embassy upon which to focus. Or it could be that Roosevelt, knowing that Porter was looking to quit Paris, wanted to ensure that one lingering project would get completed before there was a change.

The president asked Porter for an update on the search for the body of John Paul Jones. Porter had set the quest aside nearly four years earlier, when Roosevelt was still the governor of New York and before the election that had made him vice president and the murder that had made him president. Was it possible, Roosevelt wanted to know, that the body could indeed be found? Could Jones's body be moved to the United States for burial in a manner and place proper for a figure who had played such a high-profile role in the American Revolution and who had been such a key figure in the evolution of the United States Navy? And what would it cost?[16]

Porter took a few days to respond, and when he did, it was via a detailed but succinct five-page typed overview of the steps he had taken—along with Bailly-Blanchard, Vignaud, the hired researcher Ricaudy, and others—to determine where Jones had been buried. "I had pursued all the investigations cautiously and quietly so as not to excite the cupidity of the present owners of the cemetery property, but unfortunately the matter got into print," Porter wrote, choosing not to point a finger at Ricaudy. The cost of proceeding was hard to frame. "I shall have to act with great caution in obtaining any figures at which the property could be bought," Porter wrote. He estimated it could take up to $200,000 to buy the property, plus an additional budget to raze the buildings, excavate the cemetery, and then fill it all back in. Porter speculated that the vacant lot could then be sold for about $100,000, recovering about half the purchase price. So far, Porter told his president, he had paid all the search costs himself, "not feeling warranted in asking the government to make an appropriation for a purpose so problematical and which would be just as likely to end in failure." Implied was that the larger and final effort would require a federal outlay. And Porter dismissed the notion that the space should eventually be turned into a commemorative square, since the project would either prove the body wasn't there, making the memorial spot irrelevant, or the body would be found and removed to the United States. Again, not much of a reason for a park in Jones's honor.

But yes, Porter told Roosevelt, he was certain that they had narrowed the search to the right abandoned cemetery and that, if Jones had indeed been buried in a lead coffin, the remains could be found. There would be political and diplomatic hurdles to clear, though. "Cemeteries are held here to be very sacred and the idea of digging up and scattering around a great number of human bones might call forth protests from living descendants of those buried there and bring criticism upon the authorities," Porter wrote. "All this, however, could be managed quietly if done at the official request of our government."

Porter ended the letter with a note of optimism—rare for him since the death of Sophie—that he was "trusting that I may be able to find more positive proof of the location of the grave."

The ambassador had a final mission.

14

The Negotiations

PORTER'S FIRST STEP WAS to affirm what he thought he already knew: that Jones had been buried in the old Saint Louis cemetery in northeast Paris. So he and his cluster of researchers began retracing their earlier steps to make sure they hadn't missed any obvious clues that they might be on the wrong track. In October, Vignaud wrote back to the woman in Pau, in southwestern France, who had inquired a few years earlier about Jones and whom Vignaud had referred to Marion H. Brazier in Boston. Vignaud wondered whether the letter-writer had ever found out anything and might know where Jones was buried.

Porter himself sent off letters to local government officials and the national archives asking permission for Bailly-Blanchard to access their files to try to run down whatever information could be found. He also asked the Ministry of Foreign Affairs, which dealt with foreign embassies in France, whether it had any records about the establishment of the Saint Louis cemetery, which archival sources suggested had been prompted in 1762 to replace an earlier cemetery opened by the French at the request of Dutch diplomats seeking a place to bury their expatriate—and Protestant—dead.[1]

They worked through the spring, writing letters to anyone they thought might be able to shed some light—or offer contrary evidence—on what they believed they knew. A series of letters went out to people whom records indicated might be descendants of Simonneau, the Parisian official who had paid extra to have Jones buried in the alcohol-filled lead coffin. They tried to track down records through descendants of the man who served as the caretaker of the Saint Louis cemetery. No contrary information surfaced. The more they worked, the more they became convinced that they had the right cemetery and the right location.

If they were right, the body, if it could be found, would not be easy to get to. The former Saint Louis cemetery was buried deep beneath an array of buildings at the corner of Rue de la Grange-aux-Belles and Rue des Écluses-Saint-Martin "in an uninviting section of the northeastern quarter of Paris . . . covered with buildings principally of an inferior class" and several miles from the mansion-heavy sixteenth arrondissement neighborhood where Porter maintained the ambassador's residence.[2]

The property was still owned by the widow Mme Crignier, and it held three separate addresses on Rue de la Grange-aux-Belles, numbers 43, 45, and 47. The buildings had a range of uses. The largest, No. 47, was a four-story corner structure that held small shops on the street level, including a narrow grocery with a sidewalk display of wares, and in the corner space a small photography studio. The other three floors held hotel rooms owned by another widow named Mme Faidherbe. The building surrounded a rectangular courtyard accessible only through the main building. Next door, at No. 45, was a two-story building with a street-level secondhand shop and a laundry that advertised a *chambres chaudes*—a facility for drying clothes. The third building was the two-story granary owned by a man named Bassigny. It included a passageway from the street to a courtyard and large storage sheds at the back of the property.[3] From above, Crignier's property looked like a reverse image of a squared-off numeral *9*, with buildings enclosing one courtyard and the other opening to the street. The street itself descended a slight slope, so from the corner, pedestrians walked downhill past the photography studio, grocery, and entrance to the upstairs hotel,

then the secondhand shop and the laundry, and finally the granary, beyond
which were more small buildings and shops, each attached to the other,
and, a few blocks away, the Canal Saint-Martin. The Rue des Écluses-
Saint-Martin side of the property held a small tobacco and wine shop and
a property management office in rickety buildings off the end of the hotel.

It would not be an easy negotiation to gain permission for the search.
Crignier owned the property, but the tenants had significant control over
the buildings and spaces they were renting, some under long-term leases.
So Porter had a committee of people with whom to negotiate for access
to the cemetery. Each had specific interests and concerns—and, apparently, some delusions inflated by Ricaudy. At first, Porter thought the best
approach would be to buy the property from Crignier, evict the tenants,
raze the buildings, unearth the cemetery, and then, after the search was
over, sell the lot off to recoup some of the costs. No record exists to indicate what Crignier thought about selling her property; she could well have
rejected the overture. Porter noted that the idea generated "so many objec-
tions" that, added to the cost, made it unfeasible.[4] Another plan slowly
emerged in talks with Parisian excavation experts and with Crignier and
the tenants. Rather than buy and raze the buildings, Porter began to think
he could obtain short-term agreements to tunnel beneath the buildings, a
much cheaper project.

Porter tried to work quietly and managed to handle the negotiations
without notice from either the Parisian papers or the American foreign
correspondents based in the French capital. Gowdy didn't share his discretion, though. The consul general told reporters on October 17—as Porter was working on his response to Roosevelt's inquiry—that he had been
looking for the body himself, and offered a $1,000 reward to anyone who
could find it. He reiterated that the likely burial place had been narrowed
down to the site near l'Hôpital Saint-Louis. "Jones was buried in a lead coffin and his remains can be identified by his wounds," Gowdy told reporters, adding that the remains "can also be identified by certain portions of
his admiral's outfit."

Those details revealed how little Gowdy knew about Jones or the report
that Ricaudy had put together. Jones had famously never been wounded
and so had no scars that could be used to verify the corpse—the absence of

scars could be telling but not conclusive; the presence of scars could rule out a corpse as that of Jones. At the time Jones was buried, the custom was to inter soldiers of distinction in linens, saving the uniforms for public displays, which meant there likely would be no hints to be found in whatever clothing a corpse might be wearing. Still, Gowdy hoped the cash reward "would be an inducement to men of research to go to work on the question."[5]

Interest in the project was bubbling in Washington too. Congressman Bois Penrose had earlier pushed legislation to return Jones's body to the United States for burial at Arlington. Now freshman congressman Henry T. Rainey introduced a law on November 19, 1903, that would pay for a search aimed at returning the body for burial at a monument to be built at Annapolis. Three weeks later, Congressman Morris Sheppard of Texas put forward a similar bill directing the secretary of state to "ascertain the costs and submit a plan for marking the grave of John Paul Jones" in Paris.[6] Both newly proposed bills, duly reported in the press, were referred to committees, where they died. A separate movement to erect a statue of Jones in Washington faced a similar fate. Congress, it seemed, was looking more closely at the money involved than the purpose.

A few days after Sheppard introduced his bill, a correspondent for the *St. Louis Post-Dispatch* visited the Crignier property and talked with Mme Dunap, who with her husband had opened the photography studio a number of years earlier. Dunap had continued to operate the business after the recent death of her husband—making her another widow tied to the property. Dunap was well aware of the Jones legacy. A Jones portrait was hung on one wall of the shop, and she talked of the certainty that Jones was buried beneath her rented floor. In fact, she told the reporter as she tapped with one foot, "several times the floor has caved in at this spot, proving positively that a deeper excavation" had been made in the past. She also cited a rumor that Jones's head was twice the size of a normal one, which "should surely reveal the identity" if the recovered body had decayed beyond recognition. All in all, the reporter wrote, word that the US Congress might pay to dig up Jones "creates vast interest in the neighborhood."[7] It was just the kind of interest Porter had been hoping to avoid.

In fact, the sporadic news accounts made his negotiations much more difficult and dragged them out. Some of the tenants "became wildly excited as to the fabulous sums of money they hoped to receive," Porter wrote later to Secretary of State Hay, adding a presumed joke, "One tenant went crazy in brooding on the subject and is in an asylum. The demands were utterly fantastic and the negotiations . . . were so head-splitting that I came near following his example."[8]

It took months for Porter's plan to come together, even with the local prefect of the police acting as a go-between with Crignier. Porter later wrote that he persuaded Crignier that there were no riches to be made because he was paying for the project himself. Yet letters kept by the embassy indicate he presumed the US Congress would underwrite the costs. Regardless, he was able to finally persuade Crignier and her tenants—with the pressure of French officials behind him—that the goal was to disinter the forgotten body of a naval hero and rebury him with proper honors under a memorial in the United States. Surely the Parisians could understand why it was not proper to leave the historic remains mixed in obscurity with the bodies of the unknown, the leachate from the laundry, and the bones of dogs, horses, and other animals. It was to be a mission to acknowledge history and to bestow a too-long-delayed military and national honor. Slowly, the tenants came around.

While the negotiations continued, Porter sought and received the help of Parisian officials in scoping out the project. They loaned Porter the expertise of Paul Weiss, who was the governmental mine engineer and quarry inspector overseeing excavation projects for the Département de Seine, essentially the state-level government that covered Paris and its near suburbs. Porter had settled on a plan to, in effect, go mining for the body by sinking vertical shafts in open spaces and then tunneling horizontally beneath the buildings. It would be a challenge, but much cheaper than a more traditional excavation and likely to cause less damage to the neighborhood. The other option—razing the buildings and digging an open pit to expose the long dead—wasn't likely to win favor with neighbors or French officials.

In late December 1904, Crignier finally signed a contract granting Porter three months' access to the property in return for 15,000 francs. Of that, Crignier would pay 10,000 francs to Bassigny, whose granary was expected to be the most affected. Crignier would use another 4,500 francs to offset a reduction in Bassigny's rent in a new, discounted six-year lease. The remaining 500 francs would be spread among the other tenants to compensate them for anticipated inconveniences. The deal also included Porter, at his own expense, hiring the Parisian architecture firm Judin and Gravereaux to monitor the buildings for damage on Crignier's behalf.

Other than the stipend to offset Bassigny's rent reduction, Crignier kept none of the money for herself, apparently bowing to pressure from French officials. "At the instance of the French Government, she sought only to be agreeable to the American government by inducing her tenants to accept the indemnities proposed," Porter wrote. No one involved anticipated significant property damages or that the project would last beyond the spring, both of which turned out to be severe miscalculations and would lead to more than twenty years of legal disputes and claims.[9]

Weiss, the engineer, mapped out a plan to dig five vertical shafts, two of them in the street outside the property, and the rest in the courtyard or in Bassigny's sheds. The shafts would be used as access points to horizontal "galleries," excavations like those used to mine coal. To expand the search, men would poke long metal poles deep into the gallery walls, hoping to strike a solid mass that might indicate a lead coffin. Additionally, surface trenches would be dug in the dirt cellar of the corner hotel building. Weiss and Porter decided to conduct the search in three stages. The first, and most exhaustive, would be to look near the front of the old cemetery—primarily below the laundry and back to the end of the lot. It was there, Porter felt, that the odds were best, since the historical record suggested Jones's body likely was buried near the entrance or at the farthest reach of the cemetery. Those had been the last unused spaces at the time Jones died, and the cemetery was closed just a few months later, after the mass burial of the Swiss Guards killed by the mob that had attacked the Tuileries in August 1792, leading to the execution of Louis XVI six months later. The second stage of excavations would be near Rue de la Grange-aux-Belles, roughly where the southeastern wall of the cemetery had stood. The third would be along what would have been the cemetery's back wall, beneath the granary. In each case, they would begin at the outer edges of the former cemetery and then work methodically deeper, they believed, into the past.

The work would be done by Weiss's government crews, but Porter would reimburse the cost, which he estimated wouldn't exceed 130,000 francs, or $25,300, "supposing that the body should be found only at the last stroke of the pick." Another 10,000 francs would be set aside in case the buildings needed to be repaired or if a worker became injured. With other incidentals, Porter predicted the project would cost at most $35,000 and probably less. It seemed unlikely, Porter believed, that Jones would have been tucked in among the older bodies. "As the search would begin at the opposite extremities the chances are that the body would be found without having to run the excavation under the entire property and that the expense would be reduced accordingly."[10]

Porter had put a lot of thought into the likelihood of success. Even after he had received Ricaudy's report and been persuaded that Jones had been buried in the Saint Louis cemetery and never disinterred, he continued to track down leads of skepticism that came in letters from people who had read newspaper stories about the search. And he challenged his own logic and conclusions too. One of the questions was how many coffins might be found. Most of the dead, Porter reasoned, had been poor and not likely buried in coffins, let alone expensive lead coffins, as Jones had been. "It is highly probable that there are not a dozen such coffins there," Porter said. Further, it seemed likely, given the expense, that the lead coffins would have nameplates. "If the name is not on the coffin, the identification might be verified by its location in the cemetery among the last buried there" or by matching the measurements of the body inside with what was known about Jones. There had been medals made of Jones's likeness during his life and well after his death, and Porter approached one of the mints that had made them and ordered some new copies. These he tucked away in case a body was found and the likenesses could be matched.[11]

Porter put most of those details in a letter to Hay, the secretary of state, as a precursor to a request that Congress be asked to appropriate $35,000 to pay for the project. He told Hay that Crignier and the tenants would not agree in writing to a set time to start the project but that he felt he had a few weeks of leeway and hoped that Congress would act quickly.

The bigger issue was the weather. The general sense among all involved was that the dig should occur "before the approach of warm weather as there is objection here to turning up cemetery earth at that season for fear of creating sickness." Porter reminded Hay that he had underwritten the cost of the search himself, not wanting to use public funds for a speculative project. "I now feel justified in recommending an appeal to Congress. . . . Even if the whole of the collected evidence should prove deceptive and for some unaccountable reason the body after all should not be found, it seems to me that it would be well worth this small expenditure and all the trouble taken to settle once and forever the question of the possibility of discovering this historic grave."[12]

Porter wrote separately to Roosevelt, appealing to the president's always simmering sense of patriotism. "It is humiliating to feel that this famous character in American history was buried by charity and has lain for more than a century in a squalid quarter of a foreign city in a forgotten grave. Knowing the interest you have taken in this matter I feel that you will be glad to send a message to Congress asking for the appropriation I have recommended for the recovery of the body. The finding of his remains, bringing them home in a war vessel, and giving them decent sepulture, say at Arlington, in the land upon whose history he shed such luster, would, I am sure, form one of the most notable historic events of your adminis- tration." Porter suggested the country's "patriotic societies" would likely respond warmly to the project and could be counted on to rally widespread public support. "You remember how indignant you and I and all our citi- zens became thirteen years ago regarding the neglected grave of General Grant." And Roosevelt himself had played a significant role in the modern rebirth of the American navy; bringing Jones's body to America would help burnish the navy's public image.[13]

Shortly after Porter sent those letters, Crignier and the tenants informed him that they wouldn't consider the agreement valid without some cash up front—the equivalent of $3,000. Rather than see the deal unravel, Porter shelled out the money from his own pocket, then sent off a note to Hay in Washington that he had done so. "If the government, by rejecting the appropriation, decides to abandon the opportunity now offered to make the search for the body, I shall gladly pocket the loss and feel that I have done everything in my power to consummate this much desired undertaking." Then, as a nudge, he reminded Hay that the

$35,000 estimate "is a maximum. It may not require the expenditure of more than half that sum."[14]

The truth was, while Porter hoped the US government would pay for the project, he was forging ahead regardless. And he was in a bit of a hurry. In December, he had told Hay that he wanted to resign his ambassadorship and return to the United States. Roosevelt had won election to a full term in the White House that November, and he would be inaugurated in March. Porter had gone to Paris as McKinley's emissary, and while he and Roosevelt were friends and politically sympathetic, Porter felt a duty to resign and let Roosevelt appoint a new ambassador of his own choosing. He also wanted to do some writing, though his letters were unspecific regarding just what he wanted to write about.

There were personal reasons too. Elsie was spending most of her time in Switzerland with her young beau Edwin Mende, the son of her late mother's doctor, and the two were making plans to announce an engagement. They intended to settle in New York, where Porter's son and daughter-in-law already lived. With Sophie dead, Porter was longing for the contact of family and old friends. He would soon be sixty-eight years old, and, including his Civil War service, he had worked steadily for forty-four years. It was time to slow down.

On February 3, Porter sent a telegram to Hay as his official notice that he intended to resign, effective on a date to be determined by the president, and asked that Hay pass along the formal notification. Porter also sent a personal letter to Roosevelt updating the president on the status of various diplomatic projects and on French legislation that could affect American trade. Porter informed the president that he was quitting and wanted to be back home by summertime. "I cannot hope to make my sojourn here immortal by making it eternal and if I remain out of the country too long, I may find myself labeled like the liniment we buy in the drugstores: 'For external use only.'"

Porter had no intention, though, of abandoning the quest for Jones's body, he told Roosevelt. "If Congress is unpatriotic enough to reject the requested appropriation, I shall bear the expense myself, having already advanced the preliminary payments necessary to bind the options I had secured from the property owners. I have arranged to make the excavations in three sections so that I can complete the work in three or four months by giving it constant personal attention."[15]

Roosevelt replied to Porter briefly on February 6, thanking him for the Jones update and informing him that "I shall send in a message to Congress at once." In separate telegrams over the next few weeks, he and Porter set the effective date of the resignation for April 30. Roosevelt also replied to Hay on February 6 saying that he would respond directly to Porter about the resignation and asking Hay to prepare a statement the White House could send to Congress seeking the $35,000 appropriation to recover the body and to erect "suitable monuments" in Washington to Jones and to John Barry, a Jones contemporary in the Continental navy and a rival among historians regarding the question of who should receive credit for laying the groundwork for the American navy.

Roosevelt forwarded the Hay-crafted request to Congress on February 13, along with Porter's report on why he believed he could find the body. Roosevelt, who shared Porter's interest in memorializing military greatness, urged Congress to "take advantage of this unexpected opportunity to do proper honor to the memory of John Paul Jones." He also appealed to Congressional leaders' sense of patriotic pride, noting that he was moved to make the request in part due to a "sentiment of mingled distress and regret felt because the body of one of our greatest heroes lies forgotten and unmarked in foreign soil." Roosevelt's request withered and died without action, something he anticipated in a letter to Porter. "I have sent in an urgent request for Congress to act on the John Paul Jones matter, but of course I have not the slightest idea whether they will or not."

Congress might not have felt a sense of urgency, but Porter certainly did. He expected to leave France by early summer, and he desperately wanted to bring Jones's body home with him. And he wasn't waiting for Congress to act. In fact, he had already given Weiss the go-ahead to start digging—even before sending his letters and telegrams to Roosevelt and Hay. After all that time, effort, and expense in trying to figure out where Jones might be buried, Porter was about to find out whether he was right.

On the morning of Friday, February 3, Weiss and his men showed up at Mme Crignier's property and cleared out space in one of Bassigny's granary sheds to give them room to work on the first of the planned five vertical shafts. The locations of the shafts had been carefully thought out, and Porter was having Weiss play the odds. The old entry to the cemetery had been along Rue des Écluses-Saint-Martin, around the corner from the entrances to the hotel, the secondhand shop, and the granary. Visitors to the walled cemetery would have entered through a gate leading from the street into a garden holding several fruit trees, with the caretaker's cottage to the left, anchoring the street corner. The cemetery was beyond the garden's back wall, and visitors would have passed through the gate at the top of the stairs to the ground, about eight feet below the garden level. The land, sloped roughly southward, was in effect terraced. Over the years, the bodies had been methodically buried in a pattern that meant the last bodies to be interred—including Jones's—were likely buried either near the entrance or near the back wall. Porter and Weiss overlaid the old maps with the present layout of buildings on the land and concluded that the old line between the garden and the cemetery aligned roughly with the wall of the laundry building, adjacent to the hotel building. So Porter had Weiss sink the first shaft through the floor of one of the granary sheds, in a place where workers could, once they had dug deep enough, excavate horizontally beneath the laundry.

The workers, using picks and shovels, began digging through the packed earth at the surface. After the hole reached a depth of a few feet, the workers erected a hand-cranked winch to haul up buckets full of dirt, rocks, and whatever other material they might find as they gouged their way deeper. They used wheelbarrows to ferry the excavated dirt and rocks to rapidly growing piles, first in the courtyard and then in the street. The project meant the removal of tons of material, but there was no place on the property to store it until it was time to refill the holes. So Weiss and Porter rented a vacant lot two miles away and the earth was carted off on horse-drawn wagons.

It was a poor site for construction, Weiss quickly concluded. The eight feet or so of earth that had been brought in decades ago to level the cemetery with the original fruit garden had never been compacted or otherwise

The street outside Mme Crignier's property, with a pulley (right) hauling earth from one of the vertical shafts dug to explore the abandoned cemetery.
Courtesy of the Library of Congress, Horace Porter Collection, Manuscript Division

prepared to hold the foundations of buildings. Thus, below the surface compaction, the earth was loose and crumbled easily, and the workers had to use timbers and rocks to stabilize the shaft walls. Weiss discovered that the building foundations themselves were shallow and "did not rest upon the natural soil consisting largely of gypsum, which forms the substratum of the region, but upon made earth."[16]

Anxious to proceed quickly, Porter authorized Weiss to have men work the site from early morning until late into the evening, employing two shifts of diggers. Porter was confident that the research was correct, that he had found the old Saint Louis cemetery, but he was still waiting for proof. It came quickly. At a depth of about eight feet, right where they expected, the nature of the earth changed. The loose fill gave way to a denser, more compact mix of dirt, gypsum, and rock, the natural soil makeup of the region. They kept digging, ever deeper, slowed now by the firmness of the earth itself. And soon the pickaxes were striking not rocks but bones. Countless human bones. "Nowhere were any vaults of masonry, analogous to those in cemeteries of the present, discovered," Weiss later reported. "All the bodies had been interred directly in the earth." The discovery affirmed an observation Porter had found in his research: an 1804 inspection of the site reported that there were no headstones and that most of the dead had been buried in trenches rather than individual graves.

Porter felt vindicated by the lack of evidence that the cemetery might have been disturbed over the years and the bodies hauled away with others from cemeteries around Paris to join the subterranean city of the dead in the Catacombs. The first shaft, he reported to Hay, "proved that the dead had never been disturbed. Their skeletons were lying close together in two layers, one above the other, and in some places there were three. But there were few vestiges left of the wooden coffins."[17]

The men kept digging until they ran out of bones, at a depth of about sixteen feet. Then, like moles, they turned northward and "a gallery was run penetrating beneath the laundry and carried as far as the old wall of separation" between the cemetery and the garden. Everything, Porter noted, was right where the research had suggested it would be. Porter had indeed found the cemetery.

Now he had to find the right body.

15

---- ☼ ----

The Dig and the Discovery

THE WORK PROCEEDED IN ghoulish tedium. A second shaft was sunk through the street in front of the laundry, followed shortly afterward by a third shaft in the street near the entrance to the courtyard behind the granary. Two more shafts were then dug, one through the floor of a granary shed and the last in the courtyard near what would have been the back wall of the cemetery. Each shaft, beginning with the first one, was given a letter in order: Shaft A, Shaft B, and so on. The site was a hive of activity. And it was difficult work. The soil reeked of the long dead—"mephitic odors," Porter called them—and groundwater seeped in at such a pace the workers had to install pumps.

The tunnels at first were extended like exploratory tentacles, which meant they dead-ended, a design that created poor air circulation. Because of the instability of the earth, the men installed squared wooden girders to hold up a protective wooden roof and to brace sideboards that kept the crumbling dirt walls from closing in. They worked by dim candlelight amid the stench, the slop at their feet, the chill, and the stagnant air. As the men dug, they unearthed massive red earthworms, bones, leering skulls— visions they were apt to revisit in their deepest sleep.

Once the first tunnel reached the old garden wall, the workers back-tracked a bit and struck out in perpendicular directions, roughly parallel-ing the wall. In the basement of the laundry, another crew went to work in the back corner, digging an open pit in search of coffins. The crew digging Shaft B out in the street was aiming to tunnel into the property and meet up with the crews working off Shaft A. There was a logic to the scramble. Combined, the three work sites would cover the entire front section of the old cemetery, the place where Porter thought Jones's body was most likely buried.

In the first few days, they struck a cluster of corpses from a mass burial. There were three layers of skeletons, dozens of them, stacked in a crisscross-ing pattern like cordwood, "some lying facedown, others on their sides." The searchers were confused at first. Then Porter recalled journalistic paintings by Etienne Bericourt that detailed the loading onto carts of the Swiss Guardsmen killed just three weeks after Jones's death. As Protestants, the Swiss soldiers would not have been buried in any of the Catholic cem-eteries. These stacked bones, Porter concluded, were the remains of those men, and he interpreted the discovery as "another proof that although the cemetery was closed soon after [Jones's] death there was plenty of room left for his coffin at the time of his burial, for the reason that so many bodies were interred there afterward."

Porter showed up regularly at the work site, seeking updates or just watching, even as official duties kept his calendar full. Less than two weeks before the tunneling had begun, a group of about three thousand unarmed protesters in Saint Petersburg had marched toward the Winter Palace to deliver a petition to Tsar Nicholas II. They were met by the Imperial Guard, which opened fire, killing (depending on the source) anywhere from one hundred to one thousand people. The violence set in motion the events that led to the unsuccessful Russian revolution later that year, and the even-tually successful Bolshevik Revolution in 1917.

The political violence wasn't limited to Russia—the tsar's gunning down of his own people inflamed anarchists and revolutionaries across

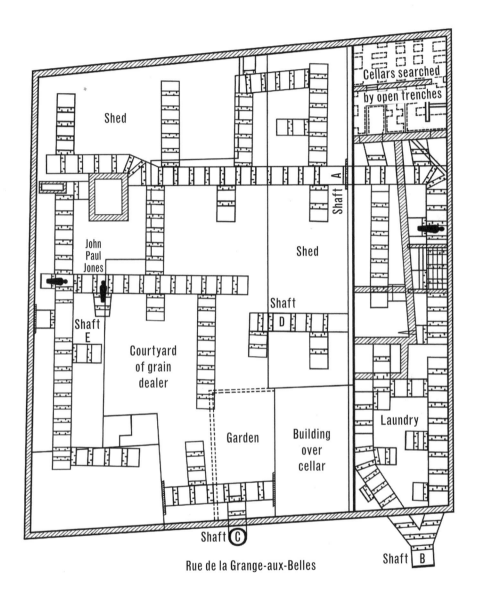

Final layout of the excavation site, within the bounds of the old cemetery.
Silhouettes indicate where the first three lead coffins were found.
Original excavation plans in Charles W. Stewart, *John Paul Jones: Commemoration at Annapolis, April 24, 1906* (Washington, DC: Government Printing Office, 1907); adapted by James Spence

Europe and the United States. In Paris, presumed anarchists placed a bomb against the outside wall of the home of Prince Troubetzkoy, a member of the Russian aristocracy and a long-standing attaché to the Russian embassy. A policeman spotted the device and snuffed the fuse before it could explode. That same night, as a meeting of anti-tsarist socialists was breaking up, someone tossed a nail-laden bomb into a throng of police officers, injuring two of them and three civilians. The attacks, along with a wave of hoaxes, set off fears that the city was headed toward another "dynamite club" era, a cycle of bombings and assassinations.

The French were dealing with their own political crises as well. A domestic showdown pitted aristocratic and conservative supporters of the Roman Catholic Church against liberals who sought a separation between church and state. And a growing number of scandals surrounding reported abuses by French officials in Africa emerged: beheading tribal chiefs, executing a tribesman by strapping a stick of dynamite to his back, and force-feeding human flesh to tribal prisoners, among other atrocities. Porter's job was to watch out for American interests amid the turmoil, and there was much to keep track of with war still raging between the Russians and the Japanese in the Far East, high-level international financial deals being negotiated in Europe, and run-of-the-mill trade issues.[1]

Porter had personal business to tend to as well. On the evening of March 2, a Thursday, the "great rooms" of the ambassador's residence, closed since Sophie's death, were opened once more for a party, a rare social celebration in Porter's life as a widower. And there was indeed something to celebrate: Porter's daughter, Elsie, was to marry Dr. Edwin Mende the next morning in a small civil ceremony, to be followed Saturday—which was also Sophie's birthday—with a public ceremony at the American Church. The focal point of the party, beyond the food and the drinks, was the presentation of gifts, and it was immediately clear that the gifts bestowed on an ambassador's daughter and her wealthy beau were not the traditional household items. The French government sent over a monogrammed Sevres tea set from the government's famous porcelain factory. George J. Gould, the railroad tycoon and son of financier Jay Gould, gave a sapphire ring. Secretary Hay and his wife sent a silver tray; Prince von Radolin, the German ambassador, and his wife gave gold *bonbonnieres* (small boxes);

Porter's old friend General Winslow and his wife gave a gold chocolate service. The parents of the couple were even more generous. Porter gave them a car. The elder Dr. Mende gave them a house in Bern, sealing the couple's decision to give up on their plans to move to New York City and instead settle in Mende's home country—a decision that Porter received with "shock," given that he had predicated his retirement on the idea that the family would be reunited in Manhattan.[2]

The wedding was the event of the season. An international array of government officials, high society expatriates, and European business leaders filed into the American church, decorated for the day with spring-like arrangements of foliage and flowers. The choir was rounded out with such voices as Bessie Abbott, the young American prima donna of the current Parisian opera season. The bridesmaids wore "dainty green and pink costumes, with broad-bred hats and sweeping plumes," the *New York Times* reported. Elsie wore a white satin dress "trimmed with lace and sprays of orange blossoms." The two-hour reception followed at the ambassador's residence in what turned out to be the last big party of his six-year stay in the City of Light.[3]

Meanwhile, Porter was planning his own departure. The White House had announced on February 10 that while Porter would likely remain in France for a few months, Robert McCormick, the current US ambassador to Russia, would be replacing him. Porter was also watching for news from Washington about Roosevelt's request for Congress to pay for the search for Jones's body. On February 13 he wired an update on the excavations and a query to Hay: "Sunk shaft. Found rows of dead undisturbed in cemetery at depth seventeen feet. What action taken on my recommendation of John Paul Jones appropriation?" He received a response from Francis Loomis, the assistant secretary of state: "The President sent message to Congress today recommending thirty five thousand dollars for John Paul Jones."

Roosevelt himself wrote to Porter the next day, thanking him for his work as ambassador. "I appreciate all that you have done in your post; and you can not be more pleased at being connected with my administration than I am at having you under me. But I understand thoroughly the pressing personal reasons you set out in your letter to Secretary Hay, which made it obligatory to leave." Roosevelt said he toyed with asking Porter to stay on into the summer but decided to accept his resignation effective April 30, a date that meshed with other anticipated diplomatic shuffles.[4]

Porter then apparently fell out of the loop of communications about his successor. In the weeks after Elsie's wedding, press accounts reported that McCormick would be heading to Paris sooner than anticipated, a development that seemed to catch Porter unaware. "I saw by press dispatch that McCormick is instructed to proceed to Paris at once and assume charge at early day," he wired Hay on March 25. "The President having written me that my resignation was accepted as of April 30, I made arrangements accordingly both here and with McCormick. What foundation for above rumor? Porter."[5]

------------------------------ ✿ ------------------------------

Throughout the private and public wedding celebrations, Porter's conversations with his superiors in Washington about when he could come home, and the daily diplomatic distractions, Weiss's work crews continued their search. Parisians gathered daily at the site, sometimes joined by Porter, even though there was little for the public to see—most of the work was happening underground. On the surface, workers came and went, and loads of dirt were moved to the street and then loaded onto carts to be hauled away to the storage field. Journalists occasionally popped in, but the newspapers had little to show for it. In fact, the Parisian press largely ignored Porter's project, and reports from the American foreign correspondents rarely mentioned the dig.

Porter had left strict orders that he was to be summoned at the first sighting of any lead coffins, and on the afternoon of February 22, nearly three weeks after the first dirt was turned, Porter received the call. He hurried from the embassy to the excavation site, crawled down the ladder (probably Shaft A), and made his way to the discovery.

The location of the coffin was encouraging: it was near where the old steps descended from the gate between the orchard and the cemetery, meaning the grave could have been one of the last to be filled, which Porter had speculated would be the case for Jones's body. The condition of the coffin itself was discouraging. It was lead, but it had been heavily damaged—the rounded "head" of the coffin had been sheared off, along with the skull of the corpse. The damage was old, and Weiss's excavators also found the remnants of a wooden barrel at the head of the coffin. Porter and Weiss surmised it had been sunk below ground as a catch basin to hold run-off rain to water a garden, damaging the coffin as the barrel was sunk into place. With the coffin split open, its contents exposed to the subterranean moisture, worms, and bacteria, the decapitated remains had been reduced to rotted flesh on bones.

The lead coffin was buried inside a wooden casket, which bore a rusted copper nameplate "so brittle that when lifted it broke and a portion of it crumbled to pieces." Working gingerly in the flickering candlelight, Porter tried to discern shadows of letters beneath the crusted green patina. None were legible. He carefully wrapped the shim of metal in his handkerchief, tucked it into a coat pocket, and climbed the ladder back out of the growing maze of tunnels. In his time in Paris, Porter had come to know the proprietor of M. André et Fil, an art-restoration business, and he headed there, where he asked the craftsman to work quickly but gently to uncover the name beneath the rust.

That night, Porter delivered a previously scheduled speech to the American Club in Paris and talked about his quest to find Jones's body. The tenor of the speech made it sound more political than historical, and it is hard to imagine that he was not counting on the foreign correspondents in attendance to wire his words to their newspapers back home. He detailed for the expatriate business leaders his efforts scouring records to find the cemetery in which Jones was likely buried, the more recent negotiations to obtain the right to dig for the body, and the need for Congress to approve the president's request to pay for the exhumation. Oddly, the *Washington Post* story on the speech did not mention that the dig had already begun, though that was clearly known both among the expatriates and the foreign correspondents. And it muddled the detail about the first shaft, implying that it had occurred a year before, at the onset of the negotiations with Crignier. If the money wasn't approved by Congress, the paper reported Porter as saying, the options would lapse and the opportunity would be lost—which was not the case.

"While other nations are gathering the ashes of their heroes in their Pantheons, their Valhallas, and their Westminster Abbeys, all that is mortal of this marvelous organizer of American victories upon the sea lies like

The search for John Paul Jones's body, during which workers made their way
through layers of skeletons and large red worms, was not for those with weak
stomachs. Note the skulls embedded in the earthen wall (left).
Courtesy of the Library of Congress, Horace Porter Collection, Manuscript Division

an outcast in a squalid quarter of a distant city, in a neglected grave, where
it was placed by the hand of charity to keep it from the potter's field," Porter told his fellow Americans. "What once was consecrated ground is desecrated by vegetable gardens, a deposit for night soil, and even the burial of
dogs. It is fitting that an effort be made to give him an appropriate sepulcher at last in the land of liberty which his efforts helped make free."[6]

Most of the news reports out of Paris focused on the found coffin and
the likelihood that Jones was in it. Speculation turned to probability. The
New York Times printed a two-paragraph story the next day reporting that
"a metal casket, which is believed to contain the bones of John Paul Jones,
has been found 16 feet below a grain shed at 14 Rue Grange aux Belles." In
addition to getting the address wrong, it said Porter and others involved with
the dig believed the bones were Jones's; while they were hopeful, they in fact

had no basis to believe it was the right coffin and made no such claim. The story went on to say that the coffin would be opened the next day—another error—and that the "time worn" nameplate was indecipherable.[7]

But those weren't Porter's only problems with the media. From the beginning of the project, Porter had been concerned about intruders at the work site. When the lead coffin was found, he sent word to the prefect of police asking that two officers be assigned to watch over the site, particularly late at night through the early morning, when the workers were gone. "Late in the evening I learned that, owing to his absence from his office and an error in getting the communication to him, there would be no guard there that night," Porter wrote later. "I could not help feeling some forebodings, and my state of mind may be imagined upon receiving a brief note early the next morning from an official saying he regretted to inform me that there had unfortunately been a depredation committed in the gallery where the leaden coffin was found."

Porter hurried to the site feeling "like a person who had delayed a day too long in insuring his property and learned that it had taken fire." But the damage, as it turned out, was minimal. "An enterprising reporter and photographer . . . had succeeded in opening the gate, getting into the yard, and entering the gallery. In the darkness they had stumbled and broken their [camera] apparatus, and in trying to use one which our men had left in the gallery had broken it also." Some camera pieces were missing, but otherwise the site was unscathed.

Porter received a report on the nameplate the next day from André, the art restorer, who had been able to work his magic on the severely damaged piece of metal. The front of the nameplate was beyond recovery, so he went to work on the reverse side, which had spent most of its time underground affixed to the wooden casket and thus was less rusted. Working carefully over two days, André cleared away the dirt and sufficient rust to read some of the engraved letters in reverse, enough to conclude that the coffin held the body of an Englishman who had died May 20, 1790, nearly two years before Jones. It was the wrong coffin, he told Porter.

By then, though, press accounts were swirling. "A reporter with a lively imagination could not wait for the deciphering of the plate and meanwhile invented a highly dramatic story," Porter recalled later. A story appeared saying "there was such certainty entertained that this leaden coffin contained the body of Paul Jones that I had summoned the personnel of the embassy and others to the scene, including the commissary of police who attended ornamented with his tricolored scarf." The coffin was opened "with great ceremony and solemnity, and the group, deeply affected, stood reverently, with bowed heads, awaiting the recognition of the body of the illustrious sailor" before it became clear that "a serious error had been made." None of that had happened, and it bothered Porter that the fictitious story had been printed. More importantly, people in some quarters believed the article, leading to criticism that the ambassador and his work crews didn't know what they were doing and were ready to conclude on the flimsiest evidence that they had succeeded.[8]

The crews kept digging, but they had little to show for it beyond a deeper and more intricate maze of tunnels. Progress was slow. The area under the laundry was explored, but no other lead coffins were found. The terrain was dangerous and unstable and beleaguered by "infiltrations of water," Weiss said, so "all the galleries were rapidly and carefully refilled and the work of exploring the property of the grain dealer begun." The other three shafts were sunk and the galleries were then expanded below ground.

Finally, on March 23, a month after the first lead coffin was found, a crew digging near what had been the back wall of the cemetery discovered another wooden casket with a smaller lead coffin inside. This coffin had a well-preserved nameplate that identified the dead man as RICHARD HAY, ESQ., who had died in January 29, 1785. Not only was it not Jones, but Hay had been buried seven years before Jones, calling into question Porter's theory that the cemetery had been filled from the center outward. If Porter was disappointed or beginning to question the project, he didn't reveal it in any surviving records.[9]

The crews worked on. Eight days later, they hit another lead coffin, this one within a few yards of the second discovered coffin, both near the foot of Shaft E, the last to be sunk. (No explanation could be found as to why it took so long to find the third coffin given its proximity to the second one.) It, too, had been encased in a wooden casket, but this one had suffered the ravages of a century underground. Little of the outer wooden casket was found beyond rotted shards. A skeleton with no coffin of its own was lying atop the lead coffin, and the wooden lid was missing altogether, which meant there also was no nameplate. Workers sifted through the earth excavated from around the coffin but found nothing. Weiss supposed that the lid had been taken up and discarded at the time the coffin-less body had been buried. The workers pulled the coffin and exposed skeleton out of the earth, then carted the metal box to an open area in the gallery. Porter again was summoned.

The ambassador, looking at the crenulated metal, decided to open the lead coffin there underground, in part to dampen public speculation. The air was already so foul that Porter was persuaded to wait, fearing that the added odors from the open coffin would be overpowering in the close, dank space. Crews got to work extending the gallery to connect with a main tunnel emanating from Shaft A, on the opposite side of the cemetery. Once they were connected, this created a ventilation circuit, and the foul air improved considerably. It delayed the opening of the coffin for a week.

Finally, on April 7, Porter was alerted that the site was ready. He brought Bailly-Blanchard with him. Weiss was there too, as was a M. Géninet, Weiss's on-site supervisor for the project. The visitors all donned long smocks over their suits, and even deep below ground all but Weiss wore bowler hats. The workers took a break and gathered around as well, curious, all, as to what they would find.

The lead coffin had been placed atop a mound of dirt in a low-ceilinged gallery. The years and the weight of fifteen feet or so of earth had crumpled it so that the coffin looked like an elongated can crushed by giant hands. The original shape was still clear, though: narrow at the feet then broadening gradually to the shoulders before narrowing again to a rounded section for the head. There was a small solder plug sealing a hole near the head, and close by was a rough and jagged hole packed with darkened earth. It looked, Porter thought, as though it had been made by the end of a pickax, and he wondered if, sometime after the burial, someone had dug down and struck through the wooden top, piercing the lead coffin below. Maybe it was whoever had buried the skeleton found atop the coffin. There was a second hole in the coffin, too, a small crack near the foot, which Porter concluded had been caused by the shifting and settling of the earth from above. It, too, was packed with darkened dirt.

The coffin had been sealed shut before it was buried, and Porter was concerned that it be protected as much as possible from further damage. So the workers took their time removing the thin line of solder from the seam. When they finished, the top was carefully pried loose and lifted, filling the gallery with the smell of alcohol. There was no liquid, though. It had apparently evaporated slowly over time through the pickax hole and the crack at the feet, which the men decided accounted for the discolored earth in the holes.

The first thing the men saw was a packed layer of hay. After carefully removing a few handfuls, they found a body wrapped in a long linen burial sheet. More hay had been jammed between the corpse and the walls of the coffin, as though prepared for a long, bumpy journey. The packing was

John Paul Jones's lead coffin, with, from left, an unidentified man; M. Géninet, a public works foreman; Paul Weiss, who led the excavation project; Arthur Bailly-Blanchard, second secretary at the US embassy; and ambassador Horace Porter.
Courtesy of the Library of Congress, Horace Porter Collection, Manuscript Division

seen as a good sign, since Blackden's letter to Jones's sister had mentioned that the admiral's body had been interred in such a way that it could be exhumed and shipped to the United States. Excitement built.

One of the men measured the body at five feet, seven inches long, the recorded height of Jones. They placed a half dozen lit candles on the dirt pile around the top of the coffin and carefully began unraveling the linen sheets from the head and upper torso of the body, revealing the face. "To our intense surprise, the body was marvelously well preserved, all the flesh remaining intact, very slightly shrunken, and of a grayish brown or tan color," Porter said. The skin was pliable and moist, as was the linen wrap, and "the face presented quite a natural appearance" except for the nose. The cartilage at the tip had been bent sharply to the side, as though the nose had been crushed by the lid.

Porter and several of the other men had with them the Jones medallions Porter had ordered from the mint while he was conducting the records search. One was pulled out and placed next to the head. Both had the same broad forehead, similar-shaped brows, the same cheekbone structure, "prominently arched eye orbits," and long, flowing hair. "Paul Jones!" some of the men shouted. Porter was ecstatic. "All those who were gathered about the coffin removed their hats, feeling that they were standing in the presence of the illustrious dead—the object of the long search."

They had found John Paul Jones. But for now, it would be a secret.

---- ✿ ----

Porter knew he needed more proof than his gut feeling and the well-preserved corpse's resemblance to a face on a medal. Before the dig began, Porter had arranged with several Parisian-based experts in forensics to look over the body should it be found. One of them was Louis Capitan, a doctor and highly respected archeologist and anthropologist. Word was sent to the École d'Anthropologie, where Capitan worked and taught, to let him know a body had been found and that Porter thought it was likely Jones. Capitan replied via messenger that he was busy that day and Porter should reseal the coffin with plaster until he could get there. The linen was replaced around the head, the coffin lid set into a bead of plaster along the bottom lip, and the body sealed away.

Capitan arrived the next day and descended the ladder to the subterranean gallery. Despite his confidence that he had the right body, Porter was too meticulous to suspend the search. So workers scurried by, and the voices and sounds of digging echoed through the candle-lit tunnels. In fact, over the next week or so the men would find two more lead coffins, one with a nameplate identifying it as someone other than Jones, and the second without a name tag but holding a corpse well over six feet in height and clearly not that of the diminutive Jones. And with Porter trying to keep the discovery out of the newspapers for the time being, it was important that the daily gathering of the curious see the site consistently busy.

Capitan looked around the gallery. It was a close, ill-lit space with no room for a proper examination table. He decided conditions were too primitive and too busy for a proper examination. He conferred with Weiss and they decided to move the coffin to the École de Médecine. Capitan went first to the local police prefecture and explained the plan, asking for discretion, and then to the medical school, where he enlisted the aid and cooperation of the key figures there. That night, after the small crowd of curious Parisians had faded away, the coffin was carefully lifted to the surface, secretly loaded onto a cart, and hauled off to the medical school.

The next morning, an august gathering of medical experts surrounded the coffin, which had been placed on a glistening steel table. Capitan was there, as were Dr. Georges Papillault, an anthropologist who would study the anatomical details of the body; Dr. Georges Herve, who oversaw the work; Dr. A. Javal, a government physician; and J. Pray, a police official. Weiss and Porter were there too, along with Bailly-Blanchard, Gowdy, and several other men. In all, a dozen men would take part in or witness different aspects of the examination and autopsy, which would stretch over nearly a week.

The plaster seal was knocked loose and the lid carefully lifted away. The first issue was how to remove the corpse from its tight packing without risk of damage. They decided the safest approach would be to cut away the lead coffin. The metal was split at the head and the feet and then pulled apart, releasing the pressure and loosening the compacted hay. Then, very delicately, the body was picked up and moved to a dissecting table, where the linen was carefully unwrapped to reveal a man clad only in a long linen shirt decorated with plaits and ruffles. Exposure to the air two days earlier had already begun to affect it. Facial skin that had been moist and soft was now sunken and leathery, with the lips pulling back from the teeth in a grimace. Capitan noted that the body was so well preserved that the ligaments and muscles still kept the skeleton intact—they were able to move the body as a whole, without it falling apart, despite the more than 110 years that had elapsed since the man's death.

The hands, feet, and legs were wrapped loosely in foil, a common burial practice in the late 1700s, when the Saint Louis cemetery was accepting bodies. The arms were folded across the chest, and the doctor straightened them to make it easier to examine the body. Porter reached out and gently picked up the right hand, as though to shake it in greeting. The knuckle joints bent easily, and the skin was soft to the touch. The face bore the stubble of a man who hadn't shaved for a few days. The right eye was closed and the left slightly open, and lines had been creased into the skin from the linen wrap. The near-black hair had gone gray at the temples, and the bulk of it, some thirty inches long, was collected at the nape, rolled into a bun and wrapped in a linen cap with an odd bit of stitching that looked like the letter "J" from one view, but like the letter "P" when turned upside down.

They removed the linen shirt, along with the remnants of the foil, and positioned the corpse in a sitting position for a series of photographs. They then carefully examined the exterior of the body and found no scars or malformations. The skin was dark in tone, and the torso was flecked with small white crystals, part of what the doctors called the "autolytic process"—the conversion of enzymes after death but before the alcohol bath could begin to preserve the flesh.

Papillault carefully measured the body, now lying flat on the table. Consistent with the initial measurement at the cemetery site, he recorded it as five feet, seven inches long. Papillault then took a series of measurements of different elements of the corpse, creating an exhaustive collection of human topography. He focused particularly on the face, taking down its length and width, the dimension of the lips, and the chin. The plan was to match those measurements against the bust of Jones created by Jean

Antoine Houdon when Jones was alive, a bust that Jones's contemporaries had described as a near-perfect likeness. Paris's Musée d'Ethnographie du Trocadéro had a copy, and Porter used his connections to gain permission to use it for comparison purposes.

It was not a perfect method, Papillault acknowledged. Allowances had to be made for artistic distortion, and a century-old corpse lacks the full-fleshed look of a living man modeling for his sculptor. "We had nothing to compare therewith but a skeleton covered with a tanned skin and shrunken tissues," Papillault wrote later. Still, any sculptor of skill and repute would deliver a bust that resembled the subject in close details, he believed, or the sculptor wouldn't have much in the way of commissions. Not perfect, no, but it would be good enough for their purposes. Especially since the bust and the corpse had an identical malformation of the earlobe—not the kind of tweak an artist would likely make for the sake of his art.

It took a couple of days for all of the measurements to be taken, checked, and double-checked. The corpse was photographed in several details, though by now the air had dried out the flesh until it looked like an ancient mummy. A hair sample was washed clean and its color noted as dark brown to black, which matched contemporary descriptions of Jones as being a dark-complexioned Scotsman, with dark hair and eyes. Capitan and Papillault also reviewed the paper trail that Porter and his deputies had amassed, including the contemporary descriptions of Jones's burial. There was nothing in their first examination of the body to suggest another conclusion, Papillault reported. The body was Jones, he felt.

Yet they pressed on, seeking certitude.

The doctors went to work on the internal organs. Not wanting to disfigure the corpse in a way that would be visible, Capitan turned the body face down and then carefully cut deeply into the back of the torso. A small amount of discolored alcohol leaked out onto the table, and Capitan "was greatly astonished" to find the internal organs contracted but preserved, like a lab specimen. He began with the lungs, which held small whitish crystals, but also "small rounded masses, hard and at times calcified," scars caused by pneumonia, from which Jones had suffered while in the service of Catherine the Great. The heart was "the color of dead leaves" yet remained soft and flexible, and had been healthy at the time of death. The spleen was larger than it should have been, but the rest of the major organs were healthy and unscarred. Except for the kidneys. They were "small, hard, and contracted," much more so than would be accounted for by the general changes in the corpse after death. Capitan concluded they were diseased, affected by interstitial nephritis, and that the damage to the lungs suggested "a patient rather pronouncedly consumptive." Capitan took small samples of each of the organs and set them aside, then carefully placed the organs back in the thoracic cavity and sewed the skin shut.

Another doctor, Cornil, reviewed the tissue samples, including a microscopic examination, and added to Capitan's conclusions. The body on the table had suffered from pneumonia (there was no evidence of tuberculosis) and severe kidney failure. The afflictions accounted for the symptoms Jones had exhibited as he neared death—the difficulty breathing, the swelling of the lower limbs and abdomen. And the kidney disease was doubtless the cause of death.

Altogether, it was a persuasive array of evidence, some direct, some inferred. There was the research trail unearthed by Porter and his deputies. The details of Jones's physical condition in his last days. The twentieth-century autopsy of the eighteenth-century corpse. All fed into the same conclusion. "Given this convergence of exceedingly numerous, very diversified, and always agreeing facts," Capitan wrote, "it would be necessary to have a concurrence of circumstances absolutely exceptional and improbable in order that the corpse . . . be not that of Paul Jones."

A week after the coffin had been found deep beneath Mme Crignier's Parisian properties, Porter prepared a lengthy telegram to Washington. It was understated, and choppily written, but unequivocal. "My six years search for remains Paul Jones has resulted in success," Porter began. He skated through the research that led him to the site, the details of the discovery of the coffin, its removal to the École de Médecine, the measurements, and the autopsy that "showed distinct proofs of disease of which the Admiral is known to have died." Porter promised to mail copies of all the reports once they were completed, but felt compelled to wire Hay with the good news: he had found the right body. "Will have remains put in suitable casket and deposited in receiving vault of American Church till decision reached as to most appropriate means of transportation to America."[10]

Porter received a congratulatory reply, and the exchange was remarkably muted given the time, effort, and expense that Porter, particularly, had put into the search. The elation came through in subtle ways. On the top of Porter's initial telegram received at the State Department, someone scrawled an undated note: "Copies made for press!"

16

The Return of the Hero

Fʀᴏᴍ ᴀ ᴛᴇᴄʜɴɪᴄᴀʟ sᴛᴀɴᴅᴘᴏɪɴᴛ, the mining for Jones's body had not gone as smoothly as Porter and Weiss had hoped. Despite the support beams and board ceilings they'd installed, the unstable ground above the tunnels had settled in places, and the walls in some of Mme Crignier's buildings had cracked. In March—in the midst of the search—Porter was summoned to a Parisian court to answer a complaint about damage filed by Crignier's tenants. Vignaud, replying on Porter's behalf, pointed out that the ambassador was not subject to French subpoenas and that, regardless, his agreement with Crignier meant that all such complaints should be made to her.[1]

The work had also taken longer than expected. Porter had predicted the project would last three months, from the first shovelful of earth to be dug out to the last shovelful to be tapped back into place. The digging had begun February 3, and some ten weeks later, when the medical experts identified the body as Jones, sections of the old cemetery remained unexplored. And only the tunnels beneath the laundry had been refilled with a mix of the original earth and large paving stones Weiss had ordered in to add stability. The records don't detail what became of the hundreds of bodies the men had encountered; presumably, they were left below ground, to be reburied with the filling of the tunnels.

The confirmation that Jones's body had been found at least allowed Porter to cut the search short. The day after Porter wired Washington with his confirmation, Weiss's crews ended their digging and began the restoration. The horse carts that had hauled away the excavated dirt to the remote storage field began the reverse process. The winch-hauled buckets that had brought the material to the surface now were used to take the stones and removed earth back below ground. Slowly, the tunnels were refilled.

There's no clear record of when the work ended, but it stretched well into summer and then fall, nearly eleven months altogether and more than three times what Porter and Weiss had predicted. Bassigny, in particular, was affected, since most of the work took up space in the property he had leased for his granary, cutting into his business. And even after the tunnels were filled, the ground continued to shift and settle, increasing the damage to Mme Crignier's buildings. The prolonged time of the project and the damaged walls created long-running problems and eventually a series of lawsuits for, and between, Mme Crignier and her tenants.[2]

The more immediate issue, though, was what to do with Jones's body. The exposure to the air had already begun drying out the skin, and what had been a remarkably preserved corpse was turning into a ghoulish apparition—head twisted to the side, skin turned to leather, lips shrunken back in that toothy grimace. And while the body was intact, it was still very delicate. After the examination and autopsy, the medical workers tried to comb out the admiral's long hair, which had become gnarled after it was unloosed from the bun and protective cap. Each brush stroke pulled locks away from the scalp, so they gave up, carefully rolled the hair into an unkempt ball, and tucked it back into the embroidered cap.

Though Jones's final resting spot had yet to be determined, Porter ordered the body packed up for the eventual trip to the United States. It was a much more involved process than simply dropping Jones back into his coffin. The medical workers rubbed glycerin onto the skin to preserve it, and sprayed essence of thymol, another preservative, as an extra protective layer over the face, before redressing the corpse in the ruffled burial shirt. They folded the original burial sheet and placed it in the bottom of the lead coffin, still split wide from the cuts at the head and foot. On top of the sheet they spread a layer of impermeable oiled silk, over which they laid cotton batting soaked in glycerin. They gently placed the body on the cotton and then added second layers of treated cotton and silk on top, from the middle of the torso down. They tucked in a small sample jar of the original packing hay near the head, and by the feet placed a sealed-up sample of the discolored earth from the breaches in the coffin. More treated cotton was tucked around the body, taking the place of the hay, and the sides of the split coffin were bent back as near as they could be to the original shape.

With Jones snugly back in his coffin, the workers turned their attention to a new lead coffin ordered by Porter, which was somewhat larger than the one in which Jones had been found. They covered the bottom with treated sawdust, then placed the original coffin lid on top of the sawdust. Gently they lowered Jones and the old coffin to rest on top of the lid, and then they sealed the new coffin's lid in place—a lid with a glass pane "which exposed to view the head and chest" so Jones could be seen without reopening the coffin. After the coffin was soldered shut, seals were affixed bearing the imprint of the US embassy. The workers then used three bands of linen to lower the nesting coffins inside a large oak casket with eight silver handles, the lid of which was then closed tight with sixteen silver screws.[3] When they were done, it resembled a morbid set of Russian *matryoshka* nesting dolls, six feet, ten inches long, two and a half feet wide, and a foot and a half high.[4]

With no pageantry and only a small entourage, the coffin was transported to the American Cathedral Church of the Holy Trinity, an Anglican parish dating to the 1830s. Pallbearers carried the coffin to the church basement, where it was draped in an American flag. Ambassador Porter, Vignaud, Bailly-Blanchard, Gowdy, and Weiss stood solemnly as the Reverend Dr. John B. Morgan (a cousin of J. P. Morgan) offered a prayer for the long-dead hero. And there Jones would stay, until Porter and his superiors in Washington could figure out what to do with him. It would be a more fraught decision than Porter had any reason to anticipate. Everyone, it seemed, wanted to claim a hero.

Porter's success was heralded in newspapers across the United States, and both his and Jones's name were invoked at businessmen's lunches and other gatherings where American boosterism could be found. The *Spokane Press* managed to squeeze onto its April 14 front page a line from a Scripps News Association wire story out of Paris that "it is announced positively that the remains of John Paul Jones have been found." An Associated Press story made it into more papers the next day, with details from Porter's report to the State Department. The *New York Tribune* and the *Evening World* in New York City carried their own front-page stories by Paris-based correspondents that included details from the autopsy, with the *World* adding a touch of biography about Jones, including how he came to rest in Paris. The *Tribune*'s correspondent, the well-connected Charles Inman Barnard, gave the discovery his own spin. Barnard's boss, *Tribune* owner Whitelaw Reid, was an old friend of Porter and had been the US representative in France under President Benjamin Harrison. Reid was also a member of the Peace Commission that Porter had hosted to negotiate the treaty ending the Spanish-American War. That connection likely helped win Barnard a coffin-side seat. In a story dated April 15, the day after Porter's telegram to Washington, Barnard wrote that "the happiest man in Paris today is General Porter, who, after six years' patient research, discovered yesterday the body of John Paul Jones. Your correspondent examined the remains this morning. There is no doubt whatever about the identity, conforming in every detail to descriptions and measurements at the time of his death."

While Porter was roundly credited with making the discovery, another man, journalist Julius Chambers, had already surfaced to claim that he, in fact, was the man who had found the cemetery. Flamboyant and self-promoting, Chambers was very much a journalist of his time, a veteran of the yellow press wars, with a ham actor's instinct for the spotlight. He and Barnard were longtime friends, and Chambers had also worked for Reid at the *Tribune* in the 1870s before he was hired away to work for James Gordon Bennett Jr. at the *New York Herald*. Bennett had sent him to France to create the Paris *Herald* in 1887. Two years later, Chambers was back in New York working for Joseph Pulitzer at the *World*.

Early in his career, Chambers was an investigative reporter and a bit of a muckraker. In one series, he conspired with friends to get committed to an insane asylum and, after his release, wrote an exposé about abuses of the mentally ill, sparking inquiries and policy changes. In 1872, Chambers followed the Mississippi River to its northernmost point, gaining credit for determining that Elk Lake, rather than the previously identified Lake Itasca, was the wellspring of one of the world's mightiest rivers. The distinction is one of splitting hairs: Elk Lake is a small pond slightly south and a few feet higher in elevation than Lake Itasca, into which it empties through a short creek. Still, the discovery earned Chambers an invitation to join Britain's Royal Geographic Society. By 1899, Chambers was out on his own, freelancing articles and traveling the world writing books, including novels.

As Porter waited for Weiss's crews to do their work and before Jones's body was found, Chambers had written an article for the *Pittsburgh Dispatch* claiming that he and Barnard, working with Ricaudy, were the ones who had read the historical trail correctly and narrowed the burial spot to the abandoned Saint Louis cemetery. They began the search, he wrote, in July 1899, and Chambers claimed that he had paid for it. By then, though, Porter had already been making inquiries, as had Gowdy. In his memoirs, published posthumously in 1921, Chambers maintained his claim but had dropped Barnard and Ricaudy from the list of credits. "At my personal expense, I had employed a friend in Paris to search the Parisian journals contemporary with the funeral of Admiral Jones, and he had thereby located the grave, beyond question, in the Protestant cemetery as it existed in 1792." Chambers noted that "I have a letter from [Porter] denying I had found the grave," but Chambers neither reprinted the letter nor refuted it, other than to restate his claim.[5] Tellingly, Barnard, Chambers's supposed partner in the search, never claimed that his role had any significance, writing in October 1899 only that he had "upon several occasions profited by M. de Ricaudy's invitations, and accompanied him during some of his most interesting researches in the heart of antiquarian Paris." Barnard notably doesn't mention Chambers. One suspects that Chambers, like Barnard, simply accompanied Ricaudy on some of his inquiries.[6]

And there were other claims. The Daughters of the Revolution (a now defunct rival to the Daughters of the American Revolution), gathered for their fourteenth annual conference in Asheville, North Carolina, in late April and unanimously passed a motion commending Porter "in his work of finding and removing to this country the body of John Paul Jones—a project which originated with the Daughters of the Revolution."[7]

The Sons of the American Revolution also claimed credit, maintaining that since Porter had been the founder and top official of the group's Parisian chapter, he had conducted the search under the SAR's banner—though Porter never linked the search with his role at the SAR.[8]

In rural western New York, the *Randolph Register* claimed that its local lawyer J. G. Johnson had prompted the search with his June 1899 letter to McKinley—which could well have been the spark that led to the discovery. Since Gowdy had made some initial queries the previous winter at the behest of Congressman Landis, it's impossible to distill a single source to credit, given the national attention paid to Jones's history in the wake of Dewey's victory over the Spanish at Manila Bay.

Porter, though, had propelled the project and financed it. It's hard to see an avenue by which Jones's body would have been recovered without Porter. Even Chambers didn't claim to have taken steps to confirm that Crignier's property was indeed atop the old cemetery and that Jones was buried within.

Similarly, there were competing claims on the body itself. Official Washington presumed space—and a memorial—would be made for Jones at the National Cemetery in Arlington. Even before Porter had found the body, speculative claims were being laid from different slices of Jones's past. Officials and boosters in Fredericksburg, Virginia, argued that Jones should be buried there, since that was as close to a home as the admiral had on American soil. Jones's brother had been a contributing member of the city in the 1700s, and Jones had lived at the house as caretaker after the brother's death. Had Jones not left to sail under the American flag against the British, they argued, he likely would have stayed there, and Jones's descendants would be living among them.

Philadelphia, too, argued that Jones's most significant time of residence was there, where he received his commission to the Continental navy and where the directives for the early days of his American naval career had been issued. New York City boosters made a case as well, given that part of

Jones's story—the discovery of some of his letters—took place in the city. Perhaps they also felt that Porter's role in finding the body would give them an edge. And while the State Department was eyeing burial at Arlington, the Department of the Navy began making noise that Jones's body belonged at the US Naval Academy in Annapolis, arguing that Jones had been among the first to advocate that the United States create a place to train and groom officers for service at sea.

Proponents of the different final resting places sent telegrams to Porter, as the man who had found the body, seeking his recommendation. "I reply that all such questions should be left to the national government for decision," he told Francis Loomis, the assistant secretary of state. Porter, in fact, didn't have a preference. He just wanted a commitment and a timeframe from Washington so he could arrange for the pageantry that would surround the transfer of the body to the United States.

Porter was also trying to finalize his own plans for moving home. As of May 1, new ambassador Robert McCormick would be in charge of the embassy and Porter would be just another American in Paris. "Mr. McCormick takes charge of the Embassy tomorrow morning," Porter wired to Loomis on April 30. "I shall have my furniture packed up during this month and will ship most of it during the month of June, of which you will be advised. I beg that you will see that the necessary instructions are given for its free entry at the port of New York."[9]

———— ✦ ————

Porter's spring exchanges with Washington were with Loomis instead of John Hay because the secretary of state was no longer in Washington. The rigors of public life had begun to eat away at the sixty-six-year-old Hay's stamina, and his health was fading. He had intended to resign as secretary of state at the end of Roosevelt's term in March, but the president urged him to stay on. He agreed but then immediately took a prolonged vacation at his doctor's urging, leaving Loomis in charge of the department.

On the morning of March 18, Hay and his wife, Clara, arrived at the sprawling White Star docks in Manhattan to board the steamship *Cretic* en route to Genoa, Italy, from which they would travel by land to other spots in

Europe. The Hays' son, Clarence, their daughter, Alice, and her husband, John W. Wadsworth, were there to help the couple get aboard, and Henry White, the recently appointed ambassador to Italy, came along to see his new boss off on the trip. The secretary had tried to leave the country quietly, without being noticed by the newspapers. Reporters were on hand at the White Star docks to record the comings and goings of the steamships—the travels of the wealthy and the powerful made for good copy—and Hay was noticed, in part because of his deteriorated physical condition. He had lost weight, his face gaunt beneath his whitening beard, and he walked unsteadily along the pier.

Passengers boarding departing ships had to climb three flights of stairs to the deck-level portion of the White Star terminal. Hay had trouble making it up the stairs without help, and he paused for a minute at the top to catch his wind before starting the 150-foot walk across the gangplank to the ship. As he moved, Hay's steps slowed until he suddenly leaned over and collapsed onto a pile of burlap stacked at the side. His family and White quickly surrounded him and the ship's doctor was summoned. Hay said he was fine, just overtired, and a wheelchair was rounded up to roll the secretary onto the ship and to his suite, No. 55, on the promenade deck. The ship's medic, a Dr. Green, told reporters that Hay was not suffering from any serious ailments and would regain his strength once at sea. Skepticism slipped into the coverage. "It was said by one of the friends who went to the pier with the secretary that no one in Washington except his family and possibly his cabinet associates realized how ill he was," the *New York Times* reported. The friend, presumably, was White.[10]

Hay tried to stay out of sight during the trip, but without much luck. Reporters met the *Cretic* in the Azores, Gibraltar, and again at Algiers, and from each spot wired to America that Hay reported he'd had a good passage and his health was recovering. After a few days in Italy, Hay and his wife went to the spas near Wiesbaden in Germany for five weeks, where Hay chafed over the inactivity. He also slowly regained strength. Heads of European states sent queries about visits, but he rejected them all, saying he needed to focus on his health. King Leopold of Belgium simply showed up, and Hay entertained him briefly and unofficially, but that was one of the few bits of work that managed to crash the walls Hay had erected. He joked about his health and his recovery in letters to friends. "My doctor here says there is nothing the matter with me except old age, the Senate, and two or three other mortal maladies, and so I am going to Nauheim to be cured of them all," he wrote to the sculptor Augustus Saint-Gaudens from Nervi, Italy, shortly after arriving in Europe. The Hays spent a few days in Paris in late May with his old friend Henry Adams, the writer, then on June 2 moved on to London. Hay had a quiet half-hour meeting with King Edward at Buckingham Palace but otherwise stayed out of sight, meeting with friends like painter Edwin Abbey rather than political figures. On June 7, the Hays boarded the White Star line's two-year-old steamship the *Baltic* in Liverpool for an uneventful passage to Manhattan, arriving on the evening of June 15.[11]

Hay looked much stronger and healthier when he landed than when he had left three months earlier. But his physical appearance masked what was the continued deterioration of a man who had been the confidante of four presidents—Lincoln, Garfield, McKinley, and now Roosevelt—as well as artists and writers, and who had helped form American foreign policy as the United States rose to the world stage.

Nine days after landing in Manhattan, Hay left Washington for his summer residence in Newbury, New Hampshire. On June 27, he fell ill with uremia—kidney failure—though he was quickly pronounced much improved after a visit from a local doctor. Near midnight of June 30, doctors were again summoned to the lakeside estate, where, shortly after retiring for the evening, Hay suddenly had trouble breathing. The descent was rapid and unstoppable. He died a short time later, at 12:25 AM on July 1, of a pulmonary embolism, ending one of the most intriguing lives of the era.[12]

17

❖

A Celebration and a Delay

S YMBOLISM CAN BE A powerful tool, and Porter and his colleagues at the
State Department were eager to surround the transfer of Jones's body to
America with as much fanfare as they could muster. Porter urged that a fleet
of US Navy ships be dispatched to arrive in France by early June, allowing
time for ceremonies and celebrations in Paris, and at the port of Cherbourg,
before the ships began the journey west, timing the delivery of Jones's body
on American soil with the Fourth of July. "When the body is borne through
the city of Paris, we can count upon the French government to provide
a military escort commensurate with his rank and to take every possible
measure to do honor to his memory," Porter wrote to Assistant Secretary
of State Loomis. But delays could cause problems. "Parliament generally
adjourns the first week in July and after July 14th, the French Independence
Day, official persons and the people generally begin to leave the city for their
summer vacations." Porter sought a quick decision, but Washington had
other ideas, and the decision lagged, much to Porter's frustration.[1]

On May 1, McCormick formally took control of the US Embassy in France, which had once again moved, this time to 12 Quai de Billy, along the Right Bank of the Seine just east of the Exposition Universelle fairgrounds. It was about four blocks from the embassy Porter had established on Avenue Kleber when he arrived in Paris. Where Porter's embassy was a functional space, the new embassy was a step toward the ostentatious; it had more in common with Porter's rented mansion than his diplomatic offices. The vestibule was walled with white and green marble and decorated with Louis XV tapestries. A grand marble staircase in the center of the room carried visitors to a bank of rooms overlooking the Seine, each decorated with ebony and gold, the ceilings covered with frescoes of Venus on a chariot and other classical depictions. The dining hall was warmed by a large fireplace, and the sixty-square-foot "festival Salon" was adorned with tapestries and frescoes as well as selections from McCormick's private collection of portraits of Napoleon, Washington, and other heralded leaders and statesmen of the past.[2]

Through the first couple of weeks of May, McCormick slipped into the ambassador's harness with the formal presentation of his credentials to President Loubet and endless meetings with high French officials and fellow diplomats. Porter, formal duties done, hit the dinner circuit, taking a seat at the head table of a series of banquets organized in his honor. He was alone in Paris and busied himself with the mundane details of packing up his possessions and arranging to have them shipped home. He and McCormick also continued to press Washington for a decision on when and how to move Jones's body. Porter, in fact, was becoming anxious over what he saw as an unnecessary delay in coming to a decision; French law, he informed Assistant Secretary of State Loomis, forbade storing a human body above ground for a protracted length of time, and he feared testing the French authorities' patience. Yet he also said that he felt he could squeeze an extension from the French, which suggests that he was using the French laws as a goad to get an answer from Washington.[3]

The decision ultimately was made by Roosevelt, reflecting his keen interest in Porter's project. On May 12, during a cabinet meeting at the White House, the president ordered that a special squadron under Rear Admiral Charles Sigsbee, who had been in command of the USS *Maine* when it blew apart and sank off Havana, be sent to France to reclaim Jones's body and return it to the United States. Loomis was planning to be in Europe in July to meet with foreign ministers in several countries, and it was decided he would be named a special ambassador to France with a single assignment: to receive the body, which eventually would be interred at the US Naval Academy at Annapolis. Which meant that the navy had won the fight over who would get the body.

Porter began making arrangements in earnest. Then he received another telegram from Washington telling him to hold off—there was a new wrinkle. Porter's frustration seeped through in his cable back to Loomis: "I would strongly recommend that if the squadron can possibly get here in time, the Fourth should be named." Porter said he had discussed the plans with President Loubet, the French minister of foreign affairs, and the heads of the French army and navy, who all "considered that day a very convenient and most fitting one for France to pay her homage to the memory of our admiral and [were] anxious to arrange imposing ceremonies if notified a reasonable time in advance, consisting of a military and a naval escort and the participation of her public men."

Since the Exposition Universelle in 1900, Paris had celebrated July 4 as "America's Day, and there is a gratifying display of American flags, etc.," which would add to the celebration of Jones were the body shipped out that day. And to wait longer, Porter warned, would conflict with French celebrations tied to Bastille Day. The Americans also risked a public relations problem. "If postponed too long, the people here and at home might construe the delay as neglect, as great indignation has been aroused by the negligence which continued one hundred thirteen years during which the body has been allowed to lie in a wretched spot in a foreign land, and they naturally would like to see it taken home as early as arrangements can be conveniently made for that purpose."[4] Washington finally agreed, though the date ultimately was pushed back a couple of days to July 6, Jones's birthday.

Another problem cropped up, however. The French had ceded the body to Ambassador Porter, who was now a private citizen, so it was no longer France's body to turn over to Loomis. And there were legal and diplomatic uncertainties over whether Porter, as a private American, could hand over the body to the new US ambassador—the kind of tempest that would seem to roil only a diplomat's teapot. The solution: President Roosevelt appointed Porter a temporary and special ambassador to France, in addition to McCormick and Loomis. Porter was once again an official representative of the United States, but with a very narrow portfolio.[5]

The squadron came together June 7 at the US Naval Frontier Base at Tompkinsville, Staten Island, in New York, under Sigsbee's command. The flagship was the USS *Brooklyn*, an armored cruiser under Captain John M. Hawley, accompanied by three other cruisers, each only about two years old: USS *Tacoma*, the USS *Galveston*, and the USS *Chattanooga*. As the ships were being provisioned, crews built an oak stage on the deck of the *Brooklyn* just outside Sigsbee's midship quarters. It was protected by a canopy and curtained with both US and French flags and a silk ensign provided by the Daughters of the American Revolution. The organizers hoped it would be a fitting place to secure Jones's coffin for the journey back.

The departure was delayed a few days as more logistics were worked out on the French end. There were concerns that Cherbourg, the planned port for transferring the body to Sigsbee's squadron, might not be large enough to handle the number of people and ships expected. By June 11 the decision was made to send the ships to Le Havre instead, because it was larger and closer to Paris.[6] Le Havre also lies at the mouth of the Seine, and the initial plan was to float Jones's body by river barge for the transfer. For reasons that remain murky, though, the French decided that Cherbourg would work after all, and the plans shifted back. That made it impossible to send Jones's body by river barge, so fresh plans had to be made for moving him by train.[7] While the organizers and diplomats wrangled, Sigsbee and his ships sat at anchor off Staten Island, the naval version of twiddling their thumbs, before finally getting the word to proceed, and the squadron steamed out to sea at 1 PM on June 18. "Because of the recently reported icebergs and floes well to the southward of the Great Bank," Sigsbee later reported, "I chose the most southerly steamship route for the passage."[8]

It was an uneventful crossing, marked by clouds, a mix of rain and mist for most of the trip, and moderate seas. The squadron encountered several ships along the way, mostly masted schooners that were duly noted in the log.[9] They came within sight on June 26 of the eastbound *Deutschland* and, a few hours later, the westbound *New York*, both steam-powered passenger ships.

Some of the crew aboard the *Brooklyn* were part of an experiment in wireless telegraphy. Only three years earlier radio pioneer Guglielmo Marconi had sent the first wireless message across the Atlantic, and two years earlier President Roosevelt sent a message via a new station in Wellfleet, Massachusetts, across the sea to England's King Edward II, the first transatlantic wireless message to originate in the United States. The *Brooklyn* was taking part in more experiments in that vein, and the crew reported receiving a wireless message 1,040 miles into the voyage, and again some 1,000 miles west of Poldhu station in southwest England.[10] Yet they couldn't get an answer out of either the *Deutschland* or the *New York*, though they could hear transmissions from the two ships.

"I asked the captain of the *Deutschland* to let me know what weather he had had," Sigsbee later reported. "He paid no attention to my message, but informed the other vessel, the *New York*, of the weather conditions. It is possible that this was done in order to give me my information indirectly. . . . I understand that vessels having the Marconi wireless apparatus are not allowed to communicate with vessels having other apparatus." Sigsbee saw the obvious problem with observing such exclusivity. "One result of the adoption of the Marconi apparatus is to set aside the ordinary helpful amenities of the sea, which is greatly to be regretted."[11]

Around 1 PM on June 29, the squadron steamed within sight of Bishop Rock, the remote lighthouse marking the eastern end of the North Atlantic steamship route. As they pressed on, the ships were enveloped by a thick fog off the tip of Bretagne, which lasted through the night. The weather disrupted their radio transmissions, and Sigsbee reported he had trouble moving a squadron of four ships in formation at 11 knots when they couldn't see each other or the approaching coast and had to make repeated and sudden stops to take soundings and make course corrections. "I have had much experience with squadrons in fog," Sigsbee said, "but this was by far the most difficult case within my experience." The ships used gun fire to signal one another, and an unintended benefit was that the blasts alerted the French port officials that the ships were near. "No landmarks were seen, nor any whistle heard, until we sighted the breakwater fort at the western entrance to Cherbourg, about two miles distant, and saw the pilot boats coming out." They had found the harbor at Cherbourg with pinpoint accuracy. "John Paul Jones himself would have applauded such an example of excellent navigation," wrote shipboard chronicler Henri Marion, a French-speaking history professor at the US Naval Academy who had come along to record the events and act as an interpreter for Sigsbee.[12] Sigsbee finally got a wireless message through to shore that the squadron had arrived, and asked that the embassy and other American officials be sent wires announcing their arrival. After exchanging cannon salutes with French military detachments ashore, the American ships dropped anchor.

Sigsbee's squadron had been in harbor less than a day when word reached Europe of Secretary Hay's death in New Hampshire. Shock and grief spread among those who had known the secretary of state, including Porter and McCormick. That was followed quickly by discussions about how the Embassy and American expatriate community should respond. The new ambassador was planning to continue Porter's tradition of hosting a massive party for American expatriates to celebrate the Fourth of July; Hay's death made that seem inappropriate. "Conceiving it to be the best expression of the sentiments of Americans in Paris over our country's great loss, I have closed my house on the Fourth of July, abandoning usual reception," McCormick cabled to Washington. But there were too many moving parts to the transfer of Jones's body to add a delay now, he believed. "Pending instructions and believing it to be in accordance with the wishes of the president," he cabled, "I have suggested no change in the functions in connection with the turning over of the remains of Admiral Paul Jones by special ambassador Porter to special ambassador Loomis, on account of the lamented death of Mr. Hay."[13]

So the party would go on.

--------------------------- ❖ ---------------------------

The ceremonies marking the dispatch of Jones's body would be a binational affair, and on the morning of July 1, a contingent of three French naval ships arrived at Cherbourg to represent the French role in Jones's life and his death. American sailors granted shore leave mingled with French sailors and local residents excited by the surprise role they were playing in what they saw as a historic moment. There were garden parties and theatrical programs, impromptu celebrations and navy-versus-navy rowing and boating contests. On the Fourth of July itself, ships from both navies anchored at Cherbourg were ablaze with lights in celebration. Mixed in with the celebrations, though, were visits to a quiet cemetery that held the bodies of American seamen who had died in the June 27, 1864, Civil War naval battle off Cherbourg between the Union sloop of war *Kearsarge* and the Confederate cruiser *Alabama*, a battle won by the North.[14]

Rear Admiral Sigsbee missed most of the Cherbourg parties. Around 5 PM on July 1, Sigsbee and a contingent of ten officers (including the captain of each of his ships) boarded a train for Paris, arriving a little after midnight, and headed directly to the small but exclusive Hôtel Brighton, across Rue de Rivoli from the Jardin des Tuileries. Hours after Sigsbee and his men left for Paris, Loomis arrived in Cherbourg on the steamship *Philadelphia*. A dispatch boat collected him and took him to the *Brooklyn*, where he spent the night before taking a morning train for Paris, arriving in midafternoon.

The American representatives spent the next few days bouncing among parties and diplomatic duties. They met with McCormick and Porter at the embassy, and French premier Maurice Rouvier and President Loubet in their offices. Loubet also hosted a Fourth of July reception at the Élysée Palace for the Americans, a fete that was more subdued than originally planned out of deference to official US mourning of Hay. Every movement by the Americans, who were invariably in their navy dress uniforms, was a small parade, complete with crowds along the streets to watch and applaud their passage. And they were accompanied everywhere by contingents of French cuirassiers, soldiers in dress uniform atop decorated horses.

Parties and receptions gave way to even grander ceremonies on July 6. A detachment of some five hundred US sailors and marines boarded a special train in Cherbourg at 3 AM, disembarking at the Gare des Invalides on Paris's Left Bank at 11:40 AM. As they left the station, they met a squadron of French infantry, with whom they exchanged salutes and then national anthems, and joined in a march to the nearby École Militaire, drawing cheers from a thickening crowd. After a luncheon, the two military contingents marched to the American Church for the 3:30 PM ceremony.

The church was decorated as though for a state funeral, with masses of flowers and plants filling the air with a light scent. The coffin had already been reclaimed from the basement cloister and placed on a stand at the head of the church, in front of the altar. *Huissiers*, French men in formal clothes and wearing large silver chains, served as ushers, and the church quickly filled with dignitaries, all present by invitation only. Throngs of the curious, without invitation, gathered on the street outside, growing to a large crowd by the time the ceremony began.

Inside the church, on the left side of the aisle, sat Premier Rouvier and most of the French Cabinet (Loubet was not present), as well as most of the foreign diplomats assigned to the French capital, each wearing the formal regalia of his home country. The right side was reserved for the Americans, including Sigsbee and the commanders of the ships in his squadron; US senator Henry Cabot Lodge, who happened to be in Paris; and McCormick, Loomis, and Porter, who was wearing a dark suit and a thick red sash of the Grand Cross of the Legion of Honor. Morgan, the pastor, delivered a short prayer, and then Porter moved from his front-row pew to the altar and stood beside the flag-draped coffin.

"This day," Porter began, "America claims her illustrious dead." He went on to talk about the length of time between Jones's death and his repatriation to American soil. "It is a matter of extreme gratification to feel that the body of this intrepid commander should be conveyed across the sea by the war vessels of a navy to whose sailors his name is still an inspiration." He thanked the Frenchmen who helped him decipher the hints of the past, thanked Sigsbee for leading the squadron to retrieve the body, thanked the French government for its support and help in honoring "the memory of a hero who once covered two continents with his renown in battling for the cherished principles of political liberty and the rights of man, for which the two sister republics have both so strenuously contended." He reminded the audience that the US Congress in one resolution both adopted the Stars and Stripes as the national flag, and gave Jones the helm of the *Ranger*. He then quoted Jones: "The flag and I are twins; born the same hour from the same womb of destiny. We can not be parted in life or in death." "Alas,"

Porter added from beside the flag-draped coffin, "they were parted during a hundred and thirteen years, but happily now they are reunited."[15]

Loomis followed, accepting the coffin on behalf of the United States, and thanked Porter for his "patient, persistent, self-sacrificing search for the grave and body of John Paul Jones." He went on to detail Jones's history, delivering a eulogy, really, more than a century late. Sigsbee followed with a much shorter speech, pointing out that Jones's naval achievements were due in large part to the support he had received from France, where he outfitted his ships and trained his crews before heading off for British waters. He, too, thanked Porter, and then accepted custody of the body from Loomis and promised to "bear the remains of John Paul Jones most reverently to their final resting place within the Naval Academy at Annapolis."

With that, a choir in robes sang "Onward Christian Soldiers" as the vocalists walked to the church doorway. Twelve uniformed men under Sigsbee's command, each over six feet tall, hoisted the over-large coffin and carried it from the altar down the center aisle and out the door to the street, where they slipped it onto the bed of a horse-drawn artillery wagon decorated with both French and American flags, a mishmash of funeral floral arrangements, and a large wreath ordered by Sigsbee on behalf of his squadron. Around 5 PM the procession began along Avenue de l'Alma to the Champs-Élysées, led by a small contingent of French police, followed by regiments of French military units and US marines and sailors—the troops who had taken the early morning train in from Cherbourg. With the exception of the caisson carrying the coffin, a handful of artillery pieces, and the horse brigade, the procession was entirely on foot "as an additional mark of respect and courtesy."

The parade moved slowly along the Champs-Élysées to the cutoff to the Pont Alexandre III, the sidewalks filled with tens of thousands of cheering people despite the solemnity of the occasion. When the parade reached the Esplanade des Invalides, the twelve pallbearers moved the coffin from the wagon to a raised bier near Napoleon's tomb, where diplomats and other dignitaries, the parading troops, and then members of the public walked past as military bands took turns playing "The Star-Spangled Banner" and "La Marseillaise." A guard remained posted while Sigsbee and his commanders joined Porter, McCormick, Loomis, and others at a dinner.

John Paul Jones's body on parade at the start of its journey from Paris to Annapolis.
Courtesy of the Library of Congress, Horace Porter Collection, Manuscript Division

As darkness fell, the coffin was moved from the bier through the Gare des Invalides to a mortuary car. A little after 9 PM, the special train started its westward journey with the body of Jones and the American sailors and marines; Sigsbee, his command staff, and the diplomats remained in Paris until the next evening for another round of receptions, including a luncheon hosted by President Loubet. That evening, Sigsbee joined Loomis for a smaller, more private dinner with some old mutual friends, and then caught a 9:10 train that night. Porter had gone on ahead earlier in the day and Sigsbee had arranged for him to spend the night on the *Brooklyn*.

By the time Sigsbee arrived back in Cherbourg on July 8, the coffin had been transferred to a dockside chapel. After a shorter program of speeches by French and American naval commanders, it was loaded onto the *Zouave* and, amid a flurry of cannon salutes, steamed out to the anchored *Brooklyn*, where the flags were at half-mast. A winch swung out over the smaller ship, and a hook was lowered carefully to the deck. French sailors attached it to a net of straps fitted around the coffin, which was then slowly lifted and swung into place on the catafalque on the deck of the *Brooklyn*. A few hours later, as the clock neared 5 PM, the American squadron weighed anchor and steamed slowly out of the port, the sailors exchanging cheers and salutes with their counterparts aboard the French vessels, and throngs of people lined up along the shore and jetty. Once clear of the harbor, Sigsbee gave the command to increase speed to 11 knots, and the ships set a course for the West and the capes of northern Virginia.

One figure missing from the *Brooklyn* was Horace Porter. Sigsbee had offered the former ambassador a private berth so he could return to America with Jones's body. Porter demurred. His role, he believed, ended with finding the body and serving as its caretaker until it could be sent to the United States. That job was now done, and his special ambassadorship had expired. He was, once again, a private American citizen. So Porter turned down Sigsbee's offer. The morning after the *Brooklyn* left Cherbourg, Porter—who had arrived in France eight years earlier with a family and grand expectations—boarded the Hamburg America liner the *Deutschland* and sailed, alone, back to America.

--------------- ❖ ---------------

Sigsbee's squadron took its time crossing the Atlantic, encountering fog, rain, and moderate seas for most of the voyage. Sigsbee set a speed of 10 to 11 knots, and it wasn't until July 20, when the squadron was within thirty or forty miles of the *Nantucket Lightship*, that the *Brooklyn* was able to get a message through to his superiors. "Report to Navy Department Paul Jones Squadron is off Nantucket light-ship and is due at Chesapeake entrance early forenoon of Saturday," Sigsbee radioed the lightship. "No stops needed on passage. All well."[16]

The *Nantucket Lightship* was anchored about forty miles southeast of Nantucket Island off Massachusetts and marked the southeastern edge of the dangerous Nantucket Shoals, which had claimed hundreds of ships over the years. The lightship also served as the unofficial western end of the transatlantic shipping lane. Sigsbee's squadron sighted the *Nantucket* about 8:30 PM on July 20, then changed course to the southwest, headed for the Cape Charles lightship off the Virginia coast and the entrance to Chesapeake Bay.

The next day Sigsbee spotted the new USS *Maine*, launched in 1901, which had been dispatched with six other ships from the North Atlantic Fleet to greet Sigsbee's squadron. At the direction of the commander of the *Maine*, Sigsbee aligned his ships one behind the other, and all eleven ships steamed around the southern tip of Cape Charles and on into Chesapeake Bay, where the *Brooklyn* and seven other ships continued northward, finally anchoring off Thomas Point Lighthouse, some seven miles from the US Naval Academy. The next morning, Sigsbee again weighed anchor, and the eight ships steamed in the midst of a furious storm to an anchorage just off Annapolis itself, where the French cruiser *Jurien de la Gravière* was waiting.

There was considerably less official pageantry surrounding the transfer of Jones's body ashore than had accompanied his departure from Paris and then Cherbourg. While Sigsbee was still at sea, the decision was made in Washington that the arrival of the body would be marked solemnly and only by the military, saving a full public ceremony for later.[17] Yet there was still considerable local excitement. After the storm passed, cottagers lined the shores to look at the ships at anchor. More than one hundred small pleasure boats and yachts, many sailing down from Baltimore, took to the bay off Annapolis to get a closer look. A floating party evolved, and more than one thousand people found space aboard the boats, for up to two dollars apiece, for a close view of the ships; a few dozen managed to secure permission to board the *Brooklyn* for a personal look at the flag-draped coffin.[18]

Around 9 AM on July 24, the USS *Standish*, a naval tug, pulled up alongside the *Brooklyn*, and the coffin was hoisted from the deck of one ship to the other. The *Standish*, with Sigsbee also aboard, then steamed between two rows of navy ships, which fired off a fifteen-gun salute and continued on to the Naval Academy, where scores of seamen and some fifty sailors from the French *Jurien de la Gravière* stood silently as the Standish docked at a float attached to the north seawall. Midshipmen carried the coffin from the ship to the float to dry land, where an officer barked the order to present colors, followed by three quick flourishes by the academy band and then another fifteen-gun salute. As the echoes died out across the bay, the pallbearers loaded the coffin onto a hearse drawn by a team of four black horses. The band launched into Chopin's funeral march as the cortege began to move, a contingent of marines and sailors first and then the coffin. They crossed the open park area to the under-construction chapel, near the Herndon Monument, where a temporary red-brick vault had been built in a rush over the previous few weeks. Hundreds of sailors and marines standing at attention lined the route and the park. After a brief prayer, a salute of three volleys was fired, and a single bugler played taps as the coffin was deposited in the brick crypt. The grated door was locked, and as an armed, though mostly ceremonial, guard took up its position, the crowd began dispersing.[19]

The morning's ceremony came just days after the 113th anniversary of John Paul Jones's first burial in Paris's Saint Louis cemetery, an act that was viewed in some quarters as temporary, but that, were it not for the dogged efforts of Horace Porter, would have become permanent. This new interment was also intended to be temporary, though there was little risk that anyone would lose track of the coffin in the vault in the middle of the US Naval Academy grounds. There would be more pageantry and ceremonies and celebrations in the year to come as Annapolis prepared Jones's final resting place. There would be delays, too, and political bickering by a penurious Congress. But the long-lost American hero was at last on American soil.

18

-------- ✱ --------

Annapolis Celebrates

T HE *DEUTSCHLAND* MADE A much faster journey west than Sigsbee's squadron, perhaps reflecting the difference between a funeral fleet and a ship seeking to make a profit. Porter landed in Hoboken on July 14, and as he stepped onto the Hamburg America Steamship Line wharf, he was accosted by a larger-than-usual gaggle of newspapermen seeking scoops and tidbits among the arriving dignitaries and celebrities. A few asked Porter about diplomatic issues, questions he waved off. The newsmen also pressed him about how he could be certain that the recovered corpse was, indeed, that of John Paul Jones. Porter ticked through the steps taken to identify the cemetery, and the list of evidence that led the French experts to conclude that the body was Jones's. "There is absolutely no room for doubt," Porter said in what was for him a rare public display of impatience.[1]

The *Brooklyn* was still at sea when Porter traveled a few days later to Oyster Bay, Long Island, to lunch with the vacationing President Roosevelt at his home, Sagamore Hill. At one level, it was a recently returned ambassador's courtesy call on his former boss. But Porter also wanted to discuss the plans underway for building a permanent place for Jones's body on the grounds of the US Naval Academy, which, despite its role as the nation's elite training ground for future navy officers, was little more than a cluster of outdated and dilapidated wooden buildings.

The academy had been established in 1845 at Fort Severn in Maryland, on a small rise overlooking the confluence of the Severn River and Chesapeake Bay. As time passed, the land around the fort had been expanded through levies and fill. Wooden buildings were added as needed, though little thought was given to the design of the grounds or the buildings, let alone maintenance and upgrades. A special naval Board of Visitors commission, chaired by academy graduate and Manhattan industrialist Robert M. Thompson, investigated conditions at the academy and issued a report in 1895 faulting the complex as unsafe and unsanitary. The Thompson report was followed by an internal investigation by five naval officers that reached the same conclusion. The reports spurred the navy to draw up plans for a modern facility, but the deterioration outpaced the planning. In November 1897, one of the campus's main buildings, a recitation hall used by some 250 cadets a day, was found to be so compromised that it was deemed too dangerous to enter. Engineers, in fact, feared it could collapse at any moment and damage nearby buildings as well. Under emergency orders, workers razed the hall, and Congress was asked for $5,000 to replace it. That was just the first of a series of discoveries of compromised buildings at the academy. The walls of several, in fact, were held in place from the outside by wooden beams jammed at an angle into the ground.

McKinley's assistant secretary of the navy at the time was Roosevelt, who reported to navy secretary John Long that the US Naval Academy was both an embarrassment to the navy and a threat to its cadets. Roosevelt noted that George Bancroft had founded the academy in 1845 with no map in mind and that "it has grown little by little in an almost haphazard way . . . so that the only note of harmony among them is their condition of utter decay and of unsuitableness for the purpose for which they are used." The secretary forwarded Roosevelt's report to Congress after adding his own voice:

If they were merely unsuitable; if it were merely desirable that they be replaced by others built in accordance with a general scheme to turn the Annapolis Academy into what it should be as a training school for the nation's naval officers, it might be advisable to wait before seeking to reconstruct them. But it is not possible to wait, because the buildings are not merely unsuitable, but are for the most part in the last stages of decay.[2]

Long asked Congress to do something bold. Rather than embark on a regimen of emergency repairs to buildings that weren't worth saving, he suggested they completely rebuild the academy. He recommended a massive project be undertaken—requiring maybe a decade or more of work—to create a campus "made primarily for use and not show, and yet one in which the nation can take the heartiest pride because it will in every way be a fit training school for a naval service as ours." The most pressing needs were for "an armory, a boathouse, and a power house," but also new officer quarters because the existing ones would be razed to make way for the new armory. And Long asked that the bay be dredged and a new seawall built to accommodate a training ship and torpedo boat. Other buildings needed replacing, as well, including dilapidated dormitories with a kitchen and bathrooms in the basement and upper-level floors of small rooms holding three cadets each. The first phase would cost about $1 million, Long estimated. The whole project would cost some $6 million (later increased to $10 million, or about $225 million in today's dollars).

Puffed up by Dewey's victory over the Spanish fleet at Manila Bay just a month earlier, Congress agreed in June 1898 to the first phase, which architect Ernest Flagg had begun designing two years earlier, after the Thompson commission assessed the dire state of the buildings and grounds.

Flagg was one of the era's most celebrated—and controversial—designers of Beaux Arts–style buildings. His portfolio included the Scribner Building and St. Luke's Hospital in Manhattan and the Corcoran Gallery in Washington, DC, among others. Yet most of his commissions were won through the favors and influences of friends—he was a cousin to the Vanderbilt fortune. Flagg was brought into the academy project by Thompson, the kind of connection that made Flagg the subject of professional envy among East Coast architects. His abrasive personality did little to help his reputation. Neither did revelations that his older brother, who had been his business associate in controversial speculative building deals in Manhattan, was running a whorehouse, a sideline that cost the brother a month in New York's notorious Tombs jail. That Flagg had already drawn up a redesign for the academy by the time the navy was prepared to make a decision spawned another round of criticisms about favoritism, just when the federal government was moving to a system of competitive bidding for government contracts.[3]

Flagg later wrote that he was surprised by how indiscriminately the existing academy grounds had been laid out, roughly on a quadrilateral facing the river, and with no consideration given to the flow of people around the campus. Cadet housing was far from the marching field and the armory, for instance, necessitating long walks to change for drills. He drew up plans that sought to make more efficient use of the space, while preserving a couple of key aspects: The integration of village streets, through gates, into the academy, and a parade ground, like a village square, serving as a commons near the riverbank. The main entrance to the grounds, Maryland Street, crested the highest elevation, some thirty feet above sea level. "Here seemed the best place for the chapel, which from its height would be the dominating feature of the design," Flagg wrote. And it would face the commons to the northeast, with a marine basin and the Severn River in the distance, the entrance marked by twin lighthouses. (The basin eventually became sports fields.)[4]

Flagg, for reasons he didn't detail publicly, had John Paul Jones's body in mind when he designed the chapel. "I have always been a great admirer of John Paul Jones, and when I made the first rough sketch for the rebuilding of the academy in 1896, I had in mind that the Chapel should be his burial place, if his remains could be found," Flagg wrote in a 1908 magazine article. He met with Long, the navy secretary, in 1900, and told him that he had included space for a crypt in the basement of the chapel and suggested "that a search be made in Paris for the body." Flagg didn't mention Porter's 1899 announcement that he believed he had found the cemetery. And Flagg didn't claim to have instigated the search. Yet Flagg's prescience was uncanny given that in 1896, when Flagg drew up his initial plans, the commodore was, for most Americans, little more than a forgotten hero of the past.

Work on the chapel began on June 3, 1904, with the ceremonial laying of the cornerstone by Admiral Dewey. A time capsule was embedded
containing signed photos of President Roosevelt and other dignitaries of
the day, including Flagg and Dewey.[5] Work then progressed very slowly.
And since Jones's body wasn't recovered until April 1905, there were no
approved plans for finishing the crypt in the basement. Navy officials had
hoped the chapel would be finished and Jones's body placed in the crypt in
October 1905. But even before the body arrived, there was talk of delaying the interment until the following spring in hopes the building would be
completed then. By the time Jones's body arrived in July 1905, the building
was only partly built, and a design for the main doors wouldn't be selected
until May 1906. More delays ensued. And more.

Flagg began lobbying for the contract to complete the design of the
crypt. He had an ambitious vision of a national shrine for naval heroes,
with Jones's sarcophagus in the middle of the circular room and niches for
the remains of other heroes built into the walls, all beneath a crystal dome
diffusing electric light into the room. A few days after Porter announced
in Paris that he had found the body and before Roosevelt had decided
where it would be interred, Flagg lobbied for his plan in a letter to Captain Willard H. Brownson, who was just finishing a stint as the academy's
superintendent:

> I know that you agree with me that the crypt of the new Chapel of the
> Academy should be [Jones's] final resting place. What more appropri-
> ate than that the ashes of the founder of the American Navy should
> repose in the midst of the institution, which is the cradle, so to speak,
> of the navy. If the crypt is made a place of sepulture by depositing
> these remains there, then the Chapel will become what it ought to
> be, and what I have always hoped it would be, the Pantheon or West
> Minster of the Navy. . . . Representing the academy as you do it seems
> as if you are the proper one to call attention to the fact that the Crypt
> of the Chapel was arranged with this very contingency in view from
> the start; that here is already at hand a most suitable burial place for
> this great hero. I fear that unless some one speaks at once, Arlington
> may be selected as there has already been talk of that.[6]

Plans for the crypt had not advanced since then, and the chapel itself would not be completed in time (it would finally open in May 1908). Amid the uncertainty, Porter, navy officials, and Roosevelt began discussing alternatives. On July 20 Roosevelt wrote to Charles J. Bonaparte, his new navy secretary, that he wanted the public celebration to be held on September 23, the anniversary of Jones's victory over the *Serapis*—a date for which Porter had been heavily lobbying. Bonaparte asked his subordinates for a report on whether that would be feasible; he was told that the crypt—which had not yet been designed, or even approved by Congress—would not be completed in time. That raised the question of whether they should hold the ceremony in the fall and then schedule another ceremony for when the crypt was done.

Porter, after his luncheon with Roosevelt at Sagamore Hill, had joined up with his friend and fellow Son of the American Revolution, Frederick W. Vanderbilt, for an Eastern Seaboard cruise aboard Vanderbilt's yacht *Warrior*, a 239-foot white-and-green-hulled steamship that held Vanderbilt's luxurious quarters (including a piano), and six other guest suites. Porter wrote Bonaparte from the "floating palace"[7] on July 25 that the president had settled on the September ceremony. "The disagreeably hot weather is generally over by that date and the weather favorable for an outdoor large gathering." Porter also noted that Roosevelt had unspecified plans for October that would preclude him from attending a ceremony then. Porter said Roosevelt wanted him, Bonaparte, and Maryland governor Edwin Warfield to oversee the planning, which would be carried out by Rear Admiral James H. Sands, the new academy superintendent. Excitement was already building. "The patriotic societies, with all of which I happen to be connected, are already beginning to organize delegations to participate in or be present at the ceremony. They will represent more than half the states, I should think."[8]

Two weeks later, Porter was staying with his friend Morris K. Jesup at the financier's Stonecliffe summer house in Bar Harbor, Maine. He wrote Bonaparte again, telling the navy secretary that Roosevelt was insisting "the celebration be held this fall. Would there be any objection to holding it a week after the anniversary of the Naval Battle [September 23] if the midshipmen are off their annual leave? I hate to break up their annual leave, and yet I would like to have them there when we hold the celebration."

Roosevelt was also writing to Bonaparte, part of a regular correspondence about naval affairs. The president took an unusual interest in the
Jones ceremony planning, involving himself in a surprising level of minu-
tiae, including ensuring that the academy's midshipmen would be on
hand for the ceremony. "But do write to General Porter first to find what
he thinks," Roosevelt wrote.[9] The president saw the event as a chance to
enhance the academy's image to the nation. "I would like to turn this celebration into something of actual benefit to the navy." In another letter
to Bonaparte, Roosevelt indicated that Sands was somewhat resistant to
the idea of calling the midshipmen back early from their leave. "I leave
it to your judgment, though I should suggest your consulting Porter, as to
whether we can defer the celebration two weeks to have the midshipmen
back, or whether we should get them back and then add on just so much to
their leave, which can be done perfectly by Admiral Sands if he is ordered
to do it," Roosevelt wrote on August 3. "He will grumble, but he will do it
and not the slightest damage will follow."

Two days later, Roosevelt wrote that September was out and the ceremony would be held in the spring. The determining factor was arranging
to have French warships take part in the celebration, a diplomatic project
that would take more than six weeks to pull off. Roosevelt asked Bonaparte
to tell Porter, but then sent off a letter himself to the former ambassador.

Porter deferred to his president and to Bonaparte. "You have many
means of judging of all the circumstances of the government's participation
which I have not, and I acquiesce fully in the views you express for the reasons
given." Porter then offered a suggestion that would prove to be the final date:
April 24, 1906. If they could not time the ceremony to mark the anniversary
of Jones's most-famous sea victory, then they could tie it to "the anniversary of
Paul Jones' next greatest victory, the capture of the *Drake*."[10]

Roosevelt's affinity for the navy extended to the midshipmen of Annapolis. He impressed upon Bonaparte that he wanted as many of the student
officers to witness the ceremonies as possible, along with active seamen in
port. "I very earnestly hope that you will make some provision by which my
speech in the occasion of the Paul Jones ceremonies shall be listened to by
some of the enlisted men from the ships. I feel very strongly, as I know you
do, that in every ceremony of this kind we should include a good proportion

of the enlisted men and make them understand that they are just as much a part of the business as the officers."[11]

Bonaparte made the public announcement that the ceremony would be held April 24, at which time Jones's body would be moved from the temporary vault and installed in one of Flagg's completed buildings until the crypt below the chapel could be completed. It would be a grand and fitting celebration, including comments by President Roosevelt, Ambassador Porter, and others. It was lightly noted that the placement of the body would once again be temporary. It would allow official Washington to wash its hands of the matter and pretend that justice had been done to the memory of the Revolutionary War hero.

So Annapolis prepared for a party. And once again, Jones's bones would be set aside and, for a time, forgotten.

———————— ✿ ————————

As April 24 neared, the yachting class of Baltimore and Washington made their own plans for attending the celebration. Boats began arriving off Annapolis a day or two early, and what had been intended as a quiet and reverent celebration began taking on the trappings of a national holiday. The Daughters of the American Revolution chartered a steamship from Baltimore to ferry its members to Annapolis, where the group had managed to arrange a separate reserved section of seating for the ceremony. The Merchants and Manufacturers Association of Baltimore similarly leased the *Susquehanna* steamship and packed some 250 members aboard for the daylong excursion, though only a few had tickets to the event itself. The ship left at 9 AM, and the passengers enjoyed Smithfield ham steamed in champagne and "other tidbits," an open bar, and music. The day was raw—chilly and strong winds kept the passengers inside—but good for sailing, and the *Baltimore Sun* noted that the *Susquehanna* engaged in an impromptu ten-mile race with a steam-powered yacht owned by R. Brent Keyser, the chairman of the board of Johns Hopkins University. When the *Susquehanna* reached Annapolis, it did a couple of turns around a flotilla of eight US and three French naval ships that had anchored about five miles into the Chesapeake as part of the celebration. Then the steamship headed for the levy, where it docked temporarily as the passengers swarmed ashore. Smaller yachts anchored offshore and ferried their passengers to the academy in small launches. Still others came by land, and as the morning progressed, the grounds slowly filled. For most, the day was an excursion, with an overlay of patriotism.[12]

Bonaparte's office had sent out six thousand official invitations to the ceremony, but most of the on-site decision making was undertaken by academy superintendent Sands. Requests poured in from passenger ship companies and private groups seeking permission to dock at the academy pier to offload passengers.

Given the historic and patriotic underpinnings of the day, newspaper reporters were dispatched as well. The *Baltimore Sun* requested seats for four reporters, and *Collier's*, the Associated Press, and several New York and Washington newspapers staffed the event as well. The American Mutoscope and Biograph Company sought permission to film the event, offering to sell the navy a copy of the film for the standard rate of twelve cents per foot. Extra trains were added to the regular services from Washington, Baltimore, Philadelphia, and New York. A special train dubbed the "Congressional Unlimited" made its way from Washington with 750 passengers, including more than thirty US senators and representatives.

Some had deep personal interest in the celebration. Henry T. Rainey, as a freshman member of Congress, had sponsored a bill three years earlier to pay for the search and repatriation of Jones's body. (That bill died in committee.) Charles B. Landis was aboard too. His letter to American consul general Gowdy in November 1898 could well have been the catalyst for the extensive search for—and Porter's obsession with finding—Jones's body. Yet questions bubbled about whether they were going to spend the day celebrating around the body of John Paul Jones or that of some unknown Frenchman. The discussion prompted a bit of satire from *Washington Post* reporter Josephine Tighe, who was aboard the train: "It was echoed and re-echoed all day, 'It is. It isn't.' The starboard piston rod plunging in and out of the cylinder said, with the escaping steam, 'It iss, it iss, it iss hiss body,' The port piston rod shrieked in angry response on the other side: 'It issn't, it issn't hiss body.' The smokestack thundered out: 'Piff, paff, pouff; what's the odds bodikins?'"[13]

President Roosevelt, with an entourage of about eighty people—including Porter, who had traveled from New York City, members of the cabinet, and France's ambassador to the United States—boarded his own special three-car train at the Baltimore and Ohio station around 11 o'clock that morning. The entourage arrived at Annapolis around 12:45 PM and was greeted by superintendent Sands and other Annapolis dignitaries. They boarded motorcars for the short trip to the grounds, cheered by onlookers as they passed in an informal parade. Roosevelt, Porter, the French ambassador, and other high-ranking officials immediately went to a private reception at Sands's house, hosted by Maryland's Governor Warfield, while others were entertained at luncheons scattered around the grounds and the village hotels. By then the grounds—in fact, Annapolis itself—were swarmed by visitors. Thousands of people crammed into the village, filling the few small hotels, bars, and restaurants. It's unclear whether those without tickets realized there would be little for them to see.[14]

The biggest room on the grounds was within the massive armory, which was some 425 feet long and 100 feet wide, a cavernous structure large enough for indoor parade exercises, a basketball court, and a second-floor running track designed as a four-sided balcony overlooking the floor below. On this day, the armory would serve as a chapel. Sands and his superiors at the Department of the Navy decided that the tone should be more commemoration than funeral, since Jones was long dead and had been eulogized several times before. So, early in the day, midshipmen retrieved the body from the brick vault and moved it with solemnity but no ceremony to a stand near the midpoint of the armory, where they laid it in front of a temporary stage that would hold Roosevelt, Porter, and other speakers. The coffin was draped with an American naval union jack—a large dark blue flag decorated with foot-wide white stars. Other union jacks festooned the front of the balcony and the stage, and chairs were placed on the main floor facing the coffin and the speakers' stand. A double row of some eight hundred midshipmen stood at attention around the armory walls, and gold strips of cloth accented the deep blue of the union jack bunting.

The program was scheduled to begin at 2 PM, but it wasn't until just before 2:30 PM that Roosevelt and his entourage entered the armory through the southwest doors, the crowd rising to its feet in a cheering mass. Roosevelt made his way to the middle of the armory then mounted the short flight of stairs to the speakers' stand, joined by French ambassador Jean Jules Jusserand; Bonaparte, the navy secretary; Maryland governor Warfield; and Porter. Before they could sit down, and as the audience members slowly gained their feet, the Baltimore Oratorio Society launched into the "The Star-Spangled Banner," their meshed voices resonating through the large open space. When they finished and as the audience settled back into their seats, Bonaparte stepped forward and in a loud, projecting voice introduced Roosevelt.

The president spoke for nearly a half hour, beginning with an endorsement of the longstanding relations between the United States and France and then offering his thanks and congratulations to Ambassador Porter "to whose zealous devotion we particularly owe it that the body of John Paul Jones has been brought to our shores." Roosevelt explained that he had finally settled on Annapolis as the resting place for Jones after lobbying from an array of cities. "I feel that the place of all others in which the memory of the dead hero will most surely be a living force is here in Annapolis, where year by year we turn out the midshipmen who are to officer in the future Navy, among whose founders the dead man stands first." For those men, he said, Jones's life and career are "not merely a subject for admiration

President Theodore Roosevelt speaks at the April 1906 commemoration of John Paul Jones at Annapolis. Seated, from left, navy secretary Charles J. Bonaparte, French ambassador Jean Jules Jusserand, Maryland governor Edwin Warfield, former ambassador Horace Porter, and Admiral James H. Sands, superintendent of the US Naval Academy.
Courtesy of the National Archives, RG 19-NV, records of the Bureau of Ships, box 1

and respect, but an object lesson to be taken into their innermost hearts. . . .
Every officer in our Navy should feel in each fiber of his being an eager
desire to emulate the energy, the professional capacity, the indomitable
determination and dauntless scorn of death which marked John Paul Jones
above all his fellows."

Roosevelt went on to summarize Jones's greatest moments, and he then
urged members of Congress and his own administration to study more history—a favorite topic of the president's—so as to recognize that national
security was defended by a robust military, including a navy. He argued
that the United States had suffered during the War of 1812 from a lack of
readiness and that the nation would again be at risk if it did not invest in its
defense. He concluded with a direct call to the navy for better devotion to
preparedness. "You will be worthless in war if you have not prepared your-
self for it in peace," the president said, leaning over the rail while reading
from a sheaf of papers in his right hand. "Remember that no courage can
ever atone for lack of that preparedness which makes the courage valuable.
And yet if the courage is there, if the dauntless heart is there, its presence will
sometimes make up for other shortcomings. . . . If with it are combined the
other military qualities, the fortunate owner becomes literally invincible."

Jusserand, the French ambassador, followed, detailing Jones's close
relationship with France, from his friendship with the Marquis de Lafayette and King Louis XVI to his reliance on French ports to mount his
raids on the British coast. "He died in France, who had proved for him
another motherland, and who honored him dead as she had alive. But he
had done his life's work, and that work consisted not only in playing splen-
didly his part in the struggle for freedom, but also in showing the young
Republic the importance of having a navy of her own. . . . His dream, or
rather, his prophecy, has been fulfilled."

As Jusserand moved to his chair, the armory filled with applause.
Bonaparte rose and stepped to the front of the stage to introduce Porter,
who in turn stepped forward to thunderous applause and cheers.

"This day America reclaims her illustrious dead," Porter began, his
words flowing over the fan-array of chairs and up to the second-level balcony. "We gather here in the presence of the Chief Magistrate of the nation
and of this vast concourse of representative citizens of the Old World and

the New to pay our homage to the leading historic figure in the early annals of the American Navy, to testify that his name is not a dead memory, but a living reality. To quicken our sense of appreciation, and to give assurance that the transfer of his remains to the land upon whose arms he shed so much luster is not lacking in distinction by reason of the long delay."

He went on, as had the others, to detail some of Jones's exploits, a history "that reads more like romance than reality. . . . He was a many-sided man. On the water, he was a wizard of the sea. On the land he showed himself an adept in the realms of diplomacy." Porter had had a lot of time to prepare his remarks, and they offered a sugarcoated portrait of the man Porter knew to have embraced many faults, from his occasionally harsh treatment of his men to his vanity, sexual dalliances, and other weaknesses. But this wasn't the platform from which to deliver the full portrait of Jones. It was the platform for extolling patriotism and for gently arranging the hero's shroud.

"Paul Jones never sailed in a man-of-war whose quarterdeck was worthy of being trodden by his feet," Porter told the crowd. "His battles were won not by his ships, but by his genius." Porter detailed Jones's victories: raids on British soil, some sixty vessels captured, the seizure of British weaponry, more than a million dollars' worth of floating prizes and cargo, and the capture of hundreds of enemy prisoners. "He was the very personification of valor. He ranked courage as the manliest of human attributes. He loved brave men; he loathed cowards. He believed there was scarcely a sin for which courage could not atone."

Porter did note that Jones's tongue had sometimes cost him friendships, and that while he was alive he had suffered from the venomous words of enemies. "He lived to realize that success is like sunshine, it brings out the vipers." And when Jones died, "by some strange and unaccountable reason he was covered immediately with the mantle of forgetfulness. In all the annals of history there is not another case in which death has caused the memory of so conspicuous a man to drop at once from the height of prominence to the depth of oblivion." Porter went on for well over a half hour, by far the longest speech of the afternoon, and his words served ultimately as Jones's final, and most detailed, eulogy.

The Maryland governor followed Porter, but his brief comments felt like an afterthought as he spotlighted Maryland's connections with the

Midshipmen at the United States Naval Academy move John Paul Jones's body to its temporary home beneath a staircase in the Bancroft Hall dormitory, where it would remain for seven years.
Courtesy of the Library of Congress, Prints and Photographs Division, reproduction number LC-DIG-ds-03055

navy. The ceremony ended with a brief prayer, and at a signal twenty midshipmen stepped forward to surround the casket. Moving slowly and with precision, the young men lifted Jones free of the bier. In silence, they carried the coffin outside and placed it on a small caisson, which they then hauled in a parade along pathways from the armory, past the unfinished chapel, then through the open park area to Bancroft Hall, the ornate dormitory building. A smaller detachment then lifted the coffin from the caisson and carried it inside, where it was placed atop two sawhorses under the front main staircase, a quiet spot away from the daily to and fro of the midshipmen training to be naval officers.

Jones was now at his third—but not yet final—resting spot.

19

---- ☼ ----

"Stowed Away Like Old Lumber"

Horace Porter, generally an even-keeled and diplomatic man, was peeved. More than five years had passed since he had recovered John Paul Jones's body from its forgotten grave deep below a Parisian neighborhood. More than four years had passed since he, President Roosevelt, and several thousand other people had gathered at the US Naval Academy armory to praise the dead admiral and his long-ago exploits, the body then moved temporarily to the makeshift mausoleum beneath a dormitory staircase. The problem was that the coffin was still there, propped on two sawhorses and draped with a blue-and-white jack, an ignominious grave despite the twenty-four-hour honor guard. Once the object of reverence, Jones had become the butt of jokes among irreverent midshipmen who scampered down the stairs and past the coffin. One popular ditty in "Crabtown," as Annapolis was called, mocked the hero of the American Revolution for his rest:

Everybody works but John Paul Jones!
He lies around all day,
Body pickled in alcohol
On a permanent jag, they say.
Middies stand around him
Doing honor to his bones;
Everybody works in "Crabtown"
But John Paul Jones!

It was, in a sense, an ignominious defeat for Porter, or at least a frustration of his ambitions. Porter was a man accustomed to achieving his goals. Nearly twenty years earlier, he had taken over the Grant Monument Association and fought long odds and disinterest to finish the tomb for his old friend and personal hero, Ulysses S. Grant. As a leader of the Sons of the American Revolution, Porter had thrown his support behind monument projects in Maryland and elsewhere. He had spoken publicly about the debts that a nation owes to its war veterans, both those killed in action and those who returned safely, and what he saw as the ingratitude inherent in failing to establish proper memorials. Jones's body was still right where the navy had stashed it after the pomp and pageantry of the Annapolis ceremony, a fate that seemed to contradict in act the respect and thanks expressed from the podium on that April day in 1906. And the root of the problem lay with Congress, which refused to spend the money to finish the crypt.

Porter was irked to the point of action. He sat down on December 3, 1910, at a desk in his Madison Avenue house in Manhattan and put his frustrations in a letter to US Representative George A. Loud, a Michigan Republican, Spanish-American War veteran, and chairman of the House navy committee, with responsibility for vetting navy funding requests. The issue, Porter argued, was no longer about creating a monument to Jones. The issue was a matter of proper respect for the dead and the symbol that Jones's coffin now offered to navy cadets. Congress, Porter wrote, had been asked several times to allocate $135,000 to finish the crypt. Each request had languished and then died from inaction. William Howard Taft had succeeded Teddy Roosevelt in the White House, and top officials in both administrations supported the project. Several, in fact, had written

Congress about the issue, as had leaders of "the Navy League, Paul Jones Clubs, patriotic societies, the press, and hosts of public-spirited citizens. All appeals to Congress thus far, however, have been without avail." Porter's outrage built as he wrote. "For 113 years the body of this great central figure in our naval history was allowed to lie neglected in a sort of dumping ground in a distant land, and when brought back to the country he so eminently served it has lain for five years equally neglected, stowed away like old lumber," Porter wrote. "The body was taken by the Government to Annapolis, believing that the memories it would awake would be an inspiration to the midshipmen at the Academy. Instead of that, it remains only as a reminder of a nation's humiliating neglect of its historic defenders and is a sad example to young men about to enter the naval service."[1]

If Congress was not willing to finish the crypt, Porter warned, other solutions were possible. "A number of patriotic gentlemen are willing to provide the means for taking the body for burial, if permitted, to a lot on a city cemetery if this session of Congress refused it a sepulcher, so that the remains may rest at least in consecrated ground." Porter reminded Loud that Jones had been buried in Paris as an act of charity, and "it would constitute a further national disgrace to leave his remains to be buried in his own country again by the hand of charity." It was not an empty threat. The man who had raised the money to build Grant's Tomb and to elect a president would have no trouble putting together an organization to steal away the body and give Jones a proper grave.

Porter didn't refer to it in his letter, but Congress was balking both from a penurious spirit and because some of them still doubted that Porter had, indeed, found John Paul Jones.[2] The questions began in Paris as the dig was underway, with local wits joking that the Americans were going to a lot of trouble to move an unidentified Frenchmen to a fresh grave across the Atlantic. The genesis of the skepticism was a general belief that a body interred for more than a century would no longer be identifiable, despite the alcohol bath in which it had been laid to rest. There also were questions about the methods Porter and his array of experts had used to identify the body. How accurate could a Houdon bust be for the purposes of making an identity by comparison, given an artist's predisposition to artistic license? And there was speculation that Porter, about to leave the country, had so wanted to find the body that he was ready to believe in the flimsiest of evidence. Other news articles put forward unsubstantiated claims that Jones's body had been moved to Scotland years before and buried near his hometown. (Porter had already ruled that out through an inquiry to the pastor of the church where the body was supposedly interred.)[3]

The *Chicago Daily Tribune,* which had followed Porter's quest closely in part through the dispatches of Charles Inman Barnard, was one of the first to publicly raise questions in the United States. In a lightly mocking editorial, the editors wondered what the misidentified corpse's spirit would be saying at his disinterment. He "may be wondering how to get even with the person who has transplanted his remains to a foreign land. Nobody wishes to find himself among strangers on resurrection day." It went on to say that "it may not be civil to investigate a gift corpse too closely," but that, indeed, such an investigation was warranted, even granting Porter's benevolent decision to foot the bill. The editorial also noted that the body had been found as Porter planned to leave Paris, which "may have made him more ready than he otherwise would have been to accept negative evidence—evidence which goes to show that the body exhumed may be that of Jones, but which does not prove that it is." According to the article, were the evidence presented in a court of law, the verdict would be "not proven."[4]

The body was still on its way to the United States when the weekly *Independent* magazine published an article by Park Benjamin Jr., a former editor for *Scientific American* and the author of several books, including *History of the United States Naval Academy,* which was published in 1900. Benjamin styled himself a Jones expert "because for a long time past I have been making a close study of the voluminous memoirs, letters, etc., left by John Paul Jones, in order to reach an appreciation of his real place in our naval history." Benjamin wrote that the *Independent* editors had sought him out "because my professional work requires constant criticism of investigations in physical science."[5]

Benjamin's article was a response to the Parisian experts' reports identifying the body as Jones, which had been reprinted in the previous week's *Independent.* Benjamin was circumspect, but his doubts were clear. He noted that little was known about Jones's physical appearance other than he was forty-five years old and five feet seven (though the source for that was dodgy), with dark hair. "No other physical data useful for present identification of the body without extraneous and inferential aid appear," Benjamin wrote. "Nothing in this inquiry is more remarkable than the total absence of identifying remarks or objects in or upon the coffin."

Benjamin also was skeptical about the story of Jones's burial and the lost cemetery, arguing that it was unlikely that the grave and coffin of such an esteemed man would go unmarked. And the absence of scars and mended bones contradicted what he believed to have been evidence that Jones had, in fact, suffered a wound in battle, based on a letter written four months before Jones's death in which he referred to a social slight. "M. de Sartine . . . did not say to me a single word or ask me if my health had suffered from my wounds and the uncommon fatigue I have undergone." Benjamin also rejected the close match of measurements of the corpse's head and the Houdon bust, suggesting that the changes in flesh after death should have made the measurements different. Like the *Tribune* editorial, Benjamin invoked the metaphor of a trial and asked readers to imagine themselves jurors. Would "you . . . bring in a verdict of guilty solely on the proof of the *corpus delecti* here advanced and thereby send the prisoner to execution?"

Other doubts followed. In 1911, six years after the body arrived in Annapolis, a biography of Houdon, the sculptor, renewed questions about the identity of the corpse. The authors, Charles Henry Hart and Henry Biddle, took issue with perceived discrepancies in the shape of the nose on the corpse and on the statue. They also argued rather thinly that the sculpture used to identify the corpse was a copy of a copy—and thus unreliable—and that it was inherently problematic to use a piece of art to establish anatomical fact.

The consensus of opinion of the most eminent of American sculptors which the writer has obtained, is against the measurements of a bust being accepted as the exact measurements of the living head reproduced, as the true artist makes but little moment of measuring and is likely to vary in his work from the measurements of nature, exaggerating parts, either plus or minus, to produce a desired effect. The truth is that the sculptor seeks to express character and general lifelikeness, not the mathematical measurements of the subject, and therefore, while Houdon unquestionably was very exact, he may have been also very inaccurate; consequently, to take a work of art to prove a scientific fact seems, to say the least, most unscientific.[6]

The sweep of skepticism, from the jokes in Paris to Benjamin's piece to the Houdon biography, is worth considering. But it dissolves under close scrutiny. That the average citizen of Paris didn't believe an alcohol-pickled corpse could be so well preserved after a century underground does not mean that it could not be so. The Paris medical experts who examined the body and conducted the autopsy had exemplary credentials, and no whispers are found about their integrity as men of science. While the corpse wasn't photographed in the moments after the coffin was opened, when it was at its best preserved, the autopsy reports are quite detailed, and some of the methods Porter and the doctors used to identify the corpse—including matching photographs of the corpse against the busts—were path-breaking techniques in forensics. Later examinations of the reports raised no fresh questions, and academics revisiting the evidence as recently as 2004 came to the same conclusion: the body was Jones's.[7]

Part of the problem for skeptics has been that much of the evidence was circumstantial. Jones had never had any reported injuries, and the corpse bore no scars. His height, set at five feet seven, came from a source—a biography by A. C. Buell—that was later found to have been heavily fabricated. In life, Jones was described as being diminutive, and biographer Samuel Eliot Morison, in his Pulitzer Prize–winning *John Paul Jones: A Sailor's Biography*, estimated he was only five feet five. A 2004 review by forensic experts found, after an exhaustive review of the evidence and the questions of the identity, that estimates of Jones's height and that of the corpse were consistent. Benjamin's point about the accuracy of the Houdon bust was also dismissible, since "Houdon described himself firstly as an anatomist and secondly as an artist."[8] Houdon took great pride in delivering precisely accurate sculptures of his subjects, and Jones was so taken with his that he had at least eight copies made and sent to friends. Jones's contemporaries, including Thomas Jefferson, described the bust as a perfect likeness. And while there were quibbles about the measurements of the face compared with the bust—deteriorated flesh versus stone depicting the full-fleshed head—those too were dismissed, since the measurements recorded at the time of the autopsy were based on bone structure. And no one has questioned a subtle but crucial match: the unusual shape of Jones's earlobe, which those present at the exhumation said was visible on the corpse and matched a malformation depicted on the Houdon sculpture. Unfortunately, photos of the corpse did not show the earlobe.

While individual bits of evidence cited to identify the body as that of Jones might be challenged, all of the evidence taken together is convincing. The coffin was found where the historical record suggested it would be; the autopsy remains unindicted; the identified manner of death was consistent with Jones's reported final ailments; the physical resemblance between corpse and bust were persuasive to those who viewed them. There is no reason, more than a century later, for significant doubt. To tweak an old joke about one of Porter's other projects: if asked who is buried in John Paul Jones's tomb, the answer surely is John Paul Jones.[9]

———————— ✿ ————————

When acting navy secretary Charles H. Darling sent his order in July 1905 to the Naval Academy that it "maintain, night and day, a guard over the remains until the final interment takes place," he doubtless didn't envision the guard would be on duty for seven years.[10] But Congress would not be moved. The original budget for the chapel called for leaving the crypt as a roughed-out space of "exposed concrete and brick work" for future completion. And that future was coming quickly, Bonaparte wrote to Congress two days after the April 1906 Annapolis ceremony. The crypt needed to be finished—and soon. He asked for $135,000 to cover the design costs—Flagg, at the navy's request, had already done preliminary designs—and construction. Bonaparte pointed out that Porter had spent $35,000 of his own money to find and identify Jones's body, and he relayed the news that the former ambassador had rejected plans to reimburse him with the suggestion that Congress spend the money on the crypt instead. Naval officials had initially thought $100,000 would be enough to do the job but were revising their estimates upward, and even with Porter's act of generosity, "this sum, it is believed, is barely sufficient to complete the work in a simple but suitable and substantial manner," Bonaparte told Congress.[11]

Bonaparte's request met a chilly reception in Congress, which should not have come as a surprise. As the dig was underway in early 1905, President Roosevelt had asked Congress to pay for the search and recovery of the body, a request that died without action, leading Porter to forge ahead on his own. Later bills submitted by sympathetic congressmen had died at the committee level in successive Congresses. This lack of support had continued once the body was tucked away under the staircase in Bancroft Hall. In session after session, the navy and the White House had requested money to finish the crypt. The US Senate had managed a vote on the measure, approving it, but the legislation died when the House failed to vote on a parallel measure.

Porter's letter in December 1910 was part of a coordinated campaign that seems to have come together after an article appeared in the April 9, 1910, issue of the mass market magazine *Collier's*. The piece was by artist and navy reserve officer Henry Reuterdahl, who two years earlier had roiled the naval bureaucracy with a scathing article about ship designs crafted amid an inflexible bureaucracy. The earlier article, in *McClure's* magazine, had sparked investigations and, eventually, changes in how the navy designed its ships.

In his new piece, Reuterdahl again sought to spur the recalcitrant into action. And the article should not have caught navy officials by surprise. In February, two months before the piece was published, Reuterdahl wrote to navy secretary George von Lengerke Meyer asking if it was true that Jones's coffin was still resting "upon two wooden horses back of the stairs in Bancroft Hall, at the Naval Academy at Annapolis, and that no money is available for the proper interment of his remains."

Meyer responded that the body was being properly treated. "No criticism of this location was offered by any of the distinguished visitors present on that occasion (when placed), who included among their number those most actively interested in the return of the Body to this country from its original burial place; nor, until the receipt of the attached communication, has any hint of such criticism reached this office."[12]

Reuterdahl was unswayed. Under the headline JOHN PAUL JONES, OUR GRAVELESS HERO, Reuterdahl drew a picture of the chapel and a second illustration of Jones's casket under a starred banner beneath the grand staircase at Bancroft. The article offered a survey of Jones's importance to US naval history and then finished with a public lament at the ingratitude of a nation. "His earthly remains are not properly cared for by the nation. It is over a century since Paul Jones died, and his body has not yet found its final resting place." The US Senate, he noted, had approved spending $135,000 to complete the crypt. "It remains for some patriot in the House of Representatives to make its members understand that it is a national shame that the founder of the American navy has not what is accorded to every decent citizen—the right to a final resting-place."

Over the next few months, members of the Sons of the American Revolution began lobbying Congress to allocate the money to build the crypt. The Vermont legislature, two weeks after Porter sent his letter, passed a resolution urging Congress to act.[13] Porter also wrote an appeal to Congress on May 28, just six weeks after Reuterdahl's article was published. "Many promises were made by the Government that the body of Paul Jones should be given a decent sepulcher, but not withstanding the urging of our Presidents, Secretaries of the Navies, 19 patriotic societies, Paul Jones clubs, and public press, etc., there has been no step taken even to place it in some consecrated place. . . . His poor body was probably better off during the 113 years of neglect in Paris, for at least there it reposed in consecrated ground."[14]

The campaign finally gained some traction in early 1911 when the House's navy committee once again sent an expenditure measure to the full House. But this time it recommended a lower amount—up to $75,000, instead of the $135,000 the navy had been pushing for. Even that amount found deep resistance. Illinois Republican representative James Robert Mann pointed out that the navy wanted Congress to pay for designing and building the crypt without seeing what those plans would be. He wondered "if it would be better to properly authorize the Secretary of the Navy to have estimates, plans, and specifications prepared and submit them to Congress before acting upon this?" His Democratic colleague, Augustus Stanley of Kentucky, was even more direct and skeptical. "I am surprised and grieved at the wanton and reckless expenditures by the Committee on Naval Affairs," he said on the floor of the House. "Of all the bills that ever came before the House, it strikes me that this one is the most reckless in regard to expenditure of the dear people's money. Now, you have proposed

the erection of a building not only to take care of all the live people in the
Navy, but you are building a gilded mausoleum for people who are not
yet dead and you do not know when they are going to die. . . . You do not
know how much it will cost, how many are going to be buried there. You
just know you are taking the people's money to start a kind of military
graveyard." Besides, he said, "nobody knows whether it is John Paul Jones
or John Paul Jones's coachman; but that does not keep the Committee on
Naval Affairs from throwing away money like a drunken sailor."[15]

Despite the resistance, the House finally approved the expenditure, and
the project let out for bids. Flagg, the original designer of the new Annapolis,
had hoped to design the crypt but found himself on the outs with the navy
after his lawyers filed a court claim for additional fees for the work already
done. Flagg's bid for finishing the crypt died, and the project eventually
went to Grand Central Terminal architect Whitney Warren and his "less
imaginative design" (in the words of Flagg biographer Mardges Bacon).

Work proceeded relatively quickly, and the unfinished concrete basement was transformed into a mausoleum, minus some of the grandiosity
of Flagg's vision. Given the lower budget, the skylight effect of the original
plan was scrapped. Warren went with eight Doric dark marble pillars encir-
cling the crypt, and a twenty-one-ton sarcophagus of Grand Antique des
Pyrénées marble resting on the backs of swimming dolphins. The names of
Jones's navy ships—the *Ranger, Alliance,* and *Bonhomme Richard*—were inlaid
in the floor, made from Knoxville and Tennessee marble. The limestone-
faced wall ringing the sarcophagus was set aside for displays and other
memorials—but not the niches for heroes that Flagg had wanted.[16]

Finally, in January 1913, the crypt was ready for Jones, bringing the
story of the search for an American hero to its end. This fourth and final
funeral was also the least elaborate. Meyer, the navy secretary, accompanied by Porter, the man who had rescued the body from beneath Mme
Crignier's Parisian buildings, led a small entourage on a train trip from
Washington, DC, on the morning of January 26, an unusually springlike
day in Annapolis. They watched as a small contingent of seamen retrieved
Jones's coffin from its sawhorse bier beneath the staircase and carried it outside to a caisson, which was wheeled through the treed park to the chapel,
where the pallbearers carried the coffin down the short flight of stairs to the

John Paul Jones's crypt in the Chapel at the United States Naval Academy, Annapolis.
Courtesy of the Library of Congress, Prints and Photographs Division, reproduction number HABS
MD,2-ANNA,65/1--23

waiting sarcophagus. After a brief prayer service in the chapel, the attendees filed downstairs to the basement crypt and became the first tourists to visit the final resting place of John Paul Jones.

Some 120 years after he slipped into death alone in his Paris bedroom, the hero was finally at rest.

---- ❖ ----

Horace Porter was seventy-five years old in January 1913 and living a relatively quiet life with five servants in his home on Madison Avenue. In the years after he left Paris, he had initially maintained a high profile. He was part of the delegation representing the Roosevelt administration at the

Second International Peace Conference of the Hague in 1907, a gathering of diplomats aimed at trying to regulate the way wars were waged. In 1908 he accepted appointment to the navy's Board of Visitors at Annapolis. He became more active in the "patriotic groups," such as the Navy League, for which he served as president, and chaired meetings of the International Law Society in Washington. He was elected president of the Legion of Honor, an association of living winners of the Congressional Medal of Honor.

In an odd juxtaposition, Porter also belonged for a time to the New York Peace Society, which began in 1906 to prod the United States and other nations to resolve disputes through mediation and arbitration, not war. Porter was accepted as a member in April 1909 at a meeting in which Andrew Carnegie warned presciently of growing frictions between England and Germany. Each nation directed a large navy sailing off the coasts of Europe, and chance encounters could easily turn into war, he cautioned. He urged the US government to lead the world in resolving disputes through the structures of international law and discussion, not weapons and invasions.

It's unclear whether Porter was present at that meeting, but after Carnegie finished speaking, another member, E. J. Malloy, rose to ask whether the Porter who had been added to the group that day was the same Porter who was serving as president of the Navy League—an organization whose sole purpose was to promote a strong US Navy. Yes, he was told, it was the same Porter. "It seems to me thoroughly inconsistent for a man to hold office in both these societies when the very raison d'être of each is determined to defeat the plans of the other," Malloy said. He accepted that Porter could well be a man of peace, "but under existing circumstances it is ridiculous for him to hold office in this society." Since there was no proscription in the Peace Society's bylaws, Porter was allowed to stay, and the chair of the meeting noted that some good might come of it. "Possibly the ameliorating effect of his association with us may induce him to stop his nefarious practices."[17]

There was nothing nefarious about what Porter was doing, though. He had long been a champion of veterans and of the military—not surprising for a West Point graduate, Medal of Honor winner, and close friend of Ulysses S. Grant. Porter long identified himself as a military man. Even after he left France, he preferred to be called General Porter, rather than Ambassador Porter. Yet he was a proponent of peace. He believed in diplomacy and mediation, but also that a big US military was a pre-requisite for peace. Why he wanted to belong to the Peace Society, whose members tended to believe a nation with a big military was more likely to use it, is lost to history. But given the broad sweep of his affiliations, he could have just seen it as another way to fill his time with a good cause.

Porter also remained active in Republican politics. During an internal party squabble over whether to nominate New York governor—and future US Supreme Court chief justice—Charles Evans Hughes for reelection in 1908, Porter's name was tossed around as a compromise candidate. Hughes prevailed with his party but lost the general election.

Porter's most visible role tended to involve eulogizing the dead at funerals and unveilings of monuments. He spoke at the 1908 Washington, DC, dedication of a statue of General Philip H. Sheridan, who was part of the Civil War battle at Chickamauga for which Porter received his Medal of Honor. The next year he offered a eulogy to Abraham Lincoln at Carnegie Hall during a celebration marking the centennial of the president's birth, and he delivered the 1909 commencement address at the US Naval Academy. He spoke briefly at the 1912 dedication of the statue of John Paul Jones near the Potomac in southwest Washington in 1912, the year before the crypt was completed and Jones was finally laid to rest. That the statue was done before the crypt had to have galled the former general, but if it did, he kept those thoughts to himself.

By the time the crypt was finished and Jones was placed within his elaborate sarcophagus, Porter was beginning to slow down. A *New York Times* reporter visited him at his Madison Avenue home in April 1913, three months after that final dedication, and found the seventy-five-year-old man vigorous, with graying hair, an erect stature, and a thick vein of humility. Noting that Porter read six newspapers each morning, the reporter asked for his thoughts on the developing issues of the day, from politics to looming war in Europe. "Individual expression of opinion does not count for much where big issues are concerned," Porter told him. "Nor would anything I might say be of journalistic importance." One wonders why Porter agreed to the interview in the first place.

As World War I unfolded in Europe, Porter lent his name to various fundraising efforts to support the troops, but he was no longer chairing meetings or running campaigns. Porter continued to make summer trips to West Long Branch, New Jersey, where his wife, Sophie, and their sons William and Horace M. were buried (soon to be followed by son Clarence in 1917). He also traveled to Newport, Rhode Island, and Bar Harbor, Maine, for the summer social season. Sometimes he rented a cottage; sometimes he stayed with well-heeled friends from Manhattan. His name popped up regularly in the society columns, as a guest at various weddings and as a financial supporter for a wide range of local causes. But as Porter neared his eightieth birthday, the pace of mentions became less frequent.

In June 1920, at age eighty-three, Porter was taken ill. Details are scant, but he was stricken while vacationing in Greenwich, Connecticut, at what was described as "his summer home" (presumably a seasonal rental). He was rushed back to his residence at Madison Avenue and Forty-First Street, a neighborhood of mansions under stress from Manhattan's growing appetite for skyscrapers. Appendicitis was diagnosed, and Porter underwent surgery to remove the failing organ. While the operation was successful, Porter never really recovered. Six weeks after his eighty-fourth birthday, Porter slipped into a coma. He died on May 29, 1921, nearly a year after he first fell ill. While the cause was ascribed to a general failure of health, the start of his decline was pinned to the bad appendix.

Before his death, Porter—whose history included arranging mass public displays of a nation's thanks to General Grant, McKinley's first inaugural parade, and the elaborate celebration commemorating John Paul Jones's contributions to both the nation's independence and its embrace of a strong navy—had ordered a simple observation of his own passing. No pallbearers. No eulogies. "I want the simplest funeral a man can have," Porter said. "A word, a song, and a prayer." And that's what he received on June 2, 1921, at the Fifth Avenue Presbyterian Church. The coffin was ferried from his home in a hearse escorted by police motorcycles and then carried to the altar, where it was draped in the Stars and Stripes with Porter's cocked hat and ceremonial sword placed on top. The ceremony began with a choir singing "There Is a Land Beyond the Setting Sun," followed by a prayer by pastor John Kelman, who managed to slip in a few words of eulogy despite Porter's request.[18]

"For all the great and noble lives dedicated to high services in Christ's name, we give Thee thanks," the minister said.

For those who have not counted their own lives dear unto them, but have jeopardized their lives in the high places of the field, entering into the fellowship of His sacrifice, who gave His life for the redemption of the world, we give Thee thanks. For the high example of all upright men who have served their generation and especially today do we thank Thee for the long life and varied services of our brother now departed, for the high responsibility loftily borne and executed, for his service on the stern field of battle and on the fruitful fields of peace, for his life-long affection for his great commander, for all the share that Thou didst give to him in the international relations of the world, and for all that he did to keep these relations sound and friendly, for the world-wide fame, his fine culture, his courtesy and great simplicity and dignity, and for his distinguished self-control, we give Thee thanks. In him Thou didst grant to his generation one of Thy great gentlemen of the olden days, and we thank our God upon remembrance of him.

The pews were filled with, in essence, the survivors of a bygone era. Porter, the obituaries noted, was the last of Grant's intimate advisors. The mourners included Elihu Root, the former secretary of war, secretary of state, and 1912 Nobel Peace Prize winner; Chauncey Depew, a lawyer for Cornelius Vanderbilt, former railroad executive, and former US senator from New York; legendary financier J. Pierpont Morgan; Cornelius Bliss, Porter's former neighbor and cofundraiser for McKinley; and scores of others.

At the end of the service, the coffin was removed from the church and taken to a train for transport to a vault at the Old First Methodist Church Cemetery in West Long Branch, New Jersey, until Porter's daughter, Elsie Mende, could make the trip from Switzerland for a small, private burial next to Sophie and Elsie's three brothers.

It was a muted end to a long and public life. And while tourists and history buffs make regular trips to the crypt below the US Naval Academy chapel to contemplate Jones and the sweep of America's birth and its history, Porter's grave is just another headstone in a nondescript cemetery near the New Jersey coast.

A NOTE ON SOURCING AND SOME THANKS

CRAFTING A STORY SUCH as this involves finding and collating a lot of fine details from a wide range of sources. I tend to cast a wide net in my research and then sift through the treasures I've caught, which can make crediting individual sources for specific details a tedious task both for me and for the reader. So throughout this work I've opted to cite the sources for major details, but in scenes that are built from a number of sources, I chose not to footnote each fine point. Also, I mention weather often in descriptions of scenes and similarly decided not to clutter the footnotes with the source material for these details. In each case, this information was gleaned from accounts in local newspapers. Also, unless otherwise noted, the details of the dig itself came from Porter's reports and related accounts. Again, I opted not to footnote every detail. And finally, given the close scrutiny that John Paul Jones's life has endured, I opted not to do much primary research on such a well-documented subject; details in the three chapters that focus on him were gleaned primarily from the published works of others, duly cited in the footnotes. Those chapters were also graciously reviewed by Mark Lardas, naval historian and member of the Nautical Research Guild, to whom I'm indebted for saving me from some rather embarrassing errors.

While writing is a solitary pursuit, research is not, and I owe thanks to my wife, Margaret, and our Parkside Pub regulars, particularly Jann Gumbiner, Katherine Jacobs, and Laura McFarland, who've exhibited remarkable patience as I've talked through this project; in-laws Joe and Helen Mercier, who let me use their attic space in Greece, New York, as a writing garret in the summer of 2012; my parents, Walter and Dorothy Martelle, for infusing me with a love of books and writing; James R. Wils, who provided research help at East Carolina University in Greenville, North Carolina; Ray and Annie Herndon, Marc Midan, and Janine Lanza, who did valuable legwork for me checking Parisian archives (and a special thanks to Ray for some much-needed translation help); Cedric Guhl, Edouard Musy, and Karin Schindler of the extended Horace Porter family in Switzerland, who shared with me unpublished family papers; the staffs in the Library of Congress Manuscript Reading Room and the Newspaper Reading Room, two irreplaceable resources; the staffs of the National Archives in Washington, DC, and College Park, Maryland, particularly David Langbart and Richard Peuser, for their patience and guidance; longtime friend and former colleague Ivan Roman for his research help at the Navy Department Library, Naval History and Heritage Command in Washington, DC; and archivist James Allen Knechtmann, for his assistance to both Ivan and me. Thanks, too, go to Sarah Hartwell of Baker-Berry Library, Dartmouth College; Paul Mercer, Senior Librarian, Manuscripts and Special Collections, New York State Library; and James Cheevers, US Naval Academy Museum, Annapolis, who all provided crucial confirmations of stray facts. Also to Richard H. Owens, who shared his hard-to-find book *Vigilance and Virtue: A Biography of General and Ambassador Horace Porter, 1837–1921* (Lewiston, NY: Edwin Mellen Press, 2002), and to Susan Noftsker, a descendant of John Sherburne, for her help in deciphering some family lore. Obviously enough, their assistance does not carry a burden of blame; any errors in this work are mine and mine alone.

Thanks are also due to my editor (and author in his own right), Jerome Pohlen, as well as Mary Kravenas, publicist Meghan Miller, and the rest of the team at Chicago Review Press; and most of all to agents Jane Dystel and Miriam Goderich of Dystel & Goderich—it's good to have you two in my corner.

Finally, it's fitting that since these acknowledgements began with my wife, Margaret, they shall end with her, too, as my first and best reader. You've made this a better book and, to paraphrase a line from a movie, you've made me a better man.

NOTES

INTRODUCTION

1. Details drawn from "Honors to Paul Jones," *Washington Post*, January 25, 1913; "Crypt Now His Tomb," *Washington Post*, January 27, 1913; and "Final Resting Place of John Paul Jones, and Persons Attending Ceremony," *Washington Times*, January 25, 1913.

1. JONES: A HERO DIES

1. Details of Jones's last days are drawn from a letter by Samuel Blackden to Jones's sister, Janet Taylor, in Scotland, August 9, 1792, reprinted in John Paul Jones, *Life of Rear-Admiral John Paul Jones* (New York: American News, 1883), 388; and *The Diary and Letters of Gouverneur Morris* (New York: Charles Scribner's Son, 1888), vol. 1, 555, vol. 2, 45–46.
2. See Samuel Eliot Morison, "The Empty Wineskin," chapter 21 in *John Paul Jones: A Sailor's Biography* (Boston: Little, Brown, 1959).
3. Details are drawn from later reports after the body was recovered, reprinted in Charles W. Stewart, *John Paul Jones: Commemoration at Annapolis, April 24, 1906* (Washington, DC: Government Printing Office, 1907).

2. A NEW PRESIDENT

1. "Weather Conditions," *Washington Post*, March 5, 1897.
2. Details drawn from Elsie Porter Mende's biography of her father, Horace Porter, *An American Soldier and Diplomat* (New York: Frederick A. Stokes, 1927), 168–69, and contemporary media accounts, including "March Down the Avenue," *New York Times*, March 5, 1914, and "President McKinley," *Washington Post*, March 5, 1914.

3. R. Hal Williams, *Realigning America: McKinley, Bryan, and the Remarkable Election of 1896* (Lawrence: University of Kansas, 2010), 170.

4. Mende, *An American Soldier*, 5–6.

5. Mende, *An American Soldier*, 9. This and Horace Porter Papers, Manuscript Division, Library of Congress, Washington, DC, are the main sources for details about Porter's pre-Civil War life.

6. Richard H. Owens, chapter 1 in *Vigilance and Virtue: A Biography of General and Ambassador Horace Porter, 1837–1921* (Lewiston, NY: Edwin Mellen Press, 2002). My thanks to Owens for sharing with me a manuscript draft of his hard-to-find book.

7. Details on Porter's West Point days are drawn from box 1, 1854–1860, West Point Grades, Appointment Papers, Horace Porter Papers.

8. Mende, *An American Soldier*, 16–17. Unless otherwise noted, the details of Porter's Civil War years are drawn from Mende, Owens's *Vigilance and Virtue*, and the Horace Porter Papers at the Library of Congress.

9. Horace Porter, *Campaigning with Grant* (New York: Century, 1897), 2.

10. Mende, *An American Soldier*, xviii; Porter, *Campaigning with Grant*, 478.

11. William Baumer Jr., *Not All Warriors: Portraits of 19th Century West Pointers Who Gained Fame in Other Than Military Fields* (Freeport, NY: Books for Libraries Press, 1941; repr. 1971); see the last chapter, "Horace Porter, Diplomat."

12. Mende, *An American Soldier*, 157.

13. Porter to *Century* magazine, November 16, 1896, box 2, Letter Book, Letters Sent, Horace Porter Papers.

14. *The Elite of New York, Society List and Club Register*, published annually by Elite of New York.

15. "General Horace Porter," *Bismarck Daily Record*, May 16, 1896.

16. "Gen. Porter Was Host," *New York Times*, June 1, 1895.

17. Lewis L. Gould, ed., *American First Ladies: Their Lives and Their Legacy* (New York: Routledge, 2001), 189.

18. Williams, *Realigning America*, 106–108.

19. Ibid., 42–43.

20. Porter to Strong, October 21, 1896, and October 28, 1896, box 2, Letter Book, August 5, 1896–October 28, 1896, Horace Porter Papers.

21. Ibid.

22. "Greatest of Parades," *New York Times*, November 1, 1896.

23. "News at Headquarters," *New York Times*, November 4, 1896.

24. Porter to Col. A. A. Woodhull of Denver, Colorado, December 30, 1896, box 2, Letter Book, October 28, 1896–January 16, 1897, Horace Porter Papers.

25. Porter to Colonel H. H. Prettyman in London, Ohio, November 12, 1896, box 2, Letter Book, October 28, 1896–January 16, 1897, Horace Porter Papers.

26. Porter to Woodhull, December 30, 1896, box 2, Letter Book, October 28, 1896–January 16, 1897, Horace Porter Papers.

27. Porter to George M. Smalley of New York City, February 18, 1897, box 2, Letter Book, January 18, 1897–April 2, 1897, Horace Porter Papers.

28. Porter to Gen. W. M. Osborne of Boston, Massachusetts, January 30, 1897, box 2, Letter Book, January 18, 1897–April 2, 1897, Horace Porter Papers.
29. Margaret Leech, *In the Days of McKinley* (New York: Harper, 1959), 116–120.
30. *Inaugural Addresses of the Presidents of the United States* (Washington, DC: U.S. General Printing Office, 1989), 101–10.
31. Details drawn from contemporary news accounts primarily in the *New York Times*, *Washington Post*, and *Chicago Tribune*.
32. McKinley official inauguration program, Frank Mt. Pleasant Library of Special Collections and Archives, Leatherby Libraries, Chapman University, Orange, California.

3. MCKINLEY, GRANT, AND AN AMBASSADORSHIP

1. Porter to Winslow, March 26, 1897, and April 2, 1897, box 2, Letter Book, January 18, 1897–April 2, 1897, Horace Porter Papers.
2. Geoffrey C. Ward, *A Disposition to Be Rich* (New York: Alfred A. Knopf, 2012), 218; Jean Edward Smith, *Grant* (New York: Simon and Schuster, 2001), 623–627.
3. Mende, *An American Soldier*, 144; for a full overview of Grant's last days, see Thomas M. Pitkin, *The Captain Departs: Ulysses S. Grant's Last Campaign* (Carbondale: Southern Illinois University Press, 1973).
4. "Tribute to E.F. Cragin," *Chicago Tribune*, April 20, 1897.
5. Cragin, both an activist supporting Cuban rebels and a future investor in a group that sought to build a canal through Nicaragua rather than Panama, had a final exchange of letters and telegrams with Porter just after the dedication ceremony. Cragin's half of the conversation is lost, but Porter's papers include an April 26, 1897, response that implied Cragin had accused Porter of taking more credit for the fundraising than he deserved. "Both telegrams received. Deeply disappointed that commemoration [illegible word] miscarried. You should have come anyhow. Please recall your first dispatch. It is not like you. My address contains full public acknowledgement of your valuable services. You should have trusted me." But transcripts of Porter's address in newspapers did not include any mention of Cragin.
6. Details drawn from period maps and photographs, including reproduction no. LC-D4-12680, Prints and Photographs Division, Library of Congress, Washington, DC.
7. "Shipping and the Mails," *New York Times*, May 5, 1897.
8. William Henry Flayhart III, *The American Line*, (New York: W.W. Norton, 2000), 137–144, 174; "America's Largest Vessels," *New York Times*, September 16, 1894; "The New Ocean Steamers St. Louis and St. Paul," *Scientific American*, August 11, 1894.
9. Flayhart, *The American Line*, 141.
10. Mende, *An American Soldier*, 176.
11. "Manton Marble, Publicist, Dead," *New York Times*, July 25, 1917.

12. "Dazian's," *New Yorker*, October 8, 1932.

13. Nelson A. Miles, *Military Europe: A Narrative of Personal Observation and Personal Experience* (New York: Doubleday and McClure, 1988), 4–7; "Prominent People Sail for Europe," *New York Times*, May 6, 1897.

4. JONES: THE SCOURGE OF ENGLAND

1. *Life and Correspondence of John Paul Jones, Including the Narrative of the Campaign of the Liman, Drawn from Letters and Papers Kept by His Sister, Janet Taylor* (New York: A. Chandler, 1830), 13–14. This is the collection of Jones letters published by his niece.

2. There have been many biographies of Jones, and many conflicting versions of key moments in his life. Unless otherwise noted, I rely mostly here on Morison's *John Paul Jones*.

3. Jones's version is included in *Life and Correspondence of John Paul Jones*, 18–22.

4. Jones's version is included in a letter to Benjamin Franklin written in March 1779 as Jones was in France outfitting the *Bonhomme Richard* for battle. See Appendix B in Mrs. Reginald de Koven's *The Life and Letters of John Paul Jones*, vol. 2 (New York: Charles Scribner's Sons, 1913).

5. See "Ships of the Continental Navy," Naval History and Heritage Command, www.history.navy.mil/wars/revwar/contships.htm.

6. *Life and Correspondence of John Paul Jones*, 65.

7. Journals of the Continental Congress, 1774–1789, Saturday, June 14, 1777.

8. Morison, *John Paul Jones*, 101.

9. Ibid., 100–110.

10. Jones's report to Congress is contained, among many other places, in *Life and Correspondence of John Paul Jones*, 82–83.

11. See the *Ranger*'s doctor's account in Ezra Green, *Diary of Ezra Green, M.D.* (Boston: private reprinting, 1875).

12. Additional details drawn from contemporary newspaper accounts collected in Don C. Seitz, *John Paul Jones: His Exploits in English Seas During 1778–80* (New York: E.P. Dutton, 1917).

13. Letter from Jones to Countess Selkirk, May 8, 1778.

14. Entry dated July 27, Green, *Diary*.

15. *Fanning's Narrative, Being the Memoirs of Nathaniel Fanning*, ed. John S. Barnes, included in *Publications of the Naval History Society* 2 (1912): 23. Fanning's then-anonymous memoirs first appeared in 1806.

16. Morison, *John Paul Jones*, 223.

17. For details of a long string of such abusive behavior, see *Fanning's Narrative*.

18. *Fanning's Narrative*, 45.

19. Pearson's report to the Lords of Admiralty, October 6, 1779.

20. *Fanning's Narrative*, 42.

5. THE AMBASSADOR ARRIVES

1. Mende, *An American Soldier*, 175–177.
2. Jane C. Loeffler, *The Architecture of Diplomacy: Building America's Embassies*, 2nd rev. ed. (New York: Princeton Architectural Press, 2011), 14–16; Mende, *An American Soldier*, 176–182, including endnotes.
3. Porter to Winslow, April 29, 1897, box 2, Letter Book, January 18, 1897–April 2, 1897, Horace Porter Papers.
4. Porter to Vignaud, April 20, 1897, box 3, Letter Book, May 24, 1897–November 10, 1902, Horace Porter Papers.
5. Porter to Sherman, July 16, 1897, record group 84, Records of Foreign Service Posts, Diplomatic Posts, France, volume 0185, National Archives, College Park, Maryland.
6. Porter to Cornelius Bliss, August 10, 1897, box 3, Letter Book, May 24, 1897–November 10, 1902, Horace Porter Papers.
7. Porter to Mark Hanna, July 13, 1897, box 3, Letter Book, May 24, 1897–November 10, 1902, Horace Porter Papers.
8. Mende, *An American Soldier*, 182.
9. Sims to his mother, July 8, 1897, Personal Correspondence, box 4, folder JL-DE 1897, William S. Sims Papers, Manuscript Division, Library of Congress, Washington, DC.
10. Porter to Hanna, July 13, 1897, box 3, Letter Book, May 24, 1897–November 10, 1902, Horace Porter Papers.
11. Jeremy D. Popkin, *A History of Modern France*, 2nd ed. (Upper Saddle River, NJ: Prentice-Hall, 2001), 132–139; Colin Jones, *Paris: The Biography of a City* (New York: Penguin, 2005), 328–330.
12. "A History of the Commune," *Literary World; a Monthly Review of Current Literature*, March 21, 1896, from a review of Thomas March, *The History of the Paris Commune 1871* (London: Swan Sonnenschein, 1896).
13. Susan Dyer diary, November 24, 1897, box 21, folder D, George Leland Dyer Papers (#340), Special Collections Department, J. Y. Joyner Library, East Carolina University, Greenville, North Carolina.
14. Dyer diary, December 21, 1897.
15. Sims to his mother, May 30, 1897, Personal Correspondence, box 4, folder FE-JE 1897, William S. Sims Papers.
16. Porter to Hanna, July 13, 1897, box 3, Letter Book, May 24, 1897–November 10, 1902, Horace Porter Papers.
17. Michael Burns, *Dreyfus: A Family Affair, from the French Revolution to the Holocaust* (New York: HarperCollins, 1991), 171–72.
18. For a deeply researched and highly readable look at the European colonization of Africa, see Thomas Pakenham, *The Scramble for Africa: White Man's Conquest of the Dark Continent from 1876 to 1912* (New York: Random House, 1991). For details on King Leopold's crimes against humanity, see Adam Hochschild, *King Leopold's*

Ghost: A Story of Greed, Terror, and Heroism in Colonial Africa (New York: Houghton Mifflin, Harcourt, 1998).

19. Porter to Hanna, July 13, 1897, box 3, Letter Book, May 24, 1897–November 10, 1902, Horace Porter Papers.

20. For a good discussion of the religious and class tensions in Paris at the time, see Geoffrey Cubitt, "Martyrs of Charity, Heroes of Solidarity: Catholic and Republican Response to the Fire at the *Bazar de la Charité*, Paris 1897," *French History* 21, no. 3 (2007): 331–352.

21. Details from Edwin O. Sachs, "The Paris Charity Bazaar Fire," reprinted in *Red Books of the British Fire Prevention Committee* (London: British Fire Prevention Committee, 1899), 16.

22. Elsie Porter Mende diary entry, October 25, 1897, private collection of granddaughter Karin Schindler.

23. For detailed analyses of the forces that led to the Spanish-American War, see David F. Trask, *The War with Spain in 1898* (New York: Macmillan, 1997) and Philip S. Foner, *The Spanish-Cuban-American War and the Birth of American Imperialism*, vols. 1 and 2 (New York: Monthly Review Press, 1972).

24. Trask, *War with Spain*, 3–7.

6. OF WAR AND HEROES

1. Porter to Sherman, July 13, 1897, box 3, Letter Book, May 24, 1897–November 10, 1902, Horace Porter Papers.

2. Porter to Bliss, August 10, 1897, box 2, Letter Book, May 24, 1897–November 10, 1902, Horace Porter Papers.

3. Dyer letter to his wife, August 18, 1897, box 13, folder B, George Leland Dyer Papers (#340).

4. "Canovas Murdered," *New York Times*, August 9, 1897.

5. Porter to Sherman, August 19, 1897, box 3, Letter Book, May 24, 1897–November 10, 1902, Horace Porter Papers.

6. Trask, *War with Spain*, 17.

7. Unless otherwise noted, the source for Elsie Porter's quotes are her diaries.

8. For a good overview of the time, see chapter 24 in James McGrath Morris, *Pulitzer: A Life in Politics, Print, and Power* (New York: Harper, 2010).

9. Mende diary entries for March 4, 1898, and March 6, 1898.

10. Mende diary entry March 8, 1898.

11. These details are drawn primarily from Trask, *War with Spain*, and Foner, *Spanish-Cuban-American*. Also see Evan Thomas, *The War Lovers: Roosevelt, Lodge, Hearst, and the Rush to Empire, 1898* (New York: Little, Brown, 2010).

12. "Dewey Praised by President," *New York Times*, May 3, 1898.

13. "Take Ship at Home," *Chicago Tribune*, May 3, 1898.

14. Details are drawn from the National Historic Landmark application for the gravesite, available at National Park Service, www.nps.gov/nhl/Spring2012 Nominations/FarragutGravesite.pdf.

7. JONES: THE FALL

1. For more details on that fascinating escape, see *Fanning's Narrative*, 72–76; and chapter 14 in Morison, *John Paul Jones*. Unless otherwise noted, Jones's life as depicted here is drawn from these two works.
2. *Fanning's Narrative*, 79–80.
3. Ibid., 112.
4. For a good overview of the history of the bust, see chapter 7 in Charles Henry Hart and Edward Biddle, *Memoirs of the Life and Works of Jean Antoine Houdon* (Philadelphia, printed for the authors, 1911).
5. Morison, *John Paul Jones*, 296.
6. Fanning provides details on these stories, but Morison, finding no other mention anywhere that they had transpired, disbelieved that they had happened.
7. Fanning stayed behind in Lorient, and Jones figures no further in his memoirs.
8. *Life and Correspondence of John Paul Jones*, 387. And for details on Catherine II, see Robert K. Massie's masterful *Catherine the Great: Portrait of a Woman* (New York: Random House, 2011). Her intersections with Jones's life are in 509–514.
9. The letters are reprinted in, among other places, Massie, *Catherine the Great*, 511.
10. The historical record has conflicting translated spellings of these Russian names; I opted for the spellings that seem most authentic.
11. There is some dispute over exactly when this occurred. I use Morison's timing, but Evan Thomas writes in *John Paul Jones: Sailor, Hero, Father of the American Navy* (New York: Simon and Schuster, 2003) that he believes it occurred on the next night, after the Turkish fleet had moved westward under the protection of the fort.
12. Details of Taylor's trip are drawn from chapter 25 of de Koven, *Life and Letters*.

8. WAR IN CUBA, PEACE IN PARIS

1. All quotes attributed to Elsie Porter Mende are drawn from her unpublished diaries, April through August 1898.
2. It's unclear who this is. She didn't identify him further in the diaries, but based on other references in her diaries it seems to have been Lieutenant Harvey Millard Horton of the 71st Infantry regiment of New York.
3. Porter to Day, May 24, 1898, record group 59, Dispatches from U.S. Ministers to France, 1789–1906, National Archives, College Park, MD.
4. Porter to Day, June 7, 1898, ibid. Porter often sent several separate reports to Washington each day.
5. Porter to Day, June 7, 1898, ibid.
6. Porter to Day, June 3 and June 7, 1898, ibid.
7. "As Seen in London," *New York Times*, June 19, 1898.
8. Porter to Day, June 21, 1898, record group 59, Dispatches from U.S. Ministers to France, 1789–1906, National Archives.
9. Trask, *War with Spain*, 424–425.

10. Porter to McKinley, September 6, 1898, box 2, Letter Book, May 24, 1897–November 10, 1902, Horace Porter Papers.

11. Captain. A. T. Mahan, "John Paul Jones in the Revolution," *Scribner's Magazine*, July 1898.

12. Gowdy to Landis, January 2, 1899, refers to Landis letter to Gowdy, November 25, 1898, included in Stewart, *John Paul Jones: Commemoration*, 195–196.

9. THE MISSING GRAVE

1. "Thanksgiving Event in Paris," *New York Times*, November 25, 1898.

2. Gowdy to Landis, January 2, 1899, included in Stewart, *John Paul Jones: Commemoration*, 195–196.

3. See the "Editor's Preface" to the 1912 version, edited and annotated by John S. Barnes for the Naval History Society; and "Monthly List" of new titles in the *Monthly Register*, March 1, 1897.

4. *Fanning's Narrative*, 44–45, 52–53.

5. James Fenimore Cooper, *Lives of Distinguished American Naval Officers*, vol. 2 (Philadelphia: Carey and Hart, 1846), 111.

6. "A Tale of the Sea—Character of John Paul Jones," *Collections, Historical and Miscellaneous, and Monthly Literary Journal*, February 1824, 54.

7. See Donald Darnell's "Cooper's Problematic Pilot: 'Unrighteous Ambition' in a Patriotic Cause," in *James Fenimore Cooper: His Country and His Art, Papers from the Bicentennial Conference, July 1989*, ed. George A. Test (Oneonta, NY: SUNY, 1991).

8. *Time Piece*, November 24, 1797; friendship detail from de Koven, *Life and Letters*, 265.

9. The spellings of the mother's and daughter's names have been scrambled in different accounts. The book the family published based on Jones's letters lists the "Janet" spelling for the mother, so I have gone with that, and assigned the "Janette" spelling to the daughter: *Memoirs of Paul Jones* (Edinburgh: Oliver and Boyd, 1830), 3.

10. "Paul Jones," *Niles' Weekly Register*, July 1, 1820, reprinted from the *New York Commercial Advertiser*. The history of Jones's letters, and what material Hyslop possessed and from what source, are blurry in the historical record. This is cobbled from the introductions to the British and American editions of Jones's letters based on the Taylor collection, *Memoirs of Rear Admiral Paul Jones* (Edinburgh: Oliver and Boyd, 1830), vi–viii; and de Koven, *Life and Letters*, viii.

11. Jefferson to Sherburne, February 14, 1825, reprinted in John H. Sherburne, *The Life and Character of John Paul Jones*, 2nd ed. (New York: Adriance, Sherman, 1861), ix.

12. "Art. XXXVII. Life and Character of the Chevalier John Paul Jones," *New-York Review and Atheneum Magazine*, November 1825.

13. *Life and Correspondence of John Paul Jones*, 4.

14. Details on Pinkham's role in renovating Jones's boyhood home are drawn from "Lieutenant A. B. Pinkham," *Dumfries and Galloway Courier*, July 30, 1834, by the unidentified editor of the newspaper, reprinted in the bound collection *The Military*

and Naval Magazine of the United States, vol. 11 (Washington, DC: Benjamin Homas, 1836), 128–136.

15. Cooper to Simms, January 5, 1844, reprinted in *The Letters and Journals of James Fenimore Cooper*, ed. James Franklin Beard (Cambridge, MA: Belknap Press of Harvard University Press, 1964).

16. "New Light Upon the Career of John Paul Jones," *US Naval Institute Proceedings* 33, pt. 1 (1907): 692.

17. Jones, *Paris*, 212–213.

18. Ibid., 70–71.

19. Some details on Read's life are available at the Virtual Museum of French Protestantism, www.museeprotestant.org.

20. "The Contributors' Club: Paul Jones's Funeral," *Atlantic Monthly*, May 1890; Charles Read, "Le Héros d'un Roman de Fenimore Cooper," *La Correspondance Littéraire*, March 20, 1859, 172–173; "Burial of Paul Jones," *Russell's Magazine*, June 1859.

21. *Bulletin Historique et Littéraire* (Paris: Société de l'Histoire du Protestantisme Français, 1877), 136–141.

10. A BRUSH WITH FAME

1. Details drawn from the US District Court–New Hampshire website, www.nhd.uscourts.gov/ci/history/jdc.asp#JSS, accessed October 3, 2012.

2. While the authenticity seems uncertain (it's based on self-reporting by previous owners of the paintings), the portraits were credited to King in Andrew J. Cosentino, *The Paintings of Charles Bird King (1785–1862)* (Washington, DC: Smithsonian Institution Press, 1978).

3. The portraits are in the possession of Sherburne descendant Susan Noftsker of Albuquerque, New Mexico, who was kind enough to share photos of the framed portraits with me.

4. *Taylor v. Sherburne*, case no. 13,805, reprinted in *The Federal Cases Comprising Cases Argued and Determined in the Circuit and District Courts of the United States*, bk. 23 (St. Paul, MN: West Publishing, 1896), 805.

5. See Sherburne's introduction to John Wood, *The Suppressed History of the Administration of John Adams* (Philadelphia: Walker and Gillis, 1846).

6. Sherburne to Polk, September 30, 1845, reel 42, Letters of James K. Polk, Manuscript Division, Library of Congress, Washington, DC.

7. "John Adams," *Southern and Western Literary Messenger and Review*, September 1847.

8. Sherburne to Webster, January 8, 1851, manuscript 851108.1, Rauner Special Collections Library, Dartmouth College, Hanover, NH.

9. Letter from Rush to Sherburne, reprinted in the second edition of John Henry Sherburne's *Life and Character of John Paul Jones* (New York: Adriance, Sherman, 1851), 370–371.

10. *Leicestershire Mercury*, March 18, 1848.

11. Sherburne to Webster, January 8, 1851.

12. For this and the ensuing quotes, see letters among Sherburne, Sands, and Graham, in John Paul Jones, ZB files, Navy Department Library, Naval History and Heritage Command, Washington, DC.

11. THE SEARCH BEGINS

1. Harry J. Sievers, ed., *Benjamin Harrison: 1833–1901, Chronology, Documents, Bibliographical Aids* (Dobbs Ferry, NY: Ocean Publications, 1969), 26–28; Charles W. Calhoun, *Benjamin Harrison* (New York: Times Books, 2005), 162–163.

2. Harry J. Sievers, *Benjamin Harrison, Hoosier President: The White House Years and After* (Indianapolis: Bobbs-Merrill, 1968), 265–272.

3. "Decoration Day in Paris," *New York Times*, May 31, 1899.

4. Letter from Johnson to McKinley, June 7, 1899, record group 59, M79, roll 1039, National Archives.

5. Vignaud to Ricaudy, February 1899, record group 84, Records of Foreign Service Posts, France, volume 0598, National Archives.

6. Vignaud to Hay, June 28, 1899, record group 59, Dispatches from U.S. Ministers to France, 1789–1906, roll 127, National Archives.

7. Vignaud to Marion Stuart Gombauld, Mayeren in Pau, France, November 15, 1898, record group 84, Records of Foreign Service Posts, France, volume 0595, National Archives. The letter was written in English, suggesting Gombauld was an American or British expatriate.

8. Vignaud to "Monsieur de Selves," prefect of Paris, June 28, 1899, record group 84, Records of Foreign Service Posts, France, volume 0599, National Archives.

9. "John Paul Jones," *New York Times*, July 30, 1899, and "W. Churchill Dies; Famous Author, 75," *New York Times*, March 13, 1947.

10. Blackden to Taylor, August 9, 1792, reprinted in *Life and Correspondence of John Paul Jones*, 543.

11. The Sims detail is from "His Grave Has Been Found," *St. Louis Post-Dispatch*, November 14, 1899.

12. Vignaud to Alfred Leroux, August 22, 1899, record group 84, Records of Foreign Service Posts, Diplomatic Posts, France, volume 0599, National Archives.

13. Unless otherwise noted, the details that follow are gleaned from Porter's report to Hay, April 29, 1905, and Ricaudy's report to Porter, October 29, 1899.

14. Letter from Porter to Bailly-Blanchard, undated in the files but apparently written after Porter left the embassy, box 5, Horace Porter Papers.

15. David S. Barnes, *The Great Stink of Paris and the Nineteenth-Century Struggle Against Filth and Germs* (Baltimore: Johns Hopkins Press, 2006), 238–240.

16. Porter wrote several variations of his hunt for Jones's body. This is from the forward to *Letters of John Paul Jones* (Boston: Bibliophile Society, 1905), 78–79.

17. "John Paul Jones's Grave," *New York Times*, Aug 4, 1899.

18. Porter to Hay, November 9, 1899, record group 59, Dispatches from U.S. Ministers to France, 1789–1906, roll 127, National Archives.

19. "John Paul Jones's Grave," article dated October 28, 1899, published in *New York Tribune Illustrated Supplement*, November 12, 1899.
20. Memorandum by Charles W. Stewart, November 4, 1911, in which Stewart reports on interview with Porter in which Porter said Ricaudy had deceived him. Contained in John Paul Jones, ZB files, Navy Department Library.
21. Porter to Bailly-Blanchard, undated, in box 5, Horace Porter Papers.

12. DREYFUS, THE EXPOSITION, AND OTHER DISTRACTIONS

1. Legend has it that the act was oral sex. There was a touch of the black widow to Steinheil. Her husband and mother-in-law were murdered in 1908 during a purported burglary in which Steinheil was found bound and gagged. Police accused her of committing the killings and trussing herself afterward, but Steinheil was acquitted by a court, and she later moved to England.
2. Walter F. Lonergan, *Forty Years of Paris* (London: T. Fisher Unwin, 1907), 237.
3. Burns, *Dreyfus: A Family Affair*, 220–221.
4. Porter to Day, April 28, 1898, box 2, Letter Book, May 24, 1897–November 10, 1902, Horace Porter Papers.
5. For a good overview of the Exposition Universelle 1900, see Richard D. Mandell, *Paris 1900: The Great World's Fair* (Toronto: University of Toronto Press, 1967).
6. Details drawn from contemporary news accounts, particularly from the *New York Times* and the *Chicago Daily Tribune*, April 13–16, 1900.
7. "Day's Events Told in Detail," *Chicago Daily Tribune*, April 15, 1900. The twentieth century, of course, would go on to become the bloodiest in world history.
8. "Disappointed Tourists," *Los Angeles Times*, May 13, 1900.
9. Mende, *An American Soldier*, 234–236.
10. Marilyn McCully, *Picasso in Paris: 1900–1907* (New York: Vendome Press, 2011), 15–25.
11. "Paris Exposition Awards," *New York Times*, August 18, 1900.
12. Porter to Hay, December 5, 1899, box 2, Letter Book, May 24, 1897–November 10, 1902, Horace Porter Papers.
13. Nathan Miller, *Theodore Roosevelt: A Life* (New York: William Morrow, 1992), 334–335; H. Wayne Morgan, *William McKinley and His America*, rev. ed. (Kent, OH: Kent State University Press, 2003), 154–185.
14. Miller, *Theodore Roosevelt*, 335, 376–380.
15. Morgan, *William McKinley*, 385–389.
16. Porter to McKinley, November 12, 1900, box 2, Letter Book, May 24, 1897–November 10, 1902, Horace Porter Papers.

13. AN ASSASSINATION

1. Unless otherwise noted, details drawn from Scott Miller, *The President and the Assassin: McKinley, Terror, and Empire at the Dawn of the American Century* (New York: Random House, 2011), 289–320.

2. To friend Herman H. Kohlsaat, quoted but not sourced in Arthur Wallace Dunn, *From Harrison to Harding: A Personal Narrative, Covering a Third of a Century*, vol. 1 (New York: G.P. Putnam's Sons, 1922), 355.

3. Hay to Henry White in Newbury, New Hampshire, June 30, 1901, in *Letters of John Hay and Extracts from Diary*, vol. 3 (New York: Gordian Press, 1969).

4. Porter telegram, September 7, 1901, record group 84, Records of Foreign Service Posts, Diplomatic Posts, France, volume 0603, National Archives.

5. John Merriman, *The Dynamite Club: How a Bombing in Fin-de-Siècle Paris Ignited the Age of Modern Terror* (Boston: Houghton Mifflin Harcourt, 2009), 206–207.

6. Hay to Jeune, September 14, 1901, in *Letters of John Hay.*

7. Mende, *An American Soldier*, 287.

8. "What Is Doing in Society," *New York Times*, May 6, 1902.

9. Details drawn from numerous contemporary news accounts; Porter's visit made for regular items in the society columns. Also, Porter to Wright P. Edgerton, April 21, 1902, NARA, record group 84, Records of Foreign Service Posts, Diplomatic Posts, France, volume 604, National Archives.

10. Congressional Medal of Honor Society, www.cmohs.org/medal-history.php; and "Army Medals of Honor," *New York Times*, July 27, 1902.

11. "Mrs. Porter Dead," *New York Daily Tribune*, April 7, 1903.

12. Mende, *An American Soldier*, 287, and "Mrs. Porter Dead," *New York Daily Tribune*. Elsie was in Germany when her mother died, and her account of Sophie's last moments—that she swooned into her husband's arms and died with her head on his shoulder—are suspect and likely romanticized. Contemporary news accounts described an unexpected and fast downward slide, and stated that General Winslow and Sophie's brother, Henry McHarg, were also at her bedside when she died.

13. Porter to McHarg, April 6, 1903, box 3, Letter Book, May 24, 1897–November 10, 1902, Horace Porter Papers.

14. Porter to Hay, April 6, 1903, record group 84, Records of Foreign Service Posts, Diplomatic Posts, France, volume 606, National Archives.

15. His absences are spelled out in a series of dispatches through the summer and fall contained in record group 84, Records of Foreign Service Posts, Diplomatic Posts, France, volumes 0197–0198, National Archives.

16. Porter to Roosevelt, October 20, 1903, series 1, reel 33, Theodore Roosevelt Papers, Library of Congress, Washington, DC.

14. THE NEGOTIATIONS

1. The letters sent out are contained in record group 84, Records of Foreign Service Posts, France, volume 606, National Archives. Unfortunately, the embassy did not record—or at least keep—copies of the responses, which are lost to history.

2. Horace Porter, "The Recovery of the Body of John Paul Jones," reprinted in *Letters of John Paul Jones*, 73. This is one of several Porter iterations detailing his search.

3. Details drawn from contemporary maps and photos, and "Relief of Madame Crignier, Message from the President of the United States to Congress," doc. no. 101,

July 11, 1921. Several earlier similar reports were made, as well, containing the same information in efforts to get the US government to reimburse Crignier some 70,000 francs she had been ordered by French courts to pay her tenants after the buildings suffered damage in the search for Jones's body. I'm drawing on this one because it was the last in the series and included the earlier reports.

4. Porter to Hay, January 24, 1905, record group 59, Dispatches from U.S. Ministers to France, 1789–1906, roll 127, National Archives.

5. "To Find Grave of Paul Jones," *Detroit Free Press*, October 18, 1903.

6. H.J. Res. 42 and H.J. 48, 58th Congress.

7. "Where John Paul Jones' Body Lies," *St. Louis Post-Dispatch*, November 29, 1903.

8. Porter to Hay, January 24, 1905.

9. French ambassador Jean Jules Jusserand to Secretary of State Philander C. Knox, January 9, 1911, included in "Message from the President of the United States to Congress." Porter wrote to Hay that the outlay was 25,000 francs; I presume the difference is the fee paid to Crignier's architects.

10. Porter to Hay, January 24, 1905.

11. "Report of General Porter," reprinted in Stewart, *John Paul Jones: Commemoration*, 62.

12. Porter to Hay, January 24, 1905.

13. Porter to Roosevelt, January 24, 1905, record group 59, Dispatches from U.S. Ministers to France, 1789–1906, roll 127, National Archives.

14. Porter to Hay, January 31, 1905, ibid.

15. Porter to Roosevelt, February 3, 1905, and Porter to Roosevelt, October 20, 1903, series 1, reel 52, Theodore Roosevelt Papers.

16. "Researches of the Remains of Admiral John Paul Jones: Report of the Engineer of Mines, Inspector of the Quarries of the Seine," May 9, 1905, box 5, Horace Porter Papers.

17. Porter to Hay, April 29, 1905, record group 59, Dispatches from U.S. Ministers to France, 1789–1906, roll 127, National Archives.

15. THE DIG AND THE DISCOVERY

1. "French Congo Atrocities," *New York Times*, February 18, 1905.

2. "Many Gifts to Miss Porter," *Washington Post*, March 3, 1905; Mende, *An American Soldier*, 291–292.

3. "Mende-Porter Wedding," *New York Times*, March 5, 1905.

4. Roosevelt to Porter, February 15, 1905, series 1, reel 337, Theodore Roosevelt Papers.

5. Porter to Hay, March 25, 1905, record group 59, Dispatches from U.S. Ministers to France, 1789–1906, roll 127, National Archives.

6. "Grave of Paul Jones," *Washington Post*, February 23, 1905.

7. "Bones of John Paul Jones," *New York Times*, February 25, 1905.

8. Horace Porter, "The Recovery of the Body of John Paul Jones," *Century*, October 1905. The article he referenced could not be found in contemporary press accounts.

9. Unless otherwise noted, details here are drawn from Porter's several written reports and articles about the project, most prominently the report contained in Stewart, *John Paul Jones: Commemoration*, and reports by the attending doctors and anthropologists included in the government reports previously cited, as well as photographs of the scene.
10. Porter to Hay, April 14, 1905, record group 59, Dispatches from U.S. Ministers to France, 1789–1906, roll 127, National Archives.

16. THE RETURN OF THE HERO

1. Vignaud to Justice of the Peace, March 20, 1905, record group 84, Records of Foreign Service Posts, France, volume 0611, National Archives.
2. See "Report of Engineer Weiss" in Stewart, *John Paul Jones: Commemoration*, 95; "Echo of Paul Jones Case," *Chicago Daily Tribune*, July 7, 1907.
3. Porter to Loomis, June 2, 1905, record group 59, Dispatches from U.S. Ministers to France, 1789–1906, roll 127, National Archives.
4. McCormick to Loomis, June 2, 1905, ibid.
5. Julius Chambers, *News Hunting on Three Continents* (New York: J. J. Little and Ives, 1921), 366.
6. "John Paul Jones's Grave," *New York Tribune Illustrated Supplement*.
7. "Proceedings of the Fourteenth Annual Meeting of the General Society Daughters of the Revolution" (1905), 48.
8. "After Search of 50 Years," *Baltimore Sun*, April 16, 1905.
9. Porter to Loomis, April 21, 1905, and April 30, 1905, record group 84, Records of Foreign Service Posts, France, volume 0199, National Archives.
10. "Hay Goes Abroad Ill; Taft Heads Cabinet," *New York Times*, March 19, 1905.
11. William Roscoe Thayer, *The Life and Letters of John Hay*, vol. 2 (Boston: Houghton Mifflin, 1915), 399–407.
12. Details gleaned from contemporary news accounts, too many to list concisely. Consult, particularly, the *New York Times*, *Washington Post*, and *New York Sun* for the spring and summer of 1905.

17. A CELEBRATION AND A DELAY

1. Porter to Loomis, April 21, 1905, record group 84, Records of Foreign Service Posts, France, volume 0199, National Archives.
2. "Our Gorgeous Paris Embassy," *New York Times*, May 7, 1905.
3. "Selecting a Squadron," *Washington Post*, May 11, 1905.
4. Porter to Loomis, May 19, 1905, record group 84, Records of Foreign Service Posts, France, Volume 0199, National Archives.
5. McCormick to Loomis, June 17, 1905, and Porter to Loomis, July 1, 1905, record group 59, Dispatches from U.S. Ministers to France, 1789–1906, roll 127, National Archives.
6. "Will Embark at Havre," *Washington Post*, June 11, 1905.

7. McCormick to Loomis, June 20, 1905, record group 59, Dispatches from U.S. Ministers to France, 1789–1906, roll 127, National Archives.

8. Unless otherwise noted, details drawn from Stewart, *John Paul Jones: Commemoration*, 101.

9. Details of ship position and discipline issues drawn from record group 24, Records of the Bureau of Naval Personnel, Logs of Ships and Stations, 1801–1946, Brooklyn, 5-17-1905 to 1-22-1906, National Archives, Washington, DC.

10. "Sigsbee Ships in Port," *Washington Post*, July 1, 1905.

11. Report found in box 16, folder 12, Charles D. Sigsbee Papers, New York State Library, Albany, NY.

12. Henri Marion, *John Paul Jones's Last Cruise and Final Resting Place* (Washington, DC: George E. Howard, 1906), 13.

13. McCormick to SecState, July 1, 1905, record group 59, Dispatches from U.S. Ministers to France, 1789–1906, roll 127, National Archives.

14. Unless otherwise specified, details of the Paris trip and ceremonies surrounding the transfer of the body are drawn from contemporary news accounts too numerous to cite individually.

15. The texts of the speeches from that day are included in Marion, *Jones' Last Cruise*, 25–41.

16. Stewart, *John Paul Jones: Commemoration*, 111.

17. Letter from the Bureau of Navigation, July 12, 1905, record group 405, Records of the US Naval Academy, box 10, folder 1, Nimitz Library, US Naval Academy, Annapolis, Maryland.

18. "Annapolis Thronged," *Baltimore Sun*, July 24, 1905.

19. Orders, record group 405, Records of the US Naval Academy, box 10, folder 1; and "Paul Jones' Body Ashore," *Chicago Daily Tribune*, July 25, 1905.

18. ANNAPOLIS CELEBRATES

1. "Porter Sure He Found Body of Navy's Father," *St. Louis Post-Dispatch*, July 14, 1905.

2. Roosevelt to Long, December 27, 1897, reprinted in Senate doc. no. 55, 55th Cong., 2nd Sess. Other details included here are drawn from the same report.

3. For a good overview of Ernest Flagg's successes and controversies, see Mardges Bacon, *Ernest Flagg: Beaux-Arts Architect and Urban Reformer* (Cambridge, MA: MIT Press, 1986). The brother reference is on page 72; the Academy project is on pages 112–137.

4. Ernest Flagg, "New Buildings for the United States Naval Academy, Annapolis, Md.," pt. 1, *American Architect and Building News*, July 1, 1908. Flagg's two-part series will be useful to anyone with an interest in how the modern physical space of the academy came into being.

5. "Dewey Lays a Cornerstone," *New York Times*, June 4, 1904.

6. Flagg to Brownson, April 15, 1905, record group 405, Records of the US Naval Academy, box 10, folder 1, Nimitz Library.

7. H. Coy Glidden, ed., *Sail and Sweep*, vol. 3 (Detroit: Sail and Sweep Publishing, 1904), 397–398.

8. Porter to Bonaparte, July 25, 1905, General Correspondence, Letters Received While Secretary of the Navy, 1905–1906, box 124 (L–Q), Charles J. Bonaparte Papers, Manuscript Division, Library of Congress, Washington, DC.

9. Roosevelt to Bonaparte, August 1, 1905, box 132, Special Correspondence with Theodore Roosevelt, 1905–1909, Charles J. Bonaparte Papers.

10. The exchanges are in General Correspondence, Letters Received While Secretary of the Navy, 1905–1906, box 124 (L–Q), Charles J. Bonaparte Papers.

11. Roosevelt to Bonaparte, April 17, 1906, General Correspondence, Letters Received While Secretary of the Navy from the White House, 1905–1906, box 126, Charles J. Bonaparte Papers.

12. Unless otherwise noted, logistical details are drawn from letters and orders contained in record group 405, Records of the US Naval Academy, box 10, folder 1, Nimitz Library; "Some Go in Yachts," April 24, 1906, and "M. and M. Had Jolly Time," April 25, 1906, both *Baltimore Sun*.

13. "With Holiday Spirit," *Washington Post*, April 24, 1906.

14. Unless otherwise noted, details are drawn from Stewart, *John Paul Jones: Commemoration*.

19. "STOWED AWAY LIKE OLD LUMBER"

1. Porter to Loud, December 3, 1910, reprinted in House of Representatives rpt. no. 2114, 61st Cong., 3rd Sess., February 9, 1911.

2. "Paul Jones Buried Here," *Boston Evening Transcript*, December 23, 1911.

3. In a fitting symmetry, the questions about the identity continue to be raised more than a century after the body was found. For a good overview of the skepticism, see Adam Goodheart, "Home Is the Sailor," *Smithsonian*, April 2006. Most of the following details are drawn from Goodheart's piece, and from Nikki L. Rogers, et al., "The Belated Autopsy and Identification of an Eighteenth Century Naval Hero—The Saga of John Paul Jones," *Journal of Forensic Sciences* 49, no. 5 (September 2004); Nikki L. Rogers, "The Identification of John Paul Jones; The First Use of Photography in Forensic Facial Superimposition," *Journal of Forensic Identification* 55, no. 3 (May 2005); and Nikki L. Rogers and Adam Goodheart, "Historic Superimposed Image of John Paul Jones Was the Brainchild of American Diplomat Horace Porter," *Journal of Forensic Identification* 8, no. 6 (November 2008).

4. "The Unidentified Corpse," *Chicago Daily Tribune*, May 2, 1905.

5. Park Benjamin Jr., "Is It Paul Jones's Body?" *Independent*, July 20, 1905.

6. Hart and Biddle, *Memoirs of the Life and Works of Jean Antoine Houdon*, 144.

7. See the Rogers articles listed in note 3.

8. Rogers, et al., "Belated Autopsy," 1046.

9. In the modern era, DNA testing could resolve the issue, a point historian Adam Goodheart raised in his article "Home Is the Sailor" in the April 2006 issue of *Smithsonian* magazine. The chapel at Annapolis also possesses a medal with Jones's

likeness and a lock of his hair, which could be compared with a DNA sample from the corpse (if one could be obtained), but that begs the question of the authenticity of the lock of hair. And down the rabbit hole of doubt and second-guessing we go.

10. Darling to USNA superintendent, July 5, 1905, record group 405, Records of the US Naval Academy, box 10, folder 1, Nimitz Library.

11. Bonaparte to Senator Eugene Hale, chair of the US Senate Committee on Naval Affairs, April 26, 1906, included in House of Representatives rpt. no. 2114, 61st Cong., 3rd Sess., February 9, 1911.

12. The exchange of letters is in record group 405, Records of the US Naval Academy, box 10, folder 1, Nimitz Library.

13. "Slow Erecting Tomb," *Washington Post*, December 19, 1910.

14. Porter to unspecified recipient, May 28, 1910, excerpted in House of Representatives rpt. no. 2114, 61st Cong., 3rd Sess., February 9, 1911.

15. See Congressional Record for February 20, 1911, 3026–27.

16. "Photographs: Historical and Descriptive Data," Historic American Buildings Survey, National Architectural and Engineering Record, National Park Service, accessible via Library of Congress, http://lcweb2.loc.gov/pnp/habshaer/md/md0900/md0915/data/md0915data.pdf.

17. "Carnegie in Alarmist Roll," *Chicago Daily Tribune*, April 22, 1909.

18. "Noted Men at Bier of General Porter," *New York Times*, June 3, 1921; unless otherwise noted, these details are drawn from contemporary news accounts of the funeral and burial.

SELECTED BIBLIOGRAPHY

ARCHIVES

Frank Mt. Pleasant Library of Special Collections and Archives, Leatherby Libraries, Chapman University, Orange, California.

George Leland Dyer Papers (#340), Special Collections Department, J. Y. Joyner Library, East Carolina University, Greenville, North Carolina.

Library of Congress, Manuscript Division, Washington, DC: papers (among others) of John Hay, Horace Porter, Theodore Roosevelt, William S. Sims.

Library of Congress, Newspaper and Current Periodical Reading Room, Washington, DC.

National Archives, College Park, Maryland.

National Archives, Washington, DC.

Navy Department Library, Naval History and Heritage Command, Washington, DC.

Nimitz Library, US Naval Academy, Annapolis, Maryland.

BOOKS

Bacon, Mardges. *Ernest Flagg: Beaux-Arts Architect and Urban Reformer.* Cambridge, MA: MIT Press, 1986.

Barnes, David S. *The Great Stink of Paris and the Nineteenth-Century Struggle Against Filth and Germs.* Baltimore: Johns Hopkins Press, 2006.

Baumer, William Jr. *Not All Warriors: Portraits of 19th Century West Pointers Who Gained Fame in Other Than Military Fields.* Freeport, NY: Books for Libraries Press, 1941. Reprinted 1971.

Beard, James Franklin, ed. *The Letters and Journals of James Fenimore Cooper.* Cambridge, MA: Belknap Press of Harvard University Press, 1964.

Bredin, Jean-Denis. *The Affair: The Case of Alfred Dreyfus*. New York: George Braziller, 1986.

Burns, Michael. *Dreyfus: A Family Affair, from the French Revolution to the Holocaust*. New York: HarperCollins, 1991.

Calhoun, Charles W. *Benjamin Harrison*. New York: Times Books, 2005.

Chambers, Julius. *News Hunting on Three Continents*. New York: J. J. Little and Ives, 1921.

Cooper, James Fenimore. *Lives of Distinguished American Naval Officers*. Vol. 2. Philadelphia: Carey and Hart, 1846.

Cosentino, Andrew J. *The Paintings of Charles Bird King (1785–1862)*. Washington, DC: Smithsonian Institution Press, 1978.

De Koven, Mrs. Reginald. *The Life and Letters of John Paul Jones*. Vol. 2. New York: Charles Scribner's Sons, 1913.

Dunn, Arthur Wallace. *From Harrison to Harding: A Personal Narrative, Covering a Third of a Century*. Vol. 1. New York: G. P. Putnam's Sons, 1922.

The Federal Cases Comprising Cases Argued and Determined in the Circuit and District Courts of the United States. Bk. 23. St. Paul, MN: West Publishing, 1896.

Flayhart, William Henry, III. *The American Line*. New York: W. W. Norton, 2000.

Foner, Philip S. *The Spanish-Cuban-American War and the Birth of American Imperialism*. Vols. 1 and 2. New York: Monthly Review Press, 1972.

Gould, Lewis L. *The Presidency of William McKinley*. Lawrence: University Press of Kansas, 1980.

———, ed. *American First Ladies: Their Lives and Their Legacy*. New York: Routledge, 2001.

Green, Ezra. *Diary of Ezra Green, M.D.* Boston: private reprinting, 1875.

Halasz, Nicholas. *Captain Dreyfus: The Story of a Mass Hysteria*. New York: Touchstone, 1955.

Hart, Charles Henry, and Edward Biddle. *Memoirs of the Life and Works of Jean Antoine Houdon*. Philadelphia: printed for the authors, 1911.

Hay, John. *Letters of John Hay and Extracts from Diary*. Vol. 3. New York: Gordian Press, 1969.

Inaugural Addresses of the Presidents of the United States. Washington, DC: U.S. General Printing Office, 1989.

Jones, Colin. *Paris: The Biography of a City*. New York: Penguin, 2005.

Jones, John Paul. *Letters of John Paul Jones*. Boston: Bibliophile Society, 1905.

———. *Life and Correspondence of John Paul Jones, Including the Narrative of the Campaign of the Liman, Drawn from Letters and Papers Kept by His Sister, Janet Taylor*. New York: A. Chandler, 1830.

———. *Life of Rear-Admiral John Paul Jones*. New York: American News, 1883.

Leech, Margaret. *In the Days of McKinley*. New York: Harper, 1959.

Loeffler, Jane C. *The Architecture of Diplomacy: Building America's Embassies*. 2nd rev. ed. New York: Princeton Architectural Press, 2011.

Lonergan, Walter F. *Forty Years of Paris*. London: T. Fisher Unwin, 1907.

Lorenz, Lincoln. *The Admiral and the Empress: John Paul Jones and Catherine the Great*. New York: Bookman Associates, 1954.

Mandell, Richard D. *Paris 1900: The Great World's Fair.* Toronto: University of Toronto Press, 1967.

Marion, Henri. *John Paul Jones's Last Cruise and Final Resting Place.* Washington, DC: George E. Howard, 1906.

Massie, Robert K. *Catherine the Great: Portrait of a Woman.* New York: Random House, 2011.

McCully, Marilyn. *Picasso in Paris: 1900–1907.* New York: Vendome Press, 2011.

Merriman, John. *The Dynamite Club: How a Bombing in Fin-de-Siècle Paris Ignited the Age of Modern Terror.* Boston: Houghton Mifflin Harcourt, 2009.

Mende, Elsie Porter. *An American Soldier and Diplomat.* New York: Frederick A. Stokes, 1927.

Miles, Nelson A. *Military Europe: A Narrative of Personal Observation and Personal Experience.* New York: Doubleday and McClure, 1988.

The Military and Naval Magazine of the United States. Vol. 11. Washington, DC: Benjamin Homas, 1836.

Miller, Nathan. *Theodore Roosevelt: A Life.* New York: William Morrow, 1992.

Miller, Scott. *The President and the Assassin: McKinley, Terror, and Empire at the Dawn of the American Century.* New York: Random House, 2011.

Morgan, H. Wayne. *William McKinley and His America.* Rev. ed. Kent, OH: Kent State University Press, 2003.

Morison, Samuel Eliot. *John Paul Jones: A Sailor's Biography.* Boston: Little, Brown, 1959.

Morris, Gouverneur. *The Diary and Letters of Gouverneur Morris.* New York: Charles Scribner's Son, 1888.

Morris, James McGrath. *Pulitzer: A Life in Politics, Print, and Power.* New York: Harper, 2010.

Owens, Richard H. *Vigilance and Virtue: A Biography of General and Ambassador Horace Porter, 1837–1921.* Lewiston, NY: Edwin Mellen Press, 2002.

Pakenham, Thomas. *The Scramble for Africa: White Man's Conquest of the Dark Continent from 1876 to 1912.* New York: Avon Books, 1991.

Phillips, Kevin. *William McKinley.* New York: Tomes Books, Henry Holt, 2003.

Pitkin, Thomas M. *The Captain Departs: Ulysses S. Grant's Last Campaign.* Carbondale: Southern Illinois University Press, 1973.

Popkin, Jeremy D. *A History of Modern France.* 2nd ed. Upper Saddle River, NJ: Prentice-Hall, 2001.

Porter, Horace. *Campaigning with Grant.* New York: Century, 1897.

Red Books of the British Fire Prevention Committee. London: British Fire Prevention Committee, 1899.

Rosenblum, Robert, Maryanne Stevens, and Ann Dumas. *1900: Art at the Crossroads.* New York: Harry N. Abrams, 2000.

Russell, Francis. *The President Makers: From Mark Hanna to Joseph P. Kennedy.* Boston: Little, Brown, 1976.

Seitz, Don C. *John Paul Jones: His Exploits in English Seas During 1778–80.* New York: E.P. Dutton, 1917.

Sievers, Harry J. *Benjamin Harrison, Hoosier President: The White House Years and After.* Indianapolis: Bobbs-Merrill, 1968.

———, ed. *Benjamin Harrison: 1833–1901, Chronology, Documents, Bibliographical Aids.* Dobbs Ferry, NY: Ocean Publications, 1969.

Smith, Jean Edward. *Grant.* New York: Simon and Schuster, 2001.

Society de l'Histoire du Protestantisme Français. *Bulletin Historique et Littéraire.* Paris: Society de l'Histoire du Protestantisme Français, 1877.

Stewart, Charles W. *John Paul Jones: Commemoration at Annapolis, April 24, 1906.* Washington, DC: Government Printing Office, 1907.

Test, George A. *James Fenimore Cooper: His Country and His Art, Papers from the Bicentennial Conference, July 1989.* Oneonta, NY: SUNY, 1991.

Thayer, William Roscoe. *The Life and Letters of John Hay.* Vol. 2. Boston: Houghton Mifflin, 1915.

Thomas, Evan. *John Paul Jones: Sailor, Hero, Father of the American Navy.* New York: Simon and Schuster, 2003.

———. *The War Lovers: Roosevelt, Lodge, Hearst, and the Rush to Empire, 1898.* New York: Little, Brown, 2010.

Trask, David F. *The War with Spain in 1898.* New York: Macmillan, 1997.

Ward, Geoffrey C. *A Disposition to Be Rich.* New York: Alfred A. Knopf, 2012.

Williams, R. Hal. *Realigning America: McKinley, Bryan, and the Remarkable Election of 1896.* Lawrence: University of Kansas, 2010.

Wood, John, and John Henry Sherburne. *The Suppressed History of the Administration of John Adams.* Philadelphia: Walker and Gillis, 1846.

MAGAZINES

American Architect and Building News
Atlantic Monthly
Century
Collections, Historical and Miscellaneous, and Monthly Literary Journal
La Correspondance Littéraire
French History
Journal of Forensic Identification
Journal of Forensic Sciences
Literary World; a Monthly Review of Current Literature
New-York Review and Atheneum Magazine
New Yorker
Niles' Weekly Register
Publications of the Naval History Society
Russell's Magazine
Scientific American
Scribner's Magazine
Smithsonian
Southern and Western Literary Messenger and Review
US Naval Institute Proceedings

NEWSPAPERS

Baltimore Sun
Chicago Daily Tribune
Chicago Tribune
Leicestershire Mercury
Los Angeles Times
New York Daily Tribune
New York Sun
New York Tribune
New York Times
St. Louis Post-Dispatch
Time Piece
Washington Post
Washington Times

INDEX